HANDBOOK OF SPECIAL EVENTS
FOR NONPROFIT ORGANIZATIONS

HANDBOOK OF SPECIAL EVENTS FOR NONPROFIT ORGANIZATIONS

TESTED IDEAS FOR FUND RAISING AND PUBLIC RELATIONS

by
Edwin R. Leibert
and
Bernice E. Sheldon

with Foreword by David M. Church

ASSOCIATION PRESS / New York

Handbook of Special Events for Nonprofit Organizations

Copyright © 1972 by
Edwin R. Leibert and Bernice E. Sheldon
Association Press, 291 Broadway, New York, N.Y. 10007

International Standard Book Number: 0-8096-1809-5
Library of Congress Catalog Card Number: 75-129437

Second Printing—1974

Library of Congress Cataloging in Publication Data

Leibert, Edwin Reisinger, 1903-
  Handbook of special events for nonprofit organizations.

Bibliography: p. 221
  1. Fund raising. 2. Promotion of special events. 3. Public relations. I. Sheldon, Bernice E., joint author. II. Title.
HV41.L415   361.7'3   75-129437
ISBN 0-8096-1809-5

Printed in the United States of America

Foreword

Special events are a major instrument in the promotion of causes and institutions. They can serve to: *(a)* create interest and understanding of a cause or institution, *(b)* dramatize a program, *(c)* provide the basis for increased volunteer participation for the cause or institution, *(d)* raise funds.

Special events may be carried on entirely by volunteer committees. Or they may be conceived by such committees and turned over to the paid staff for operation. If volunteers carry on alone, they lose the help that the experience of the professional staff could provide. If the staff is given sole responsibility, then it becomes just an added task to their already heavy burden of work. The most successful special events are those carried out in close cooperation by volunteers and staff.

To avoid the dangers inherent in all public affairs, special events demand careful planning, good timing, and a close study of possible gains and losses. To encourage careful planning, with operations based on past experience, the authors of this book have set forth guidelines of inestimable value to all who contemplate operating a special event.

DAVID M. CHURCH

Mr. Church, formerly Executive Director of the American Association of Fund Raising Counsel, has spent much of his professional life working with and for volunteers in fund-raising campaigns, social welfare organizations, hospitals, colleges, and in such national efforts as the USO and its predecessor, the National War Work Council.

Contents

III. FUND-RAISING SPECIAL EVENTS

IV. IDEAS FOR SPECIAL EVENTS

Figure-Skating Ice Show . . . Art Auction in Connecticut . . .
Raised More Than Money . . . Thousands of Miles of Spaghetti . . .
Annual Benefit Dinner . . . Annual Emerald Lake Dinner . . . Din-
ner Meetings for Prospects . . . Pancake Breakfast . . . "Bunny
Girls" for Breakfast . . . Cooking Demonstration . . . Bacon and Eggs
Meeting for Media . . . Parisienne Holiday Show

List of Illustrations

Introduction

Simply stated, a special event is a dramatized effort to promote an idea, a cause, or a program. Its purpose is to improve relationships with an organization's public, develop understanding, and strengthen support through increased effort and contributions.

Specifically, then, what *is* a special event? It may be a kickoff dinner for a fund-raising drive, a charity ball, a theater party, a fashion show, or a pancake breakfast. It may be an annual dinner, an open-house program, a public meeting to debate a community problem, the dedication of a building, or an anniversary. Or, again, it may be keyed to some current program, activity, or service to interpret the organization's purposes and effectiveness.

Special events are important to the 500,000-plus private nonprofit organizations throughout the United States that serve thousands of communities ranging from metropolitan cities to small towns. Depending upon their nature, these organizations may serve broad segments of the population or special interest groups. They operate in every conceivable field—social welfare, health, medical, mental, youth, labor, science, charity, religion, higher education, public education, adult education, conservation, recreation, the arts. They are social, civic, political, religious, cultural, and professional.

This book is for all of these organizations. They can—if they will make the effort—take advantage of even more occasions to plan and stage special events. Those who have made the effort, following the steps and methods which lead to success, know the values that result from well-conceived and carefully planned special events. Lack of man- or womanpower—i. e., staff and volunteer workers—is probably the most frequent reason why many organizations fail to take advantage of what special events have to offer, reluctant lest it be opening a Pandora's box. So golden opportunities are lost.

The Indispensable Volunteers

Volunteers are the backbone of every successful voluntary organization and institution. This has been demonstrated for decades. They number more than fifty million. They are the people in every community who give generously of their time and effort, their moral and financial support to serve their favorite

15

causes. Backing up every successful organization is a strong, loyal corps of citizens contributing their time and talents.

Without this volunteer help and understanding no special event will ever get far. Success depends upon the joint efforts of volunteers and staff. Most staff workers realize these facts of life, and know that they must learn to work with and appreciate volunteers.

In turn this handbook has been developed for the more than 500,000 organizations that can profitably make use of it. And primarily for the two groups of people who, the authors believe, will find it an invaluable how-to-do-it guidebook, with directions and mileposts clearly marked:

1. *For volunteers*, to help them learn the steps and methods which must be followed to make special events successful.

2. *For staff members*, to ease their way so they can make the fullest possible use of volunteers. Most staff workers have had only limited experience in planning special events. Thousands of local organizations with small staffs must depend upon one person to jump in and carry the extra responsibility for staging a special event. The work of volunteers makes possible the success of the staff worker who directs their efforts!

There is, however, a third group (the pros) who will find this handbook useful: professional people in public relations, advertising, and communications. They are experienced and seasoned in most areas of public relations, but many of them only occasionally draw assignments to handle a special event. This book includes stimulating ideas, checklists and other important information which they ought to know but which would take them much time and tedious effort to work out, compile, and organize. The book should, therefore, be extremely useful to these people—especially those in business and industry who, as individual citizens, can make a valuable contribution as volunteers.

What This Handbook Offers

Working guides, manuals, and handbooks dealing with many areas of program activities, public relations, and fund raising have for many years been used widely and successfully by organizations for staff and volunteers. Lack of such a working tool for special events stimulated and challenged the authors to develop this working guide based on proven practices and successful experiences in the field.

This is a how-to-do-it book. It doesn't just tell *what* to do. The text, checklists, case studies, experience reports, sample materials and ideas for special events provide the *how*.

Experience reports are included in many chapters, describing successful special events. Case studies document more fully some of the major events. Many more appear in Part IV, under the heading "Brainstorming Ideas." All of these will be found listed in the Table of Contents.

The authors sincerely hope this handbook will serve as a practical and valuable working guide for volunteers as well as for staff members given the responsibility—and the *opportunity!* we insist—to be in charge of special events for their organizations. If you come to feel the warm glow of satisfaction that follows a successful special event, we will consider our efforts well rewarded.

E.R.L.—B.E.S.

PART I
BASIC PLANNING FOR
SPECIAL EVENTS

1: Some Guidelines for Success

It is essential to know what is meant by the term "special event." So let us begin with some dictionary definitions.

A special event should always be related to some important *occasion* or *purpose,* for some *special* reason. *Webster's New Collegiate Dictionary* lists these capsule definitions:

SPECIAL (1) "Distinguished by some unusual quality: uncommon, noteworthy"; (2) "having an individual character or trait: peculiar, unique"; (3) "designed or selected for a particular purpose, occasion, or the like."

OCCASION (1) "a favorable opportunity"; (2) "A juncture: point of time, one made critical by a concurrence of circumstances"; (3) "an occurrence: the immediate, inciting circumstance as distinguished from the real or fundamental cause"; (4) "a happening, occurrence, now usually time of happening"; (5) "a special event, ceremony, or function."

Broadly considered, a special event should in some way be identified with the purpose of an organization or institution*— its reason for existing and for seeking public understanding and support.

How Important Is the Event?

The most important guideline is: Determine whether the proposed event is important enough, is identified sufficiently with a purpose or service of the organization and justifies the effort and cost necessary to assure the event's success.

Some events which could be important for an organization are listed below.

---

*The words *organization* and *institution* are synonymous. A YMCA is usually designated as a youth organization. A museum, hospital, college or school is termed an institution. *Organization* will be used in this book as applying to both.

The range is wide.

- Reporting the results of current activities, services, or projects.
- Introducing new activities or services.
- Reporting the completion of long-range services or projects.
- Interpreting policies, practices, program activities—either those in effect, or perhaps even new or proposed, related to controversial problems of public concern. The format might be a symposium or forum, with authorities as participants and opportunity for discussion and conclusions.
- Dedication of a new building, perhaps honoring the donor.
- Open house to make members, contributors, community leaders and other interested individuals more familiar with the organization's purposes, activities, and services, thus leading to their more active involvement.
- Annual dinner or meeting, lively and entertaining in format and program, but also a "trusteeship" report recounting accomplishments during the year and telling of plans for the future.
- Testimonial dinner or meeting to recognize outstanding services or achievements of individuals—board or committee members, volunteer workers, professional and staff personnel.
- Inauguration or retirement of a president or chief officer.
- Observance of an anniversary, be it 5, 10, 25, 50, 100 years or more, honoring an organization's progress and future goals.

Special events are vital and essential during fund-raising campaigns, for interpretation, publicity, and cultivation. They may take the form of:

- Kickoff dinner or meeting for an annual fund drive or a capital campaign.
- Kickoff dinner or meeting for a membership drive.
- Charity ball or dance for a scholarship fund or to benefit some other special project.
- Theater or movie benefit for some special project or purpose—a concert, art auction, tour of historic homes or gardens, a sale, bazaar or festival to raise funds.
- Fashion show, bridge party, wine-tasting party, or some other occasion of a social nature, the proceeds to go for some special project.
- "Work program" manned by volunteers—car washing, collection of paper, clothing, furniture, a Christmas tree sale, pancake breakfast, strawberry festival.
- Recognition or "appreciation" dinner or meeting honoring volunteers, to which volunteers, contributors, trustees, and staff are invited.

One important purpose of a special event is to educate and motivate volunteers. To repeat for emphasis two key sentences in the Introduction: "Volunteers are the backbone of every successful voluntary organization. . . . Backing up every successful organization is a strong, loyal corps of citizens contributing their time and talents."

Volunteers must be informed and enthusiastic to be most effective. They cannot attend all functions by any means, but should be encouraged to go to major events such as an open house, an annual dinner, or the kickoff for a campaign where policy matters, accomplishments, problems, and future plans are to be discussed. Volunteers also should be on a must mailing list to receive important publications, bulletins and announcements of meetings to keep them informed.

They Are All Different

No two special events are alike. There is no simple formula, no one set of rules or specifications that can be relied upon. But there are some basic principles and tested methods which must be followed.

Every event will have its own different and peculiar kinds of problems—sometimes developing into near crises that have never come up before. These problems will call for alertness, imagination, thoroughness in planning, and constant attention to details. One oversight, error, or failure in even a small detail can mar an event and may seriously minimize the results desired. A series of fumbles can multiply the damages out of all proportion.

Here is an example of such a painful experience: A motion picture *Give Us the Earth* had been produced for release to theaters throughout the United States as one of Herbert Morgan's *Theater of Life* series. It told the story of a YMCA rural work project, thus providing an unusual opportunity for interpretation of the YMCA's World Service program.

A premiere showing of the film was scheduled at an international convention in Atlantic City attended by several thousand delegates. A large auditorium served as a theater. A fireproof booth and union projectionists were required at considerable cost. The hour arrived and the auditorium was packed with nearly a thousand delegates.

After a brief introduction to promote bookings through local theaters the lights were turned down. Nothing happened as one . . . two . . . three minutes passed. The audience, sitting in the dark, became restless. Five minutes passed, which seemed an eternity to the hapless staff member in charge. Impatient people began to leave amid sounds of scurrying in the dark and mumbling voices. By the time the trouble was located—some seven or eight minutes in all—half the audience had disappeared. The trouble? The power cable from the projection booth to a wall outlet near the floor had been kicked out by some innocent person in the audience.

So the most important watchwords are: (1) plan carefully; (2) proceed according to plan, alert to see that every detail is handled; (3) check and double-check in advance, and once again on location; (4) don't relax until the final curtain is down.

"Time and Timing"

One of the most successful public relations and special events experts in New York City over a period of three decades, the late Manny Strauss, held constantly before himself and his clients the importance of "time and timing" in realizing best results. He demonstrated the wisdom of this principle, or rule, in staging many special events.

Obviously, not everything can be made into a special event. But in the course of any given year every organization has in its activities and services, its growth and planning, or in its development and history, the components for some special event important enough to warrant public interest and promote public support. The problem is to evaluate the possibilities with awareness of "time and timing."

Planning and Promotion

In short-range perspective *time* is important—allowing enough time for careful planning and effective promotion. Many a special event has turned out to be a borderline success, a near failure, or even a flop because of a late start resulting in poor planning and promotion.

With many details to be handled, pressures build up and may prevent the proper handling of arrangements. Unexpected problems develop—the unpredictables that inevitably seem to happen. Then, when everybody is in a frenzy trying to meet the deadline, oversights and errors occur which may be disastrous if not caught in time.

There is another facet to the time factor. What about the date? When should the event be held for best attendance? Does the date avoid holidays or holiday weekends? Are there competitive events scheduled which might affect publicity and attendance? In a New England community recently an art auction was scheduled without realizing there would be a high-school band rehearsal going on at the same time in the next room.

In most communities the chamber of commerce or some other organization acts as a clearinghouse for registering advance dates and should be consulted. Even then, you should check coming events in the building to be used!

The Long-Range Perspective

The timing factor is most important in relation to major events, such as an anniversary observance, capital campaign, announcement of an important change in policy, launching of a new service or activity. Is the timing right as measured against the organization's milestones and stage of development?

There are many other events that do not require such critical judgment. These lesser events are obviously important in their relationship to current activities— an annual dinner, a membership drive, open house, theater parties and other benefits for special fund-raising projects.

If the purpose of the event is groundwork cultivation leading up to a financial campaign, it may be held as a private dinner on special invitation or a small private meeting. If it is for launching a membership drive, it may well be an informal dinner or luncheon (plenty of action and humor) with attendance by invitation or through promotion and publicity. If the event is to interpret and promote some program activity or service, an even more informal program may be most successful. If it is a problem of current public interest or concern, a forum, debate, or symposium may be the best format.

Questions to Be Answered

Before reaching a final decision to stage a special event, there are some important questions: Exactly what is the event expected to accomplish? Are the objectives agreed upon and stated clearly? Is the event planned to reach special groups—and, specifically, what groups? Will it report or deal with some identified result or objective attained or sought? Does it seek directly or indirectly to bring in new members, increase attendance or participation, develop financial support? Or will it be direct cultivation preceding or during a fund-raising campaign? Who should be involved in the planning and arrangements?

Planning Comes First

Someone has said, "Your public relations, good or bad, provide a barometer reading of success or failure." A special event successfully staged provides an opportunity to brighten and sharpen an organization's image, improve the climate and public response which contribute to its success. It is a painful fact, known to those who have suffered, that an event poorly handled can tarnish the image, chill the climate, and sour public response to the point of back-fence criticism and "Letters to the Editor"—or worse, negative reactions from members, volunteers, contributors and trustees.

Following these broad considerations, there are specific steps and methods to be learned (by hard experience sometimes) and followed. The first and most important of these is planning ahead.

David M. Church, in his booklet "How to Succeed With Volunteers," published by the National Public Relations Council of Health and Welfare Services, Inc., says:

Where professional and volunteer work side by side as partners, with mutual respect for each other's skills and abilities, voluntarism thrives and the agency thrives. Everybody benefits. The professional is freed from time-consuming tasks and given opportunity to bring his professional techniques into full bloom. The volunteer achieves not only usefulness but a sense of satisfaction. The public reacts to the apparent satisfaction of the volunteer, while the professional is making full use of his or her knowledge and consequently the agency gains public respect and support. Such successful voluntarism requires planning ahead.

The success of any special event depends upon the group of people who are charged with responsibility for all planning, arrangements, staging, promotion, and publicity. The Planning Committee, or whatever it may be called, is that group of people "where professional and volunteer work side by side as partners" to produce a successful special event.

Planning Committee—Key to Success

No matter what the event, it should be the product of intelligent consideration by a carefully selected Planning Committee. The size of the committee will depend upon how complex, how widely involved, and how extended the event will be. To be most effective, the committee should be made up of carefully chosen individuals who have some knowledge of the organization's policies, program, and services. Needed are one or more people with imagination whose good judgment and flexibility in dealing with problems can be relied upon, along with an ability to plan intelligently—which means a combined sense of timing, organization, and detail. Other added qualities will help—persistence, patience, and a sense of humor. This is a big order, but it's worth trying for, counting on the combined abilities of a number of people.

The chairman of the Planning Committee is the key person, as with all committees. He or she should be a strong, respected leader from the organization, one who has a broad knowledge of the organization's purposes and program. Equally important, he should have a good knowledge of the community, recognized experience and leadership in business, industry, education—a person who has what is termed "good public relations sense."

It will be fortunate if one or two people can be enlisted with professional experience in public relations, advertising, or communications. Such a person will usually make a competent chairman for a special events Planning Committee. The best sources for these people are the public relations departments of corporations and local business firms, or some public service organization.

Many corporations and business firms encourage their personnel to participate in the activities of voluntary agencies. They recognize this policy as part of being a good "corporate citizen" and are glad to approve the participation as part of their community relations program. Many kinds of talent are available. Most organizations will find, if they make an inventory, that they already have in their membership some of these people who will be glad to serve.

In their areas of competence people should be sought who are willing to operate on their experience. It adds nothing but confusion to have a man or woman who comes on a committee to "spread wisdom," impressively outlines a list of what-to-do items, and then goes home to tell everyone about all the help given and who feels that his or her advice is a golden contribution. Try to select people who have a reputation for delivering. They are the people who come in with ideas, ask "Are they practical? Have you the staff to carry them out?" and then proceed to enlist the help needed.

The Planning Committee for a major event, such as an anniversary observance or a capital campaign, should be expanded to represent community leadership—both men and women. Included should be a civic leader, an active and respected business leader, a socially prominent man or woman, an educator, a religious leader, along with one or more professional leaders—architect, engineer, lawyer, etc.

The makeup of the Planning Committee will vary, of course, depending upon the nature of the organization, its field of service, and the leadership available for recruitment. The most important considerations are: (1) a well-balanced committee; (2) a committee not so large that it becomes unwieldy; (3) with subcommittees, if necessary, for a major and extended observance, such as an anniversary or a capital campaign.

When such a committee begins planning for a special event it must determine what will make the event appealing, practical, and appropriate for the occasion and purpose in mind. Sometimes the nature of the occasion will determine the type of event and how it should be programmed. This is often the case when public relations or cultivation is the purpose. But if the event is for fund raising —a benefit, or a testimonial dinner—good entertainment is a first consideration. For it will be the deciding factor, more so even than the purpose, in drawing an attendance to sell out the house.

If the event is a campaign kickoff, appropriate entertainment becomes the "icing on the cake" for serious program items that endeavor to explain, interpret and convince in order to win a favorable response from potential contributors at some later date.

Whatever the occasion, imaginative ideas that will spare the audience dullness and sleep-inducing boredom are at a premium. The ideas may have to do with program content, how the event is staged, or how it is to be publicized and promoted. Even one small, imaginative idea in each of these areas can play an important part in creating the atmosphere for a successful event.

A committee "brainstorming" session early in the planning stage will some-times produce good ideas. But often imaginations are slow and the committee may well become desperate in trying to reach agreement on anything. That is the time when tested and proven imaginative ideas can prove useful.

This book offers a variety of such ideas in its reports of successful events. These tested ideas and events can be of great help to a Planning Committee in reaching decisions. Or they may trigger some variation or combination of ideas that will meet the basic requirements of the occasion. The reports are of value for much more than their suggestion of ideas, however. Many state the purpose of the event, explain what was done, and evaluate results. Part II deals with special events held for public relations and cultivation purposes. Part III deals with fund-raising events. Part IV deals with promotion and publicity, and we give a roundup of new and imaginative events put on by organizations in many cities and diverse locales.

Promoting Special Events

In chapters throughout this book specific references are made to the importance of publicity and promotion. Lest there be any confusion, *publicity* suggestions usually apply to the communications media—the press, radio, television, etc.

Promotion for special events should be kept in mind for both public relations and fund-raising events, for some kinds can be used successfully in either case—anniversaries and open-house events are examples. Events such as a building dedication, annual meeting, award dinner, charity ball or campaign kick-off usu-ally depend upon publicity. Here are only a few of the multitude of promo-tion materials that can be considered if they are appropriate: posters, bumper stickers, exhibits, displays, car cards, billboards, announcement cards for store counters, balloons, postage meter imprints, envelope stuffers. Every promotion is based on an unusual idea.

Department stores and utilities—telephone, lighting and water companies—will often enclose stuffers with monthly bill statements for fund-raising events—even stuffers which include contribution blanks for fund-raising efforts. They rec-ognize this policy as an essential part of their own community relations efforts.

The above comments are a "bridge" reminder, therefore, for all organizations to make use of both methods when possible. For specific suggestions regarding publicity see Part IV. For promotion, develop whatever ideas, methods and ma-terials your committee can dream up in brainstorming sessions that may prove appropriate and acceptable.

Basic Checklist for Planning Committee

Below are some over-all considerations that must be understood and kept in mind by a Planning Committee from the time of its first meeting to the filing of a final report when the event has been successfully completed.

● The event must be important enought to attract the attention of the groups the organization wishes to reach.

● It must be the right kind of event, suited to the tastes of the audience, in order to draw attendance in competition with other events.

● It must be significant—identified clearly with some aspect of the organiza-tion's over-all program, policies, and purposes—to warrant the time, effort, and cost involved.

● It must be interesting—presented in an entertaining or dramatic form that will hold the attention of the audience.

● It must be convincing—creating a desire in people to respond in some way, to make a decision, to join or participate, to support through volunteer service, or to make a financial contribution.

● It must be interpreted—promoted effectively in advance through printed pieces and other methods to build attendance.

● It must be publicized through communications media—covered or reported by newspapers, radio, television to arouse interest and encourage response.

● Thank-you letters should go to volunteers, local business firms, and groups who have contributed in any way to make the event a success.

● There should be a final report, telling of the mistakes and successes, for use in planning the next special event.

● Follow up with cultivation materials to reach members, volunteers, contrib-utors, and people on other mailing lists beyond the range of local publications. The follow-up may be for information or cultivation purposes, or may be a direct appeal for funds or volunteer service.

● Producing an event without adequate insurance coverage is asking for trouble. While the majority of events take place without mishap, accidents can occur. Consequently, the planners of an event should have a down-to-earth talk with a reliable insurance broker who can offer sound advice regarding proper insurance coverage.

● Checklists are a must. They provide a step-by-step guide and serve as a working tool. Those included in the chapters which follow are based on experi-ence, either of the contributing individual or organization or of the authors. Other of the lists combine items from several sources.

These lists should be used as a basis for developing, item by item, a final checklist tailored for the event that is being planned. Thus they can most effec-tively serve their purpose. Remember, every special event differs in certain as-pects and details from previous ones.

A Veteran Volunteer's Testimony (Mrs. Leonard H. Bernheim)

It seems appropriate that readers of this handbook should have an opportunity to hear from an experienced and widely respected volunteer worker. Mrs. Leon-ard H. Bernheim speaks with the knowledge gained from many years of dedi-cated service with a score of local and national organizations. A partial list of these organizations includes: Association for the Aid of Crippled Children, Fed-eration of Jewish Philanthropies, National Jewish Welfare Board, National So-cial Welfare Assembly, United Neighborhood Houses, Social Work Recruiting Commission of Greater New York, Community Council of Greater New York, New York School of Social Work, Columbia University, Community Service Society of New York, National Conference of Social Welfare.

Mrs. Bernheim has been the recipient of numerous awards, including: New York State Welfare Conference Award, Columbia University Bi-Centennial

Medal, National Jewish Welfare Board, Frank L. Weil Award, 1960, Blanche Ittleson Award, 1963, and Naomi Lehman Memorial Foundation Award.

Mrs. Bernheim sums up her experience as follows:

It is axiomatic that every volunteer, whether a service volunteer, a board member or a fund raiser must know his or her agency, and have empathy and excitement for it. I have found in my many years with both small and large organizations that there is not sufficient orientation for new lay workers and not enough continuing education for the more experienced ones. I would suggest that one or two initial meetings in a well-respected board member's home, over a cup of tea or a cocktail, can be most helpful—giving people a chance to learn, ask questions about program and financing, and meet some of the other volunteers and professionals in the agency.

Social events, such as dinners and cocktail parties, which bring together lay people with their spouses and members of the professional staff usually bring about a better rapport and understanding. No one can interpret or fund-raise for an agency without actually seeing it in action and the people it serves. Today it is not sufficient to learn only about one's own organization, but it is important to know how it dovetails, parallels or is different from governmental and new anti-poverty agencies. It is important to know how one fits into the community fund, federation, health and welfare council.

No one is so altruistic that he can work for years without some recognition. I love every honor I have received, whether it has been a citation, an award, a party in my honor, or my picture in the newspaper. Committee chairmen will get best results by making volunteers feel important and needed.

Loyalty is of utmost importance. It's very American to criticize everyone and everything. It may lose you a large gift and give the agency a bad name by airing complaints in the A & P or at the country club. Constructive criticism, however, should be welcomed in meetings by both staff and board alike.

All my life I have received encouragement, guidance and inspiration from professionals. One executive director gave me much social welfare literature to read, and encouraged me to take courses at the Columbia University School of Social Work. There is no doubt, although it is most time consuming, that a sensitive, warm and educating member of staff can do miracles to keep a lay person interested and enthusiastic—which of course makes for a more successful agency.

It is wonderful to have an amateur profession that you can begin at school age and never have to worry about forced retirement at sixty-five!

2: Expense Underwriting and Sponsorship

Many organizations fail to take advantage of underwriting possibilities. On the other hand, some "beat to death" the patience of business and industrial firms by too much pressure or too frequent appeals. Merchants especially are besieged, feel under pressure and may become resentful. It is important to use good judgment, lest your organization minimize or lose contributions for annual fund drives and capital campaigns. There are a variety of ways in which an organization may seek underwriting for expenses required to stage fund-raising benefits and other special events.

Patrons' List

The patrons' list is a frequent method of guaranteeing costs for charity balls and theater benefits, through the generosity of individuals who are usually closely related to an organization. Business firms and corporations are sometimes on patrons' lists, but more often subscribe for space in souvenir programs and "journals." Underwriting of expenses can take other forms, such as the contribution of merchandise or services for door prizes and raffles, food costs and other direct expenses. It is reassuring to ticket purchasers for a benefit event to know that their contribution will be used fully for the purposes stated—and also an indication of the agency's concern for good management in keeping fund-raising expenses at the lowest possible amount.

Underwriting by Business Firms and Corporations

Support for community projects—to help underwrite expenses for program activities and services, as well as benefit events—has been provided increasingly during the last twenty years by corporations and local business firms. A program or service to help meet a community need or problem may become quite special in its importance. Inevitably it will include one or more special events, large or small, keyed to a special need or purpose that lifts them to a priority position above normal activities or services of an organization. Management has recognized, by and large, an obligation and responsibility as a corporate good citizen to support activities of voluntary organizations that are enriching community life. One form of support is in contributing to help underwrite the cost for special projects. Cosponsorship is another form.

Partial underwriting of expenses, or even financial sponsorship of special events is usually given consideration by Contributions Committees of corporations and business firms. Proposals of several kinds may be made:

1. Cosponsorship with a community organization, publicly acknowledged, and underwriting all or a portion of the costs for a program project carried on by the organization—a project that will help promote and develop a constructive community service. Within the framework of the project, there will usually be various kinds of special events—for large audiences or small groups—which will allow opportunity for public identification and recognition.

2. Cosponsorship and underwriting for a major special event that gives consideration to a problem of community-wide concern (and to ways of dealing with it), such as drug addiction, race relations, crime, juvenile delinquency, conservation, pollution, etc.

3. Underwriting of expenses (with or without identification) or sponsorship for a benefit event, the proceeds to be used for a particular activity, service or purpose of an organization. This kind of support sometimes may take the form of an unrestricted contribution toward the over-all operating costs of the organition.

Required, of course, is a carefully thought-out and well-presented case (summarized in two or three pages) explaining the service or activity or event, and how it will help meet a community problem and contribute constructively to community life. The presentation should be backed by a detailed budget showing just what the money is to be spent for in mounting the event—decorations, extra personnel, promotion, etc. In the case of national corporations a favorable response is most likely for projects proposed by organizations operating in plant communities. Often a proposal made locally must be referred to the corporation's headquarters along with a recommendation for its approval.

Here are some examples of underwriting, which are reported in more detail later.

● Summer Scenic Flights are sponsored in California for a local American Cancer Society chapter by Southwest Airlines, with proceeds going to the American Cancer Society.

● The Narragansett Brewing Company, in Rhode Island, sponsored Boston Symphony "Hi-Neighbor" Pops Concerts for ten years, with proceeds from the benefits going to six hospitals and four other organizations.

● In Florida, the Used Car Dealers Association sponsored a Used Car Auction for the Duval County Cancer Society which brought in $3,520.

● The Midland Mall Shopping Center in Providence, R.I., sponsored an Arts Festival Week for the Federated Arts Fund, providing a budget of $1,000 for expenses.

● In New York City the United Hospital Fund has for twenty years staged a Hospital Week rally at Rockefeller Plaza sponsored by fashion stores, magazines, wholesale houses, and other fashion organizations.

Examples of Corporate Sponsorship

Special events are not always mass audience events, although the term has come to be thus associated in many people's minds. An anniversary observance, which continues over several months or even a year, is generally considered to be a special event. A convocation for a capital funds drive may include a combination of several adjunct events.

Program projects and services of any nature or size, in another sense, can be considered special events, even though they may continue over an extended period of time, if they contribute to solving community problems and meeting human needs. At the community level such co-operation on the part of corporations and local business firms in the cosponsorship of worthy projects with voluntary organizations will be appreciated and given recognition as good community relations. Increasingly, business and industry are realizing the importance of supporting programs, projects and institutions to improve the communities in which they operate.

Celanese Corporation Projects

In a recently published booklet, the Celanese Corporation speaks as follows:

We are sometimes asked what a corporation like Celanese is doing, above and beyond its role as a supplier of useful products, to improve the quality of life for all of us. We try to answer that question in this booklet, not because we think we have done enough or cannot do more, but because we believe it is a question that deserves an answer these days.

The Celanese Corporation is doing something about the problems of our times in a variety of programs and projects related to environment, education, equal opportunity in employment, assistance to small businesses, low-income housing, and consumer information. Below are several examples of educational programs directly related to the urban crisis, which are funded by Celanese:

—An eight-week secretarial training and liberal art program, now in its fourth year, at Hampton Institute in Virginia for black high-school graduates. At the end of the course they receive positions at Celanese.

—A twelve-week special training program, designed to prepare disadvantaged young people—both black and white but predominantly black—for jobs as laboratory assistants. This program, inaugurated in its research facility in Charlotte, N. C., was broadened to train these young people at Greenville (S. C.) Institute of Technology as lab assistants for jobs at the nearby Celanese plant in Greer, S. C.

—The Stevens Technical Enrichment Program (STEP) is a summer program for educationally and economically disadvantaged high-school students with promising educational potential. The program is run by Stevens Institute of Technology with support from various corporations, including Celanese. The program has graduated thirty students, twenty-five of whom have enrolled in college.

—As a member of the New York City Urban Coalition, Celanese has taken an active role in the Educational Task Force which is conducting a wide range of programs designed to aid education. One of these has included funding community groups such as the Bronx Parents Association, providing funds and staff support for the Ruppert Renewal Committee, a group of parents and teachers who are designing a new high-school complex, and new community participation curricula.

—Another Celanese project is designing an experimental curriculum to be used on the junior high-school level in New York City's Clinton Program, an attempt to extend formal education beyond the classroom walls. Celanese also produced a film for the New York Urban Coalition documenting Dr. Galeb Gattegno's techniques for teaching young children reading and arithmetic.

Other Projects

In addition to the illustrations of co-operation listed above, we are summarizing four outstanding examples below. The reports—issued by American Business Press, Inc., the Dayton Hudson Corporation, the General Electric Company and Xerox Corporation—suggest the possibility of similar cosponsorships that might be developed in many communities throughout the United States.

Solving the Crisis in Our Cities.   American Business Press, New York.

This report is a summary of corporate programs designed to help alleviate urban social problems. It is a workbook of ideas to help companies plan their investment in the future of their cities. Seventy or more brief case histories describe programs and projects initiated by companies, full of ideas that community service organizations might initiate in cosponsorship with business and industry firms and corporations. For a free copy of the booklet, as long as they last, write to Charles S. Mill, President, American Business Press, Inc., 205 East 42nd Street, New York, N.Y. 10017.

100 Small Beginnings.   General Electric Company, New York.

A 58-page booklet of brief case studies describing how G. E. people are trying to help disadvantaged minority groups in cities across the nation. In many cases the efforts are clearly company activities and personal activities making contributions to the needs of communities. The booklet contains a multitude of ideas, and illustrates how business and industry can work for and with community organizations, directing efforts where they will do the most good in terms of local needs. For a free copy, write to General Electric Company, 570 Lexington Avenue, Room 801, Attn. L. W. O'Brien, New York 10022.

Toward Fulfilling Our Social Responsibility.   Dayton Hudson Corporation, Minneapolis, Minn.

Two annual reports are available—1970 and 1971. The Dayton Hudson Corporation, through its Foundation, contributes nearly $2 million annually to improve the communities in which it operates department stores and specialty stores. Projects, programs and institutions were awarded grants ranging from $100 to $100,000 in the categories of Environmental and Social Action, Cultural Support and Educational Support.

These two reports describe a wide range of support for community organizations and voluntary agencies through seventeen operating companies in nineteen states. Write to Robert W. MacGregor, Executive Director, Dayton Hudson Foundation, 700 Nicollet Mall, Minneapolis, Minn. 55402 for a free copy, as long as they last.

"240 Man-Months a Year"   Xerox Corporation, Stamford, Conn.

A most enlightened and advanced step taken by Xerox Corporation offering a new and valuable kind of "underwriting" support for a worthy cause beyond the point of cash contributions was reported by Denny Griswold in *Public Relations News* (Sept. 27, 1971) as "what is even *more needed*—the donation of business know-how."

"It is for this reason," the report reads, "that we applaud the recent decision of Xerox Corporation to *contribute part of its employes' paid time to social service projects*. In brief, the public relations-oriented company will donate 240 man-months a year to any such 'public or private, non-profit, legitimate, existing organization' anywhere in the world. Anyone who has worked for Xerox for at least three years, regardless of whether he be an executive or paid by the hour, is entitled to participate for any period up to a year without loss of compensation or 'status and opportunity for advancement' upon his return.

"Whether projects qualify will be determined by a seven-member evaluation committee (a 'representative cross-section of Xerox people') with rotating membership. Employee identification is to be removed from applications and no decisions can be reviewed or amended. Xerox's president, C. Peter McColough, keenly observes that most public service programs are handicapped by a shortage of 'people of talent, dedication, imagination, and competence.'

"This personnel-lending program is clearly ploughing new ground and it will be followed closely by PR executives. It is an effort which supports *the basic concept of business PR* that a corporation is an integral part of society and must contribute to the social good if it is to continue to operate."

How much can be accomplished in this new direction can be determined if companies will follow the example of Xerox, encouraging employes to give to the organization of their choice full time for a month, six weeks, or more to help guide to a successful finish a special program or project, or a special event—a membership or fund-raising drive, an anti-pollution campaign, a theater or dance benefit, an annual dinner or anniversary.

Everything was a new idea once upon a time. This one might originate from *your* side of the street. Why not broach the matter to a large, public-spirited company in your community for an important special program or special event you are planning?

CASE STUDIES AND EXPERIENCE REPORTS

"Hi-Gear," Training for Jobs

This project to help solve the problem of the hard-core unemployed in Hartford, Conn., was sponsored in 1968 by Aetna Life & Casualty with the assistance of the Urban League of Greater Hartford and the city's school system.

The project was undertaken when the company discovered that twenty-five job openings for licensed automobile drivers were going unfilled every month in the Hartford area, but that, at the same time, only fifteen of a representative group of 311 disadvantaged young men had driving licenses. As the project developed, four courses were held. Each lasted six weeks and each provided thirty-six hours of classroom instruction and eight hours of driving in dual-con-controlled cars. Classes were held either within or on the fringe of the Negro district. Upon completion of each course there was a "Graduation Day" when students took their license tests, administered by special arrangement with the state motor vehicle bureau. Fees for tests and driver's licenses were paid by Aetna.

Of the sixty-nine candidates enrolled, fifty-three completed the course and 90 per cent of these passed the driver's examination (70 per cent is the general public average). As complete a survey as possible was subsequently made of graduates. This indicated that 70 per cent had landed jobs dependent upon their having a driving license. Expenses for the program, exclusive of salaries of regular personnel but including those of instructors, were $11,450.

(Case Study No. 1205, Vol. XXV, No. 23,
Public Relations News, June 9, 1969)

Concerts and Ballet in Philadelphia

The Philadelphia Gas Works contributes generously to the performing arts. During the last two seasons, it has financed thirteen free performances by graduates of conservatories. Through these "Franklin Concerts" the performers find engagements "at a dignified fee" before they become established professionals. PGW has sponsored 84 such performances in the neighborhood of its main office, distributing at each an eight-page booklet which it developed and which illustrates the instruments used, tells about the origin of each and explains how the elements of a symphony orchestra are co-ordinated.

"The Dance Happens in Philadelphia" is a PGW-originated program in which performances by the Philadelphia Civic Ballet Company of all kinds of ballet— folk, modern, jazz, classical—are presented in schools and recreation centers, mainly in depressed areas. More than 20,000 persons have attended the events, many seeing such performances for the first time.

(Case Study No. 1248, Vol. XXVI, No. 17,
Public Relations News, April 27, 1970)

High-School Choir Sounds a New Note for Soviets

When an unusual corps of "ambassadors" recently made a unique visit to the U.S.S.R., they were accompanied by John Canning, manager of Press Relations, American Oil Company, Chicago, Ill., who handled relations with the media for the group. The ambassadors were the 108-voice Viking Choir from Homewood-Flossmoor High School thirty miles southwest of Chicago. It is believed to be the first time that a U.S. high-school has performed in the Soviet Union. (Austria and The Netherlands were also visited during the trip.) The overseas activity reflects the school's philosophy that it "must do far more than transmit information and develop skills," the "ultimate measure of its success" being "*the extra shares* that its graduates contribute to a free society."

(Vol. XXVI, No. 17,
Public Relations News, April 27, 1970)

Service Centers Aid Women's Clubs

In New Jersey the Trenton Trust Company searched for ways in which it could offer women beyond-the-call-of-duty services. It was discovered that their clubs (PTA, church, patriotic, social, etc.) were having difficulty in building programs which would attract good attendance at meetings and encourage members to participate in community service work. To assist these clubs the Service Center for Women's Clubs, headquartered at the bank, was developed. Club programs and needs were analyzed. News media were studied for timely subjects to build meetings around and information about speaker's bureaus was collected. Then, with the aid of the Greater Trenton Chamber of Commerce and the Trenton Public Library, a list of women's groups was compiled. A registration card was sent to each group describing the new service and informing them that the reference file contained material on fifty-five subjects and would be "continuous in growth." The groups were invited to make an appointment to discuss programs and speakers.

Each spring a "Program Sampling Day" is staged. Representatives of all Center-registered clubs are invited by letter to assemble at 10 A.M. to meet persons who have programs to offer. The session continues through a sandwich luncheon (which costs each participant $1.50) and ends at 2:30 P.M. Since the Center was established in 1966, nearly 200 clubs with more than 45,000 members have received assistance in planning programs and special events.

(Case Study No. 1157, *Public Relations News,*
June 3, 1968.)

PART II
PUBLIC RELATIONS
AND CULTIVATION EVENTS

3:   Anniversary and Annual Events

Anniversaries offer organizations and institutions unusual opportunities for special events of significance. They should be seriously considered, therefore, and observed for their potential promotional value. How important and valuable they become depends on level of approach, planning, and action.

Frequently an upcoming anniversary is seen as an opportunity for a great celebration—a chance to sing songs of praise, beat drums, and point with pride to the organization's history, including everybody and everything identified with all its glorious accomplishments. Enthusiasm blows up the balloon. Then ambitious plans begin to take shape. Well and good, *but . . .*

An anniversary *is* an important occasion, a milestone along the tenuous road of progress and growth. The milestone may mark 5 years, 25, 50, 75, 100 or more. The longer the span of years, the more important the occasion. There is justification for celebrating the past, with due credit and banners to declare what has been accomplished. But that is not enough. The real point is that an anniversary calls for some degree of dignity and vision, some depth and perspective, along with the fanfare. It should be linked with the future as well as the past, with a more serious note which will make the observance—whether a week, a month, or longer—more significant and rewarding. With this in view it then becomes a medium for presenting a panorama of facts and information made colorful, interesting, and convincing, dealing with the organization's future as well as its past—its plans, its problems, its hopes, its goals.

We all know the old and well-worn saying that "nothing is deader than yesterday's news." This is truer these days than ever before, with our instant worldwide communications. Likewise, nothing presents to most people a duller, less important picture than the history of an organization's yesterday displayed for glorification alone. *But* when the history becomes a background for plans and goals in charting the future, the minds of people whose approval, participation, and support your organization needs are challenged.

If you expect your anniversary observance to be successful and valuable to your organization, your Planning Committee will do well to keep before it that line from *The Tempest* which is inscribed in the National Archives Building in Washington, D.C.: *What is past is prologue.*

How Significant Is Your Anniversary?

In terms of years, is the anniversary significant enough to warrant observance? Two important factors here are *time* and *impact*. How much stature can be claimed, how much impact and influence on your publics, over how long a period of time?

Most organizations, whether working at a community level or with publics more widespread, can justify a tenth anniversary observance. Even five years of progress can be noteworthy, depending upon how much of importance has been accomplished that can be interpreted and reported.

Hospitals, health, welfare, and medical organizations dealing with the personal problems of large segments of the population can relate with a strong emotional appeal to individuals. Five or ten years of service may provide a remarkable story that can be documented, especially in these times of amazing advances in science and medicine.

Institutions such as colleges, churches, and other religious, educational, and cultural organizations may require a longer period—say 20 or 25 years—to bring their impact into sharp focus.

A 50th anniversary holds significance for any respected organization. And when it has been active and successful for 75 to 100 years, or even longer, the milestone is indeed worth noting. This is especially true, and convincing, if a good balance of past accomplishments and future plans can be presented.

Your Anchor Date and Key Events

Both time and timing—to repeat what has already been pointed out—are important factors in planning an anniversary observance. The timing can be flexible as to the period of time marked by the observance. It doesn't necessarily need to be 10, 25, 50, or 100 years. It can just as appropriately be a span of 5, 15, or 85 years if the timing is right in terms of the story you have to tell. And here the old saw comes to mind: "The case is bigger than the institution."

There must, however, be substantial and significant progress that can be documented. Research, consultation, and agreement by a group of competent people will determine whether a major observance is justified. If so, a series of events over a period of a week or month, or even longer, will probably be required. The over-all program must combine interest and drama, dignity and significance. Each event must have public appeal and be effectively planned, promoted, and staged. Only by meeting these requisites can a proper showcase be provided that will invite good participation, attract wide attention, and leave a positive impact.

It is necessary, within reasonable limits, to be opportunistic. The anchor date for the period of time the observance is related to can be flexible—so long as it is legitimate. It may be keyed to the date of founding, granting of a charter, formal organization of a board of trustees, actual beginning of operations, or the formal beginning of an operating program, activity, or service. This is an important consideration, in order to assure the best date for the actual observance. The summer period, as well as the Christmas and Lenten periods, should be avoided, naturally. So several significant dates connected with the founding should be considered, with the best one to be selected as the anchor date.

How long will the period of observance extend? A day does not do it justice. A week offers opportunities for depth, and is a practicable period for sustaining interest, participation, and publicity at high levels. A month? Perhaps, for a large, well-established organization, with wide public acceptance and support. Six months, however, is a long time to keep activities, public interest and publicity alive.

An "anniversary year" would be the exception, only possible for a national and widely known organization, perhaps for a centennial or bicentennial. It might be keyed to some major development such as a capital campaign or some other once-in-a-century goal. And for such a long period there must be high points—an opening week, a midway point, and a final week to bring into the spotlight the over-all objectives. Public interest cannot be sustained for so long a period without such high points.

Whatever the specified period of time to be covered, key dates should be carefully set so as to avoid other major occasions or events as much as possible. Such conflicts will limit the participation of public officials, and inhibit the key talent and committees you will need to enlist. Conflicts will also affect attendance and publicity.

Precautions can be easily observed for anniversaries in a given community or local area. If statewide, regional, or national participation is involved, the problem becomes more complex. Care should be taken not to schedule key dates during a national, state, or local "white-heat" election period. Widely observed religious or national holidays will likewise interfere with attendance, public interest, and news coverage.

Conflicting dates and events to be avoided can be checked accurately, even a year or more in advance, in most instances. In nearly every community the chamber of commerce or some other clearinghouse for scheduled events can be consulted. There are also sources for checking state and national holidays, special "weeks" and "days," and other widely observed occasions. These reference sources include the *World Almanac,* the *Directory of National Days and Weeks,* etc. The public library will be your source for such information.

If the dates that must be projected are several months or a year or two years ahead, wish for good luck. When the centennial observance of 1,300 YMCA's throughout the United States was planned, it was keyed to the founding date of the organization in London, England, on June 6, 1844. No one could have possibly anticipated that the actual date for the national and worldwide observance would fall on June 6, 1944—D-Day!

Saving factors in the YMCA's predicament were: thorough planning which had begun three years in advance, good organization, advance date deadlines set for all materials and publicity coverage, and the participation of hundreds of local "Centennial Public Relations Committees," staff, boards and Program Committees in following through to see that all was made ready. As a result, the only serious loss was Page One newspaper coverage on June 6—D-Day. Offsetting this loss was the nature of the anniversary observance programs on that date by several thousand YMCA's in the United States and around the world. D-Day provided the "perspective point" for assessing both past accomplishments and the future goals of an organization whose services to youth for 100 years had provided a constructive influence welcomed by people in fifty-two countries of the world.

One of the most significant special events for coverage was the world premiere of a "Youth Symphony" composed by Morton Gould and performed in Carnegie Hall by the New York Philharmonic Orchestra. The program was heard worldwide over the Columbia Broadcasting System.

Organization and Planning

The first step in planning is the most important one—the appointment of an Anniversary Committee. Success will depend largely upon how well this committee functions. It is the key committee responsible for the planning, organization and all other over-all aspects of the affair. It is the control group in seeing that plans are carried out on schedule. Staff and volunteer workers on various committees must fulfill their assignments, but there must be a final authority to coordinate, keep morale and effectiveness at high levels, and to bear down hard if necessary to get results. That final authority must be the Anniversary Committee and its members who carry the key posts of responsibility. The committee must be carefully selected—that goes without saying—with preferably no fewer than five or more than twelve members for a local organization, made up of the best people you can enlist.

When should preparation begin for an anniversary observance? That depends upon a number of factors. Is it a tenth or a fiftieth anniversary, a centennial, or a bicentennial? The longer the span of years, the more time required for research, for advance planning, organization and buildup. Sufficient time must be allowed for documenting historical dates and facts, for other fact-finding to develop important current information, for over-all planning, for the recruitment of leadership and committees, and for proper organization to assure smooth-running events and activities.

Within this framework there must also be enough time for the planning, production, and distribution of cultivation, interpretive, and promotion materials; for the arrangement of programs and the mechanics for staging events; for the enlistment of outstanding key-noters, headliners and other talent for major events; for the scheduling of best dates to avoid conflicts, as already noted, and for the booking of theaters or auditoriums if necessary.

The extent of participation geographically may also become an important factor in the planning time required. Will the anniversary activities be confined to a community or will they be statewide, regional, or national? Is the participation of many affiliate branches or chapters involved? The more extended and larger the participation, the more time needed for good preparation.

The nature of the organization, if it is national, is another factor to be considered in allowing time for preparations. Is it streamlined "from the top down" —with over-all direction and signals called from national, regional, or state headquarters? This means easier control, and less time in making decisions, planning, organization, distribution, etc.

If there is local autonomy, calling for the participation of several hundred or even several thousand local chapters, branches, or units, the whole process of communication and the steps which must be followed in preparations will require a much longer time schedule.

A final important factor is available staff. Is your organization well staffed or must it depend upon volunteers—as is the case with the National Tuberculosis and Respiratory Diseases Association, with some 2,700 local associations most of which are manned by volunteers? Working through volunteers is bound to require more time every step of the way.

Make It Significant!

The following statement by Harold Weiner, formerly executive director of the National Public Relations Council for Health and Welfare Organizations, tell what a community organization may do to add significance to its anniversary observance. Inherent in his statement is the fact that whatever course of action may be decided upon will still justify an appropriate special event to announce "an uncommon goal"—its special anniversary gift to the community.

Special events, such as anniversary celebrations, too often are narrowly self-conscious and self-serving. As such, they tend to lack appeal and meaning to all but those most involved in an organization's constituency. The event comes and goes, doing little or nothing to advance understanding of, or interest in, the event's sponsor. An opportunity to widen public knowledge and appreciation of the organization is consequently lost.

Why not view an organization's milestone as an opportunity for offering some extra dimension of public service? In addition to, or instead of, the benefit or dinner or organizational history, why not conceive a way to share the organization's expertise or resources more widely, even on a one-time, short-term basis? Instead of seeking a special anniversary gift *from* the community, why not give a special anniversary gift *to* the community?

Acquiring additional funds and/or column inches and air time is commonly viewed as an appropriate public relations objective for the celebration of a milestone. And I'm not arguing against the legitimacy of such an objective. But the contribution of an added dimension of community service by a social agency to celebrate its special time is a far more vital—not to mention uncommon—goal. And the pursuit of this kind of public relations goal is likely to produce unusual benefits to the uncommon agency that conceives it.

The Barton Gillet Checklist

CHECKLIST OF CONSIDERATIONS
FOR
CELEBRATING ANNIVERSARIES
(Courtesy of Barton-Gillet Company,
Baltimore, Maryland)

Whether an anniversary celebration is day-long or year-long, it must have unity. To help provide unity:

1. Consider adopting a theme for the celebration. The theme, preferably, should be expressive of some aspect of the purpose of the institution.

2. Consider the creation of a graphic symbol that expresses the theme. This anniversary symbol should be used in as many different places as possible: on letterheads and stationery, in publications, as part of exhibits, in movies and filmstrips, etc.

In organizing for an anniversary celebration, the first step generally is the formation of an Anniversary Committee, whose primary purpose is to consider how the anniversary is to be commemorated:

3. In addition to key members of the institutional staff, consider including on this committee at least one representative from every constituency of the institution. Then, if this is to be a lengthy celebration, make each constituency responsible for a single event. This will help all constituencies to experience a sense of participation and will help to take some of the burden off the staff member in charge, and/or the committee general chairman. Each constituency, however, must be responsible to the staff member in the conduct of its assigned duty.

As a rule, every celebration is centered around one or more major events. As the major events, consider:

4. A special program to be held on Founder's Day, the day on which the institution was incorporated or the day it opened its doors. This day provides the opportunity for speakers to contrast the past, the present, and the future of the organization.

5. The dedication of a new building or a new addition. Today, many institutions are in the midst of a development program. By careful planning several years in advance, a building can be brought to completion during the anniversary year, and the dedication of that building can be a major event.

6. A convocation. On such occasion an educational institution can confer honorary degrees on distinguished guests, and other institutions can confer special awards on eminent local, national and international figures.

7. A two- or three-day symposium to which distinguished scholars are invited for an interchange of ideas on a subject important to the institution.

8. A social event—a banquet or ball—to which the institution can invite many of its own constituents.

9. An arts festival—an extended program featuring music, art, drama. Although this may be particularly fitting for an educational or religious institution, with a little thought the idea can be applied to other institutions. For example, a hospital might present an art exhibit of paintings done by patients or by doctors—or paintings about medicine. There are numerous plays that center around medicine or medical practice, and much great music has been written or performed by doctors.

10. Traveling seminars. Some institutions have reasonably large groups of constituents in widespread areas. Because these people rarely can journey en masse to the institution, a team of representatives can go to them. This program can be planned for a weekend, which will enable the constituents to attend without interfering with their work and will enable members of the staff to leave the institution without neglecting their duties.

11. Consider a lecture series, with each lecture pertinent to some aspect of the theme of the celebration, the purpose of the institution, or a current national or international problem relating to the institution. Such lectures—frequently as many as six—are usually spaced out over several months and are delivered by nationally known figures.

It is essential that an anniversary celebration be designed for as many of the constituencies of an institution as possible. A religious-oriented institution should consider how the church—or members of the church—can be drawn into the celebration:

12. Can the head of the national church group be induced to issue a special church-wide proclamation regarding your institution—or a declaration setting aside a specific Sunday observance by member churches?

13. Can plans be devised for sermons or services to be sent to all ministers who might use them in a Sunday church service?

14. Within the institution can a special anniversary thanksgiving or celebration service be planned to which church members can be invited?

15. During the anniversary year can your institution be made the seat for church conferences or conventions?

16. Can an "open-house Sunday" be arranged—with a day-long program—to which members of your religious denomination can be invited?

17. Is yours the type of institution that could celebrate an anniversary by having an "old time revival meeting" or a "camp meeting"?

On the other hand, for a municipal, state, or federally supported institution:

18. Consider inviting the highest political figures in the city, state or nation to speak to a gathering of the total constituency—or as many as can be accommodated.

19. Consider a "taxpayers' open house" for the general public, the people whose taxes support the institution. Such an open house should provide guided tours, and—possibly—include snacks and soft drinks at the end of the tour.

Donors—those persons who have contributed to the financial support of the institution —and prospective donors form an important audience. For those persons whose support was, or could be, sufficiently great to merit recognition:

20. Consider a special banquet, preceded or followed by a guided tour which will enable guests to learn what their money has done—or can do—for the institution. In addition to donors and prospective donors, it occasionally is good public relations to invite the descendants of deceased donors who made outstanding gifts, even if those gifts were made 100 to 150 years ago.

The present members of an institution or organization—students, patients, members, staff, etc.—should also participate as much as possible in the celebration:

21. Many of these persons get a sense of participation merely by serving as volunteer workers to perform some of the endless chores involved in the celebration. Although this may seem like work, if such chores are properly organized they build camaraderie among the participants, a spirit that can be invaluable to an institution and to the success of the celebration.

22. Consider anniversary lectures, conferences, and souvenir publications that are directed solely to those persons who are a part of the institution today.

23. If present members of the institution publish any periodicals—such as student publications, internal house organs, etc.—encourage them to put out anniversary issues.

24. For those events that take place every year—commencement, annual meeting, etc. —plan a special anniversary program to give that particular occasion an out-of-the ordinary distinction.

An anniversary, of course, frequently provides the vehicle for getting former members —alumni, former patients, etc—to return to the institution. For these groups:

25. Consider specifying certain Homecoming Days when former members will be entertained and educated by a special program, planned for their particular tastes and followed by a tour of the institution.

26. To as great an extent as possible, staff emeriti as well as current staff should be present at such homecoming occasions, and should be encouraged to mingle with and talk to the alumni, former patients, etc.

27. For an educational institution with alumni clubs scattered throughout the country, consider taking the celebration to the alumni. Form teams of professors—three or four to a team—and take an interesting program, complete with film strips or some form of photographic coverage, to each alumni club.

A constituency that too often is forgotten is the community in which the institution is located:

28. Consider a special day on which homage is paid to the community and to all the contributions the community has made to the institution. In one sense, this should be a "mutual admiration day," for the institution must not lose this opportunity to let the com-

munity know how much the institution does to support the community. The day may be capped by a civic dinner honoring key political, cultural, professional, and business leaders of the community.

In many institutions, particularly schools, colleges, and universities, the summer is a relatively slow period during which dormitories and other facilities can be used to forward the celebration:

29. Can a national or regional conference be organized on a subject of basic interest to your institution? Or a forum based on a problem of basic concern to the community and your institution? Can nationally known figures be invited to speak at such an event?

30. Can a summer theater be planned, to present a cycle of plays, all having some bearing on your institution's main purpose?

31. Can a summer music festival be held, perhaps with radio or TV coverage, expressive of the purpose of the institution?

Successful anniversary celebrations, of course, bring large numbers of guests to the institution, many of whom are not well enough acquainted with physical facilities to find their way around without help of some sort:

32. Consider establishing and staffing a permanent "welcome desk" where visitors can get the necessary information. This welcome desk also should be able to supply first aid equipment, aspirin, etc.

33. Furnish conferences and conventions with maps of the institution and its grounds. These maps should be sent out to all registrants before the event and a supply also should be kept at the welcome desk.

34. Memo pads, descriptive folders and booklets, pencils—all containing information about the institution's name—should be made available for registrants and other guests.

Because an anniversary celebration presents an unparalleled opportunity for an institution to educate constituencies and guests in regard to its history, its purpose, and its objectives, all media of communication should be used to impart this information:

35. Consider the publication of a history of the institution. Such histories can range from well-done brochures to casebound books. They must be interestingly written and should contain sufficient photographic coverage to interest the lackadaisical reader. If the institution has a particularly good photographic file, this history could be made a pictorial study.

36. Both films and film strips provide an excellent means of relating an institution's story. A film, however, generally is expensive (a rule of thumb being that a film costs $1,000 for each minute of showing time). A film strip can be almost as effective as a movie, and costs only a fraction as much.

37. For an institution that is in the midst of a development campaign, an anniversary provides an opportunity for getting a development brochure or casebook into the hands of many prospective donors.

38. A superlative president's report or trustees' report, covering a specific period of time, oftentimes receives better readership among a wider audience in an anniversary year than at any other time.

39. Some institutions have staffs who "publish." Encourage those staff members to hold up publication in the year preceding the anniversary so that a larger number of books and articles may be published during the anniversary year.

40. Collections of lectures, addresses, etc., are frequently published for specific constituencies of an institution.

41. Special anniversary issues of existing institutional periodicals can carry the anniversary story to their readers. Make sure that the anniversary seal and information about the anniversary are included in literature of this sort.

The success of an anniversary depends to a great extent upon how well it is publicized. People can't attend a celebration they know nothing about:

42. To make sure that all constituencies are fully acquainted with the anniversary, consider publication of a complete anniversary program to be mailed to the total constituency of the institution. Such a publication can range from a low-cost "calendar of events" (which usually includes an institutional map, a list of accommodations, etc.) to an elaborate and very complete brochure of the year's events.

43. If located in or near an urban center, consider the purchase of a supplement in the Sunday or daily newspaper. It sometimes is possible to sell enough space to advertisers to pay for the cost of the supplement, and the remainder of the space can be devoted to an explanation of your institution.

44. Press kits should be prepared for distribution to newspaper, radio, and TV personnel, providing them with sufficient information to interpret the institution to their audiences.

45. Throughout the year special emphasis should be given to preparing tapes for radio and television feature stories for newspapers.

46. A traveling exhibit can be prepared for display at churches, other institutions, showroom windows, conventions, etc.

47. Depending upon the nature of the institution, specialties such as music albums and records (recorded by institutional choral or instrumental groups) help to publicize the institution and the anniversary. Make these records available to local radio stations.

48. Use the newspapers and other mass media to advertise those anniversary events that are open to the public. On "Community Day," if plans call for inviting the entire community to an open house, an outdoor seminar, or any event of that nature, use newspaper advertising for your invitation to the public.

49. Be sure to make budget provisions for invitations, tickets, and programs for each of the events directed to a specific audience.

Some of these considerations, naturally, will not necessarily apply to your specific institution, and financial considerations will determine which ideas can become realities and those which will have to continue as dreams. Remember, however, that it is better to carry out a small number of ideas extremely well than it is to do a large number in a mediocre fashion. Guests during this anniversary year will judge your institution on the quality of its presentations rather than on the quantity.

No matter how limited the anniversary celebration, there is the likelihood that staff and volunteers will not be sufficiently large to carry out all the anniversary burdens in addition to their regular responsibilities. For this reason:

50. Consider retaining the services of a knowledgeable public relations or communications firm. Such a firm can help to mold the individual events into an integrated anniversary program that truly reflects the character of your institution, reduce the burden on staff members and volunteers, eliminate the necessity of hiring additional staff, and give you the benefit of experienced personnel who have an outside viewpoint.

CASE STUDY

Brown University's Bicentennial Celebration

Very few colleges and universities in the United States—or organizations of any other nature—have had the opportunity to stage a 200th anniversary observance. Brown University, the nation's seventh oldest institution of higher learning, met its opportunity with distinction and success. This brief summary of special events during the observance, which extended over the period from September 1964 to June 1965, is based on an interview with Howard S. Curtis, Secretary of the University, who was in charge of the over-all plans and series of special events.

While this is by no means a case study in depth, it should serve as a guide and stimulus to colleges and other organizations with a significant milestone ahead and an opportunity that may be realized or lost. The key anniversary events reported briefly illustrate important points that are stressed throughout the text of this chapter. They are events basically related to a significant and successful observance for any college or other institution—whether it be a 200th, 150th, 100th, or in some instances perhaps even a 75th or 50th anniversary.

TESTING POINTS IN PLANNING

Three basic points were the testing ground for planning the six major special events during the period of the Brown Bicentennial Observance:

1. What is the significance of the event in relation to the organization, the observance, and the timing and spacing in the over-all anniversary schedule?

2. Who are the most important people to honor? The more famous the individuals sought as key speakers and recipients of honors, the more interest aroused in people who may attend and the better the opportunities for interpretation through communications media.

3. What is the best avenue to pursue in seeking the best chairman for the occasion—a distinguished person who has access to the important people desired as key speakers, and to other individuals who will have major functions or responsibilities connected with the occasion? (See also Chapters 6 and 7.)

SIX SPECIAL EVENTS

The six special events to be described were the framework for the over-all observance. They were spaced throughout the year in their relationship to: *(1)* the sequence of actual dates and the university's calendar for the year; *(2)* public relations and communications aspects and impact important in relation to the true image of Brown University in higher education and the world of today; *(3)* cultivation and preparation for long-range development and financial support through future endowment and capital fund efforts. A brief description of each event follows:

1. *Brown University Exercises, Commemorating the First Meeting of the Corporation, Colony House, Newport, Rhode Island, Wednesday, September 2, 1964.*

The first paragraph of the text in the program for this occasion reads: "Today's meeting of the University Corporation is held in the first floor chamber of the Colony House where the Corporation first met two hundred years ago, on September 5th, the first Wednesday of the month." Thus the opening, preliminary event in the anniversary year was significantly held on the same day of the week and same place as the original meeting.

The parchment cover of the program, with embossed wax seal of the University, reproduced in text the first paragraph of the actual minutes of the original meeting; the back cover reproduced the first fifteen lines of text of the Preamble of the Corporation Charter. The program, with two pages of brief historical text, won a national American College Public Relations Association award.

The Order of Exercises (Fig. 1) was keyed to commemoration of the occasion and unveiling of a plaque presented to Colony House. A reception held at a historical landmark, The Elms, was attended by 2,000 guests, providing an opportunity to include citizens of

The Order of the Exercises

PROCESSION FROM NEWPORT COUNTY COURTHOUSE TO COLONY HOUSE

> The Newport Artillery Company, chartered in 1741 and the oldest surviving military unit to have served actively under both British and American flags, will form a cordon of honor. The procession will begin at 4:00 p. m.

CALL TO ORDER

OFFICIAL PROCLAMATION

> *John H. Chafee*, GOVERNOR OF RHODE ISLAND

PRESENTATION OF TABLET

> *Cornelius C. Moore*, PRESIDENT OF THE NEWPORT NATIONAL BANK

> The Bank, since 1803, has occupied the Colonel John Gardner House, where the Rev. James Manning, in July of 1763, first "made the design known" for the founding of the College which later became Brown University.

ADDRESS   "NEWPORT'S GRACIOUS GESTURES"

> *Carl Bridenbaugh*, UNIVERSITY PROFESSOR, BROWN UNIVERSITY

UNVEILING OF TABLET

> *Barnaby C. Keeney*, PRESIDENT OF BROWN UNIVERSITY

> The tablet for the Colony House commemorates the first meeting of the University Corporation on September 5, 1764.

The audience is requested to remain seated until the procession has left the building.

Fig. 1.   Order of Exercises from Brown University Program

Newport and prominent leaders from the Northeast. Advantage was taken of the coincidental America's Cup Races and invitations issued accordingly.

2. *The Opening Convocation, Sunday, September 27th, 1964, First Baptist Meeting House, 2:30 P.M.*

This was the pinnacle event in the series of special occasions. The academic procession included some 200 delegates from colleges, universities, museums and learned societies. The address for the occasion was delivered by the Honorable Lyndon B. Johnson, President of the United States of America. Greetings were extended by John H. Chafee, Governor of Rhode Island, and Nathan M. Pusey, President of Harvard University. Barnaby C. Keeney, President of Brown University, extended the welcome and conferred honorary degrees upon eleven distinguished leaders from the academic world. Following the ceremonies a buffet luncheon for delegates and invited guests was served in Alumni Hall.

. . . .

4. *Symposium, First Session, Monday, September 28th, Meehan Auditorium, 2:30 P.M.*

The over-all theme and topic for the first of three sessions was "Future Directions of the University." A panel of five college presidents examined "ways in which institutions of higher learning may meet the challenge created by the rapid expansion of knowledge."

Second Session, Monday, September 28, Meehan Auditorium, 8:30 P.M.

The topic was "The Influence of New Scientific Knowledge," with six distinguished scientists addressing themselves to "the specific problems posed by the accelerating pace of research in the various scientific fields, and its impact upon teaching."

Third Session, Meehan Auditorium, Tuesday, September 29th, 9:30 A.M.

The topic was "Future Directions of the Human Studies." Six noted scholars discussed the theme of the Symposium with regard to their own fields of scholarship, and the humanities in general. A buffet luncheon for all delegates and invited guests was served in Alumni Hall.

Total attendance at the three sessions was 13,000.

5. *The Bicentennial Alumni Convocation, Meehan Auditorium, Saturday, February 6, 1965.*

This brought scores of alumni and alumnae of Brown and Pembroke back to the campus for: *(1)* an impressive formal Convocation, *(2)* a reception following the ceremonies, *(3)* a colorful weekend of reunion meetings.

The Convocation program featured the award of a specially designed bronze Bicentennial Medallion, honoring 26 alumni and alumnae. The bronze medallion (Fig. 2) was designed by Richard Lippold. It consisted of a circular piece of polished gold clasped by a ring of twenty interlocking bronze V's. Taken together, the V's form twenty Roman numerals X's, symbolizing two hundred years. The medallion is three inches in diameter. The printed program noted that those honored "have demonstrated exceptionally high levels of attainment in their fields—not only attainment acknowledged by public recognition, but the quiet attainment that too often goes unnoticed. . . . Not all of those to be honored have been touched by fame. Some are widely known only within their professions, and some are known only within their own communities. But the common denominator is that all have helped to demonstrate that Brown University today is living up to the goal expressed two hundred years ago in its Charter, by preserving in the community a succession of men (and now women) duly qualified for discharging the offices of life with usefulness and reputation."

Fig. 2. Brown University's Bicentennial Medallion

The medallion, in the symbolism of its design, was of unique significance. Undoubtedly it is highly treasured by each individual who received it as an appropriate and well-deserved permanent mark of appreciation and recognition. One of the medallions was also presented to the Museum of Modern Art in New York City, for the collection of the designer, well-known sculptor Richard Lippold.

6. *Commencement*

Since the Commencement pattern at Brown University is a composite of traditions established over two hundred years little was done to change it for the 200th anniversary celebration. It was keyed to the bicentennial theme through speeches and by conferring honorary degrees only upon Brown graduates. Class reunion attendance was larger and there was a corresponding increase in gifts to the university as part of the bicentennial development campaign.

In retrospect it was felt that the plan to focus the celebration on a limited number of key events was a sound decision.

EXPERIENCE REPORTS (ANNIVERSARY OBSERVANCES)

Memphis Sesquicentennial Promotes Health Services

Tie-ins with public events as community-wide observations are useful ways to further public understanding of an institution. The sesquicentennial celebration of Memphis, Tenn., provided the Memphis and Shelby County Health Department with a special opportunity for a public information program and events about its origins and functions. It built the information effort around the story of the area's yellow fever epidemic in 1878, the event which precipitated the establishment in the following year of a Board of Health.

As a contribution to the city's anniversary celebration, the health agency constructed a 12-foot exhibit containing four lighted dioramas, depicting the story of the yellow fever epidemic and the health cleanup aftermath. The yellow fever theme also was used as the subject of talks and slide presentations to civic groups, and in the development and distribution of other special material, and also for newspaper and magazine feature stories. The exhibit was later accepted by the city's Pink Palace Museum as a permanent addition to its Memphis Historical Collection.

(Courtesy of *Channels*)

40th Anniversary Probes Future

"Agenda for Tomorrow" was the theme of a series of public events sponsored by the Community Council of Greater New York to observe its 40th anniversary year. As the theme suggests, the focus of the anniversary was on the future. It was hoped that the series of activities would highlight the problems and issues that the council and the city's health and welfare agencies should tackle in the years ahead. The first of the events was a public debate between the two major candidates for mayor of New York. The second event was an open board meeting to involve interested representatives of other organizations in answering the question: "What should be high on New York's agenda for tomorrow?" The last special events were a series of workshops on eight basic problem areas and a concluding luncheon featuring several of the state's top political leaders.

(Courtesy of *Channels*)

20th Anniversary Recruits Student Volunteers

In Washington, D.C., the United Cerebral Palsy Association invited more than 200 high-school and college students to participate in its 20th anniversary meeting. The young people, who participated as speakers as well as observers, indicated their interest in participating in voluntary agency work, but they requested their right to make their own mistakes.

(Courtesy of *Channels*)

"Open-House Week" Merged with Three Anniversaries

An anniversary observance year provides almost any organization with an opportunity for a special open-house program better organized, more significant and with more planning than the usual annual open-house event as described in Chapter 8.

The McBurney Branch YMCA, in New York City, took advantage of its opportunity in 1969, setting the theme and activities for its Open-House Week within the framework of the 125th anniversary of the YMCA movement, the 100th anniversary of the opening of the first YMCA building in New York City, and the 40th anniversary of the 23rd Street YMCA (now the McBurney Branch).

Paul Stone, chairman of Open-House Week and a board member, co-ordinated a complex organization of more than 200 volunteer laymen and staff members in a week-long program of special events, lobby demonstrations, building tours, awards and recognitions. The program reached out and drew in several thousand people as participants and guests. The outline of the events as given below illustrates the imagination, good organization, interest, and visibility which resulted from careful planning of the Open-House Week committee members.

Monday. (noon) Reception honoring longtime members with an Anniversary Luncheon. Good Neighbor Award, Honorary Life Membership Award, and Quarter Century Awards to 25-year members. (evening) New members' reception, lobby demonstrations, door prizes, building tours. Second Group Theater (branch members) present an original one-act comedy.

Tuesday. (noon) Luncheon meeting. Salute to the financial community focused on the role of banks and other financial institutions—their influence and responsibilities, Community Service Award to executive director of Hudson Guild. (evening) Lobby demonstrations, door prizes, building tours. Second Group Theater play.

Wednesday. Bunnies-Sports-a-Rama. Bunnies from the Playboy Club and prominent sports figures participating in a demonstration of calisthenics, jogging and other physical agility tests, in Auditorium, 5:35 to 8 P.M. Second Group Theater play.

Thursday. Teen-age Career Contest and Forum—"What I Want to Be and Why." Participating groups include guidance counselors of high schools, McBurney Y parents group, YMCA vocational counseling service, afternoon, 3:30 to 5:30. (evening) Lobby demonstrations, door prizes, building tours.

Friday. (noon) Brotherhood Luncheon (by invitation). Tribute to community relations officer, 10th Police Precinct, as "the person who has done much to create and foster brotherhood in the community among all nationalities, races and religions." (evening, lobby, 7-8 P.M.) Demonstrations, door prizes, building tours. International Department reception and festival—member groups of the department presenting a cultural evening of songs and dances. Sale of native foods by each participating group, for benefit of YMCA World Service. McBurney Y International Award for individual making significant contribution to International Department.

Saturday. (noon to 2 P.M.) Youth Celebrates. Founders Day physical fitness program—push-ups, broad jumps, running, balance, agility, muscular endurance and strength. Special invitation to children.

Sunday. (afternoon) The Boston Terrier Club of New York, presenting an All-Age Match (puppy show). Children's Handling Class; trophies, ribbons in all classes. Public invited.

(Courtesy of McBurney Branch YMCA,
New York City)

EXPERIENCE REPORTS (ANNUAL EVENTS)

Y Week Luncheon Builds Clergy Goodwill

A special YMCA Sunday luncheon for participating ministers was held by the Newton, Mass., YMCA. It turned out to be one of the most successful Y Week events ever held. It was also the largest gathering of Christian ministers the town had ever witnessed. The meal was served by the Women's Auxiliary. The program included slides of local Y programs, a YMCA National Council film *What's in a Name?*, presentation of complimentary full-privilege memberships to ministers who attended and tours of the Y building.

(Courtesy of National Council, YMCA)

Y Week Puts 1,000 Kids on Skates

For several years the Elizabeth, N.J., YMCA put on a roller-skating party for other YMCA's in the northern part of the state. As many as 1,000 boys and girls turned out. All arrangements were made through the America on Wheels Roller-Skating Arenas, which offered their rink to the Y without charge and also contributed prizes to the event. Admission was free. They could borrow clamp-on skates for nothing. Shoe skates could be rented for 40 cents. Each Y that participated had to *(a)* provide a leader, *(b)* transport its own members, *(c)* check its own members into the arena, *(d)* contribute one dollar toward general expenses, *(e)* notify the Elizabeth Y if they intended to participate.

(Courtesy of National Council, YMCA)

Y Week Dinner Honors Club Officers

The president and youth chairman of each service club in Abington, Penna., are invited to a special Y Week dinner each year. The dinner meetings and interpretation programs have benefited the Association in many ways. One year a highlight was the presentation to the local YMCA of a brand-new Chevrolet carry-all by one service club.

(Courtesy of Abington, Penna., YMCA)

Special Week for Volunteers

For the fourth year in a row, Philadelphia's health and welfare volunteers were honored in a week-long observance sponsored by the Council on Volunteers. Called "Volunteer Recognition Week," the event was given an official proclamation by the mayor's office and was boosted through the co-operative efforts of a number of agencies. Special events were spotted during the week, and exhibits showing volunteer service were on display throughout the city and suburbs.

(Courtesy of *Channels*)

Volunteers Run Health Education Day

Health Education Day is a public relations project initiated two years ago by the Auxiliary of the Guernsey Memorial Hospital in Cambridge, Ohio. The event has two objectives: to acquaint newcomers in the community with the hospital, and to provide the public with information on some of the more crippling diseases and the progress in combating them. This year's special day, as reported in *The Auxiliary Leader,* journal for hospital auxiliaries, featured tours of the hospital, talks about heart disease and poliomyelitis, as well as hospital costs, exhibitions of paintings and other art by adults and schoolchildren, along with free lunch for all registrants. More than 400 persons attended the affair. A newly published brochure describing the hospital's services and facilities was distributed. The Auxiliary reports, in addition, that it recruited many new members.

(Courtesy of *Channels*)

Variations for Senior Citizens' Month

In a guide to activities on observing Senior Citizens' Week, annually held in May, the President's Council on Aging and the Federal Administration on Aging prepared a number of interesting special events. Although designed to spotlight the field of aging, the events can be considered for other fields as well.

Here is a sampling of the activities suggested: Schedule ground-breaking, dedication, and other ceremonies for new housing projects, new centers and recreation programs for the aging. Honor your Congressman, Senator, or other Government official for his important contributions to the aging. Call on your state or local medical association to sponsor a conference on health frauds and quackery. If your community has any of the 13,000 centenarians in the United States, do something special for them. Inasmuch as May is in the baseball season, arrange for a Senior Citizens' Day at the ball park. Arrange a "Recognition Day" to present awards to older persons who have made special contributions to their community. Encourage your local health department to promote a "Keep Healthy" campaign for senior citizens. Campaign to combat discrimination in employment because of age and establish placement centers for older workers looking for jobs. Schedule talent shows and concerts featuring older persons.

(Courtesy of *Channels*)

4:   Annual Meetings

During a given year annual meetings held throughout the United States by voluntary organizations total in the hundreds of thousands. The people who attend them number into the millions. The people who fall asleep bored by dull meetings, if laid end to end, would probably stretch around the world.

Interesting or dull, annual meetings hold important public relations values, positive or negative, for every voluntary organization. These values are ultimately reflected in the support provided by people when they are appealed to for contributions.

Annual meetings need not be dull, should not be dull! Neither should they be ignored or avoided. A survey of voluntary organizations would probably reveal an amazing number that never hold annual meetings, yet the annual meeting is or should be an essential part of the life of every voluntary agency or institution.

Their Uses

The annual meeting can be used as an instrument for answering criticism and counteracting dissatisfaction. For instance, an agency was subject to whispered criticism that it was not getting its money into the community projects which needed it most, but instead was favoring old standard institutions. The annual meeting was pushed ahead in date and certain individuals were primed to ask questions. The board and the chairman were able to put forth the information which served to hush the whispered criticism and bring the matter of community service out into the open in a natural way. This annual meeting served the organization by providing a platform, and it served the constituency by letting them be heard.

The question and answer period can be used to handle such situations. It often serves to clarify important facts which have not been covered in the formal program or are misunderstood by some of the people.

Various other devices can be used to make the program lively, for instance, by including some form of entertainment related to the organization, such as a performance by the theater group of a youth agency. Demonstration groups can make activities and services more vivid. But if not well presented and varied, they will become monotonous. A program based on a series of demonstrations is subject to many hazards and may become deadly dull. Atttractive exhibits can add color to what might otherwise be somewhat drab surroundings.

Annual Meeting or Annual Dinner Meeting?

Which is better? With the objective of attracting as large an invited attendance as possible, an evening meeting probably offers better possibilities for most organizations. A noon meeting (which must be a luncheon) limits time for the program, and the attendance of women and family groups will be affected. Breakfast meetings are rarely held for reasons that are obvious.

Dinner meetings, therefore, offer the best opportunities for most organizations. They provide a social occasion, a relaxed and friendly atmosphere, opportunity for a more effective and colorful program, and possibilities for the largest attendance of a mixed audience. Some people will be certain to have conflicting social engagements scheduled (which they may be willing to change) and some folks simply don't like to go out evenings. But if people receive their invitations early and anticipate a pleasant evening, attendance problems can be minimized.

Successful annual meetings build up interest from year to year. The real test of attendance—keeping in mind *next year* and how many people will come again —lies in how interesting the program is and how enjoyable the evening. For more documentation of these points see Chapter 10. Whether the purpose of a dinner is direct fund-raising cultivation or public relations and interrelations, the arrangements are equally important and the theme song is the same. People must go home with a favorable impression that leads to pleasant recollections and supporting convictions.

Many organizations hold their annual meetings in an auditorium, gymnasium, or other large hall, if one is available. This is a good second choice, and not necessarily a drawback to an interesting program. Such a meeting will lack, however, the friendly atmosphere of a dinner meeting and groups of people enjoying a good meal and conversation with friends. The annual meeting and open house are "family" occasions. Their broad purpose is to create and cultivate a friendly feeling toward the organization.

Cost does loom as a problem for many agencies in considering a dinner function. But perhaps the cost can be covered by the sale of tickets and a partial budget subsidy, or underwriting by a few board members and contributors who have a deep interest in the organization.

If the annual meeting is a dinner event, it may prove wise to hold the meeting prior to the dinner, particularly if cocktails are being served. The dinner should be simple and not too elaborate. Too many frills that imply unnecessary expense may tempt some individuals to criticize. So far as arrangements are concerned, whether the attendance is 100 or 1,000, equal care in handling details is important. The Award Dinner checklist included in Chapter 10 is complete in every detail related to a large special event dinner. For all organizations—especially those not accustomed to planning dinners—it can prove invaluable, omitting sections that may not apply.

Some Guidelines

Following are the essential over-all points which apply for annual meetings:

● The Planning Committee should be a small group of key people including the paid executive, a staff member or volunteer who will probably be assigned responsibility for the event, one or two board members, and the chairmen of two or three key committees. The number from the latter groups will depend upon the size and nature of the organization. Avoid dates that may conflict with events of other organizations and thus affect attendance.

● The original planning group should continue to operate throughout, plus any additional members needed to handle the details of arrangements, program, ticket sales, and publicity.

● The Arrangements Committee takes care of all details, catering, dinner service, seating decorations, etc., seeing that they are completed on time. A special note to the Arrangements Committee: See that board members, staff, and key volunteers who are knowledgeable about the organization are well distributed. Place a host at each table to introduce guests and keep the conversation lively.

● The Program Committee has responsibility for seeing that the program is built around current policies, activities and services, problems and needs. There should be some emphasis on plans for the year ahead, and certainly on financial needs in general terms.

● The program must be streamlined and not too long, and well organized as to subject matter, change of pace and buildup. And need it be said again—*interesting*.

There will be activity groups to consider, and demonstrations of services which should bring into participation representative members and volunteers. Imagination (and rehearsing) will be needed to see that these segments of the program provide variety and liveliness to balance the more serious talks and reports. Organizations with experience in staging annual meetings realize that the program is crucial—getting across the story in an interesting and convincing manner.

Every effort should be made—and this will not be easy—to see that the program does not run longer than 60 minutes. Perhaps 75 minutes can be allowed, depending upon the type of program, pace, and over-all time schedule. The climax (and effectiveness) of an otherwise successful meeting can be marred by the distraction and confusion of people leaving before the program is ended.

● Advance promotion should be done *well* in advance. It is acceptable practice for the invitation to be made by a form letter or printed announcement. Special guests should receive personal invitations.

● A live-wire committee should be in charge of ticket sales, to sell and also enlist more people to take responsibility for purchasing or selling five or ten tickets each. Seek table groups for business and industry, related organizations, committee and/or membership groups, special groups of contributors and friends.

● *Advance publicity stories.* First announcement, with date and committee names, should be made as soon as available; second story should give program details—speakers, etc.; third story the day before or day of the dinner.

● *Coverage publicity.* Press—reporters and photographers—and radio representatives if part of the program can be broadcast. Television is rarely practical because of its distractions, unless the speaker is a distinguished person with public appeal and a message of special significance to the community. Personal invitations to those people, and a last-minute check to be certain someone is covering. A press table, well located, and someone seated there with a fact sheet and other information.

• *After the dinner.* Thank-you notes to all individuals who were actively involved in planning, arrangements, program, ticket sales, publicity, press coerage, etc. A final report to evaluate the event, with suggestions for next year.

• *Follow-up.* A report sent to cultivation mailing lists with a newspaper clipping, a publication of the organization reporting the event, or in some other form.

CASE STUDY

Evaluation of an Annual Dinner

For many years the Annual Dinner of the Young Men's Christian Association of Greater New York has been an assignment of its Public Relations Committee. Members of the committee assume complete responsibility for planning and staging the event. Planning begins a year ahead, following a review and analysis of the current dinner.

The committee has operated actively for more than twenty-five years, meets monthly and is in the mainstream of all major public relations considerations having to do with YMCA policy, program, membership personnel, administration and communications. All of its twenty or more members, including several women, are prominent professionally, identified with public relations and communications organizations and media, and participate in a wide variety of YMCA activities.

François L. Sheats, Director of Public Relations, in response to a request, supplied an evaluation of the New York City's Annual Dinner. His analysis provides food for thought as well as suggestions that will be of interest to any organization, large or small, in assessing its own annual dinner (or lack of one) and the values that accrue from a well-planned and successful event held consistently over a period of years.

Organizations in small communities should not be overawed by the evaluation of an annual dinner held in the nation's largest metropolis. All things are relative. The implications in Mr. Sheats' statement are clear and can be applied within a framework of any size by an organization that has the desire to "go and do likewise."

The Annual Dinner is the one time throughout the year when representatives of all our Branches participate simultaneously in a YMCA-sponsored event. Traditionally we have used it to launch the Current Expense Finance Campaign, but it is not conducted as a fund-raising event. Essentially we see it as a family reunion, helping to rally staff and leadership to go forth and expend their efforts according to the inspiration and stimulus which accrue at the Annual Dinner. We have found that there is a degree of unification taking place around the Annual Dinner. We know of nothing else which accomplishes this so effectively.

Over the past ten years we have had top speakers and guests of honor. The YMCA is established in the minds of the audience as a prestige institution when they see that prominent political figures like Senator Mark Hatfield or Sargent Shriver will come to

Program

MASTER OF CEREMONIES
William P. Epke
Vice Chairman, National Board of YMCAs and
Director, YMCA of Greater New York

GREETINGS and INTRODUCTIONS
Dais guests to be introduced as they march on

"AMERICA THE BEAUTIFUL"
Mrs. Irene B. Handler, Eastern Queens YMCA Committee of Management
(Guests are invited to join in singing)

INVOCATION
Stephen Arnold, Youth Division Member, Harlem YMCA

DINNER

STATEMENT FROM C. W. CARSON, JR.
Chairman, 1972 Finance Campaign
Alger B. Chapman, Treasurer, YMCA Board of Trustees

SERVICE TO YOUTH AWARD
Recipient—Big Wilson, Station WNBC Radio
Presented by George Heinemann, Vice-President for
Children's TV Programs; and Director, YMCA of Greater New York

"MAN-OF-THE-YEAR" AWARDS
William A. Howes, Executive Vice President, YMCA of Greater New York,
will install the 1971 Chapter, YMCA Men-of-the-Year

PRESIDENT'S COMMENTS
Herbert B. Woodman, President, YMCA of Greater New York

ADDRESS
The Honorable Louis L. Levine
New York State Industrial Commissioner

BENEDICTION
Jack Raber, Dinner Committee Chairman
and Past Chairman, Greenpoint YMCA Board of Managers

Fig. 3. Program for Annual Dinner

New York to speak at our Annual Dinner. Likewise, when eminent figures from the sports or entertainment field attend the dinner and, as is so often the case, acknowledge that the YMCA had a meaningful relationship to their growth and development, the audience cannot help but feel a lift because they see themselves as a part of this dynamic institution. For example, Art Linkletter, Mitch Miller, Frank Gifford and many others have stood at the rostrum and paid tribute to the influence of the YMCA on their lives.

An integral part of our dinner is the Man-of-the-Year ceremony. The dinner, therefore, serves as an important instrument for giving recognition to voluntary leadership over a wider range than the immediate constituency with which the volunteer works throughout the year. The Man-of-the-Year from Staten Island is paraded before people from all five boroughs. Chances are that he is well known and commensurately applauded on Staten Island, but he doesn't often stand before the other four boroughs and have his turn in the spotlight.

The Annual Dinner is an event which engenders personal involvement and enthusiastic interest on the part of people in our branches who, because of the nature of the YMCA administration, are prone to provincialism and hold dearly the doctrine of local autonomy. Furthermore, we have found that a slowly but steadily increasing number of branches have begun to hold their own annual dinners and pattern them after the format of our city-wide dinner. The result has been an elevation of the standards of the local events.

We have found the Annual Dinner to be an excellent occasion to introduce new prospects to the YMCA. Contributors of money and voluntary services have had their appetites whetted to support the Association after attending the Annual Dinner. The dinner is also an excellent way of demonstrating the inclusiveness of the YMCA membership and its co-operative relationship with other agencies, private and governmental. We always have a splendid cross section of people from diverse categories on our main dais.

And, finally, we have found the dinner to be an event which attracts an ever-widening attendance from representatives of the mass media. This has been particularly true since we inaugurated the practice of including husbands and wives in our invitations to representatives of the working press. We usually have about five tables, or a total of fifty guests who attend as a result of our invitations to the newspapers, radio, and television stations in the city. We have made some excellent contacts with media people at the dinner. Needless to say, these people come as guests of the Association.

Last year we inaugurated the practice of having a longer reception for the guests of honor and put this into the hands of a women's committee. This encouraged a much greater interest and participation on the part of the women, most of them having previously attended the dinner escorted by their husbands.

EXPERIENCE REPORTS

Promoting an Annual United Way Meeting

To let people in the Baton Rouge, La., area know that the United Givers Fund there wanted their direct involvement in its affairs, the agency decided to promote attendance at its annual meeting on a much wider scale than ever before. The basic promotional piece was a poster mailed to every business and industrial firm in Baton Rouge, city offices, Federal building, universities, and other public places. Many business firms put up the posters in their show windows, stores posted them near check-out counters, etc. The mass media also gave good pre-meeting coverage. Explaining the reason behind the heavy promotional effort, Myron Falk, director of the agency, stated: "We are convinced that we cannot overemphasize the local autonomy factor in the administration of our United Givers Fund. This fundamental principle can be safeguarded by well-attended annual meetings at which contributors exercise their privilege to vote for board members who guide the activities of the Fund."

(Courtesy of *Channels*)

Annual Meeting Report Dramatized by Tour

How an agency's annual meeting became an unusual public relations vehicle was reported at a public relations institute sponsored by the Philadelphia United Fund for its member organizations. Wanting to do more than give its annual meeting audience reports of its work by talks or even slides, as it had done in the past, the Philadelphia United Neighbors Association organized a bus tour to the neighborhoods served by its various member settlements. Four buses took scores of board members and other community leaders on the "see for yourself" tour. Acting as tour guides, staff members gave running descriptions of the neighborhoods over public-address systems on the buses as they rolled along. At each member settlement, a neighborhood leader boarded the bus to talk about achievements, problems, etc. Occasionally the touring volunteers witnessed demonstrations involving youngsters.

(Courtesy of *Channels*)

5: Building Dedications and Ground-Breaking Ceremonies

Three Possible Kinds of Events

New buildings provide opportunities for three special events:
1. Ground-breaking ceremony.
2. Laying of the cornerstone.
3. Dedication of the completed building.

All three are more intimate "family" occasions than most special events. The people formally invited are those most intimately and actively related to the organization.

If the building is the gift of one donor, that individual is the honored guest. If there are several major donors they should receive special invitations and be recognized during the program.

Others to be invited, if the organization is a college or school, will include trustees or board members, faculty, staff, parents, alumni, contributors, students, and community leaders. For a community organization the list will include board members, committee chairmen and volunteer workers, staff, members, contributors, persons who will use the building, representatives of related institutions, and community leaders.

The press—newspapers, radio and TV representatives—should be notified in advance and supplied with background information about the new building and the program for the occasion, along with invitations to the luncheon or reception if one is planned. Assign someone to see that they have facts and information about the event itself in typed form—often called a fact sheet—and access to people they would like to interview or photograph. They may have a tight press deadline to meet. These occasions offer opportunities for good feature and news photographs.

Who Participates in the Program?

Individuals representing the "family" publics are usually invited to take some part in the ceremonies. For a college or school these will include the chairman of

61

the board of trustees and the president. Also individuals representing faculty, students, parents and alumni should make brief statements. For community organizations the list might include volunteers representing key committees, membership groups and community leaders.

Top place on the program is, of course, reserved for the donor, or two or three major contributors. The speakers should be as few in number as possible, strictly held to brief statements to avoid the deadliness of an overlong formal program.

Laying of the Cornerstone

It seems that cornerstone layings are being abandoned these days in favor of ground-breaking ceremonies and dedications. One reason obviously is the clutter and confusion that detract from the program when a building is under construction. A question also comes to mind. Has the symbolism of the cornerstone as a rock of Gibraltar faded away, lost in the fog and smog of the twentieth century? Until the last two or three decades there was a cornerstone laying for almost any church or public building, with an appropriate ceremony. At least this was so in smaller, tightly knit communities. It is still appropriate if the time of year and other factors make it desirable. If the cornerstone ceremony is decided upon, make sure the things that are deposited in the cornerstone have wide interest and present a picture of the times. The ground-breaking ceremony and dedication—one or both during the period of construction—are considered important by most organizations. They yield important publicity, public relations and cultivation dividends when carefully planned and staged.

The Ground-Breaking Ceremony

This can be quite informal and offers more opportunity for participation than the dignified and impressive dedication of a completed building. It is usually briefer, smaller, simpler to plan and stage, with less expense involved.

There is a personal and satisfying appeal to the donor, chairman of the trustees and others who may be asked to turn over the first spadefuls of dirt to break ground. Whether this is done with a trowel, a spade, a steam shovel, or a bulldozer it is fun—enjoyed by the audience—and with possibilities for news and feature photos. Some private schools even provide small trowels so every pupil can take part and carry the trowel home for his mama or papa to use in the garden.

In setting up newspaper coverage check to see if a photographer can be sent to cover, talk with the news or photo editor if possible and suggest some ideas for shots with kids, personalities, and candid pictures that will have feature photo appeal.

A private luncheon or small reception can appropriately be held before or after the ceremony for a group of invited guests.

BREAKING GROUND WITHOUT BREAKING YOUR BACK

Building dedications, ground breakings, mortgage burnings, naming ceremonies and like events are an unfortunate necessity in today's college and university community.

True, there are people who work long and hard to achieve the construction of a new facility, and praise, honor and recognition should be their due. This praise, honor and recognition, however, can be applied with a little common sense mixed in.

Ground breakings are basically non-events. If a ground breaking must be held, it should be as simple as possible. A danger to be avoided is the tendency to permit it to become a true non-event. This can occur when a designated dignitary makes a few cursory scratches at the earth with the traditional spade for the benefit of the TV and news photographers. Following this symbolic gesture, the invited guests are left to find their way to a luncheon. To ask your friends to brave the possibility of inclement weather to witness such a non-occurrence is to stretch friendship to the straining point. To ask the same of your acquaintances is risking the possibility of making enemies.

A ground breaking can make use of a little of the publicity man's hoopla. An example is the traditional chrome- or silver-plated spade, engraved for the occasion. A little imagination may turn up a more suitable implement such as the 2,000-year-old spade used by the University of Florida at its Florida State Museum ground breaking.

Rather than risk damage to the implement (an engraved, chrome-plated spade can cost as much as $150), a bed of earth should be pre-shoveled, raked and sifted for rocks, roots, nails and other common obstacles.

Some type of ceremony is in order. A focal point should be prepared beforehand, if only four stakes outlined with ribbon. A bullhorn or portable lectern should be on site so that the speaker's words may be heard.

The release of gas-filled balloons adds color to an event and doesn't impinge upon its dignity. By attaching a slip to each balloon, the institution can assure itself even more press attention. The finder of a balloon who lives the greatest distance from the ground-breaking site is awarded some sort of prize.

(Reprinted from *American College Public Relations Association Technics*, Vol. 4, No. 6)

Building Dedications

Several important purposes are served when a new building is dedicated. A program wisely planned and mercifully brief, followed by an open-house tour, will produce good publicity, important public relations visibility, and lasting cultivation values.

Good taste and brevity are essential. The program should be limited to a very few speakers, selected because they have the knowledge and ability to make brief statements interpreting values and services the building can contribute to the community life and to the organization's purpose.

A key speaker who is a distinguished leader noted locally, statewide or nationally will add significance to the occasion and increase news media coverage. Select the key speaker early and get a firm commitment, thus avoiding a frantic search a few weeks before the event and ending up with a second-choice speaker. Usually, for this kind of an occasion, there are a number of individuals quite close to the organization or college who are distinguished speakers. The hope is to select one who is a good speaker.

Who Participates in the Program?

If an individual (rather than a company or foundation) is the principal donor that person will, of course, be given formal recognition and appreciation at some point in the program. Other speakers, limited to brief statements, will likely be

The Board of Trustees and President

of

Fordham University

cordially invite you to the

Dedication

of

The Leon Lowenstein Center

in honor of

Mr. Leon Lowenstein

Fordham University Campus at Lincoln Center

Thursday afternoon, May the fifteenth
Nineteen hundred and sixty-nine
at three o'clock

Guests are requested to enter
the Fordham Campus from the
62nd Street stairway entrance

Dedication Program

3:00 p.m. *Presiding and Master of Ceremonies:*
               JOSEPH A. KAISER, Chairman of Board of Trustees

Band:
               NATIONAL ANTHEM

Invocation:
               HIS EMINENCE TERENCE CARDINAL COOKE

Remarks:
               THE HONORABLE JOHN V. LINDSAY
               THE REVEREND MICHAEL P. WALSH, S.J., President

Tribute to Leon Lowenstein:
               THE REVEREND LEO McLAUGHLIN, S.J., Chancellor

Response:
               LEON LOWENSTEIN

Benediction:
               DR. JULIUS MARK, Rabbi Emeritus, Temple Emanu-El

Band:
               ALMA MATER

*General Tours and Reception at Plaza Lounge and
Cafeteria*

Fig. 4. Invitation and Program for Building Dedication

64

selected from among those who have been intimately identified with the building project.

Music performed by a group related to the organization can provide warmth and variety to the program. But this honor should be extended only to an orchestra or vocal group which has achieved recognition for the quality of its performances. Otherwise, keep the program that much shorter.

The printed program can serve as a permanent record, and also help keep the program brief, by including recognition and appreciation to groups and individuals who have played an important part in the building project. This investment is well worth two extra pages in the program and the nominal cost involved. The printed program should be formal, reflecting in design and typography the dignity of the occasion.

Invitations (formal printed invitations) should be extended to much the same "family" publics suggested for ground-breaking ceremonies. The dedication ceremonies will justify, however, a larger invitation list and more personal efforts to see that prominent contributors, representatives of related organizations, and community leaders receive personal invitations.

Likewise, more attention should be given to press coverage than for a ground-breaking ceremony, following the same procedures already suggested in setting up news and photo coverage. Make every reasonable effort to obtain from the key speaker or speakers, in advance, a copy of the speech to be delivered, for use with the press. This is often difficult but worth trying to accomplish.

It is appropriate to suggest to newspapers the possibility of a feature story, illustrated, describing the purposes and services of the building. A suggestion from the chairman of the trustees or anyone who has a really personal acquaintance to local newspaper editors or editorial page editors may result in an editorial. Tread lightly, however, since this is sometimes a sensitive area. Offer to provide background information if such is desired.

Why an Open-House Tour?

Here is an opportunity that should be capitalized on fully for public relations and cultivation values. Guests will be more impressed by observing activities, services, and facilities and having them explained by guides than they will be by secondhand newspaper reports, photos or printed brochures.

Take particular care to see that enough personable and well-informed guides are available to conduct small groups through the building. Refreshments served during the tour at some attractive location graced by charming hostesses will add a pleasing social atmosphere and encourage guests to mingle in groups.

For additional suggestions that will help assure a smooth-running tour see Chapter 8.

CASE STUDY

Dedication of a College Academic-Athletic Building

Western Kentucky State College, like other colleges in the state-assisted system, is involved in an expanding building program to increase the educational opportunities for Kentucky's youth. The dedication of a $3 million academic-athletic building, the E. A. Diddle Arena, on December 7, 1963, was a special event planned to inform the public about the wise use made of their tax dollars which provided for this multipurpose structure.

Much needed classroom space was provided for three academic departments, in addition to facilities for the physical education department, including an indoor swimming pool and an auxiliary gymnasium, and a modern athletic arena, seating 8,500 for basketball games, which can be expanded to seat more than 13,000 as an auditorium for musical and theatrical events.

An all-day dedicatory program was designed to fully inform the public and acquaint it with the multiple functions of the building. The tri-part event consisted of a formal dedication of the academic portion in the early afternoon, with the Honorable Bert T. Combs, governor of Kentucky, officiating. Faculty and staff wore their academic regalia for this event which was attended by the general public. An open house, with tours of the building, followed. The evening program to dedicate the basketball arena included an address by the lieutenant governor, along with the first basketball game to be played there. Half-time ceremonies honored basketball coach E. A. Diddle, whose teams, in 42 years, had won over 700 games and whose name the arena bears.

OBJECTIVES

To make the citizens of the state aware that the building existed, that there was a need for it, that its multipurpose nature contributed both to the college and the area in many ways, that it was a milestone in the college's development in less than ten years from a teacher-training institution with fewer than 2,000 students to a great college offering liberal arts education and both professional and pre-professional training with a student body of 6,000. To enhance the prestige of the college and to reflect favorably on its over-all progress. To call attention to future needs for increased educational facilities to match increased enrollment and a rapidly expanding educational program, and to spotlight Western Kentucky State College's role in the total state educational program of Kentucky.

PERSONNEL

The responsibility for the entire program was vested in a committee appointed by the president of the college, under his over-all supervision, with specific duties assigned to various areas including that of public relations, directed by Robert Cochran.

BUDGET

(Not indicated.)

CHRONOLOGY

June 9, 1960—appointment of committee to make study of recommendations concerning construction of new building.

May 13, 1961—announcement that construction would start in November.

November 11, 1961—news release concerning forthcoming construction.

November 14, 1961—bids opened and contract awarded.

November 15, 1961—news release on ground-breaking ceremonies.

December 1, 1961—scheduling of Vanderbilt University as dedication game opponent (in December, 1963).

December 9, 1962—all TV networks contacted about possibility of nationwide telecast of dedication game.

April 14, 1963—announcement made of dedication date and basketball opponent.

June 25, 1963—ad hoc committee formed to raise money to purchase new automobile for Coach Diddle.

August 29, 1963—Dedication Committee appointed.

September-November 1963—dedication promoted through radio interviews during football games.

September 4, 1963—first meeting of Dedication Committee.

September 5, 1963—Governor and lieutenant governor invited to speak at dedication.

September 23, 1963—prospective brochure advertisers contacted.

September 25, 1963—dedication ticket design approved and order placed.

September 27, 1963—William McCrocklin, Western Kentucky State's first basketball all-American, now a Buick Motor Co. executive, agreed to make presentation of automobile to coach.

October 11, 1963—formal invitations ordered.

October 18, 1963—arrangements made for local telecast of dedication game.

November 4, 1963—invitations mailed to over 3,000 people.

November 7, 1963—bids received for printing dedication brochure.

November 9, 1963—news release concerning opening of ticket sales.

November 11, 1963—tickets placed on sale.

November 14, 1963—design approved; press kits ordered.

November 18, 1963—invitations to President's Dinner mailed.

November 26, 1963—arrangements made for broadcast to be taped and turned over to the school for future use.

November 27, 1963—information sent to Buick Motor Co. for publicity purposes in connection with presentation of a new Buick to Coach Diddle.

December 2, 1963—announcement of dedication program and speakers.

December 3, 1963—Coach Diddle appears on Nashville TV to promote program.

December 4, 1963—special dedication issue of *College Heights Herald* distributed.

December 5, 1963—game and dedication program discussed on Nashville radio program, with both Western Kentucky State and Peabody College officials on program.

December 7, 1963—Dedication Program

1:00 P.M.   Coach Diddle interviewed on TV
1:30 P.M.   Academic processional, dedication
3 - 5 P.M.   Open House
5:00 P.M.   President's Dinner
6:30 P.M.   Arena dedication
8:00 P.M.   Basketball game
8:45 P.M.   Half-time ceremony honoring Coach Diddle
December 9, 1963—brochures mailed to invited guests who could not attend dedication and to alumni.

SPECIAL PROBLEMS

Handling of a crowd of nearly 10,000 in a building with which no one was thoroughly familiar presented a few problems. Another problem was that the city's annual Christmas Parade was scheduled for the same day, but this was taken care of by starting the parade from the parking lot of the new building so that remote TV equipment could cover both events without moving.

Since the Western Kentucky State football team was scheduled to appear in the Tangerine Bowl on December 28, this was an especially hectic period, with many demands on the public relations office.

MEASUREMENT AND RECOMMENDATIONS

Invitations to the dedication did not make it clear that the invitation included complimentary tickets to the basketball game and so probably cut down on attendance.

Failure to supervise student assistants properly resulted in extensive wastage of invitation envelopes.

All reactions to the event were on the plus side. The color brochure, distributed to all in attendance, was designed as a souvenir and provided useful information about the new building, such as a seating chart, as well as spotlighting the college's entire growth program.

Recommendation to others is that extensive planning, be done down to the minutest detail, with enough flexibility to permit last-minute changes and refinements.

(From American College Public
Relations Association Case Studies)

6: Citation Awards
and Testimonial Dinners

College and University Ceremonies

Recognition ceremonies are held by many colleges and universities to honor alumni and alumnae for outstanding achievement and service in their particular field of endeavor which reflect credit upon the alma mater.

These ceremonies are often held in connection with alumni reunions, less frequently at Commencement time, or may be held on another occasion planned as a special event for public relations purposes to improve the image of the college.

Citations are also awarded by some colleges and universities to citizens of the community, county or state for notable achievement or service in their field of endeavor. In some instances a distinguished leader of national prominence may be so honored. Honorary degrees, another form of citation, are usually conferred as an even higher mark of distinction and recognition.

Citations are frequently awarded by colleges and universities as a cultivation event in connection with a capital campaign. (See Chapter 7.)

Recognition of Citizens by Community Organizations

Many community organizations award citations to citizens for outstanding achievement or service of benefit to the community. These special events are usually dinners honoring one or more citizens. They are also held as evening meetings in a public auditorium or armory, depending on the nature of the awards, the prominence of awardees, and the attendance anticipated.

The importance and prestige values of citations awarded by community organizations should be carefully protected. The occasion should be of special significance to the organization and related to community interests. An organization should give recognition to an individual for outstanding leadership, achievement and service to the community and/or to its own purpose and service on behalf of the community.

Be Cautious About Citation Awards

If citation awards are made too frequently they will lose significance, and the occasion will no longer have the importance or public interest required for a successful special event. Colleges and universities have a wider field and more individuals to screen in making their selections than is the case with communities. They also have more occasions than community organizations when award ceremonies can be justified and logically held.

A community organization might make special awards in its own field of service as part of an anniversary observance or on some other significant occasion. Or it might make awards in its own field of service in conjunction with a community's centennial or bicentennial observance, in a tribute to a community leader or leaders.

This is, then, not the type of special event to be considered often by a community organization, and certainly it should be decided upon only after careful study. Chapter 10 contains information, guidelines and item-by-item suggestions which are important for any community organization to consider.

The Brown University citations were awarded as part of a convocation program preceding a campaign, when the purpose was public relations impact and cultivation of a constituency to interpret the accomplishments of the university, with no direct emphasis on fund raising. This was true also of the Bucknell Convocation, reported in Chapter 7, which gave recognition to honor students for their academic achievements as part of the program.

CASE STUDY

Brown University and Pembroke College

SUGGESTIONS FOR AWARDS OF
ALUMNI AND ALUMNAE CITATIONS
(Courtesy of Marts & Lundy, Inc.
New York, N.Y.)

The award of citations to outstanding alumni of Brown and alumnae of Pembroke should be one of the most popular and gratifying events of the entire Convocation. To be most effective, the citation plan needs careful planning and complete follow-through to the actual awards at the Convocation and to newspaper stories to the hometown papers of those who receive the awards.

CRITERIA FOR SELECTION

A request for nominations for these awards was mailed to all Brown and Pembroke alumni in August. The committee appointed for making the final selection of the persons to be cited should set up the rules by which final selections can be made. We suggest the following for your consideration:

1. Since the purpose of the citations is to honor alumni who would not be

honored by the University in some other way, the following might be deemed ineligible:

    (a) holders of honorary degrees from Brown;

    (b) present faculty members;

    (c) present members of the Corporation;

    (d) officers of the alumni association;

    (e) holders of other Brown awards which are limited to only a few alumni.

2. Citations might be awarded on the basis of the following factors:

    (a) the nominee's record in his chosen profession;

    (b) his record in public service—either in government, or in nonpolitical activity in his community, his state, or the nation;

    (c) his contribution in service to Brown or Pembroke;

    (d) unusual or outstanding service in a unique profession or perhaps his record of faithful, effective service in a profession like teaching.

3. Although important, the number of nominations received by any one person should not be the deciding factor in his choice for an award. This is not a popularity contest. The final decision should be made by the judges on the basis of all other rules for eligibility. The judging committee itself should be permitted to add names to preclude overlooking any outstanding candidates.

4. If possible, geographical distribution of the nominees should be considered. It is preferable to have awardees from several sections of the country rather than from just one or two sections.

5. Some care should be taken to present awards to representatives of several fields of service, e.g., Law, Medicine, Science, Government, the Arts, Teaching, Business, Religion, Public Service. The obvious purpose is to show the wide horizons of a liberal arts education and the wide scope of Brown's training.

6. The number of awards should be limited if they are to have real meaning and significance. Twenty awards seems to be an adequate number for a university of Brown's size.

PROCEDURES

When the selections are made, each awardee should be notified immediately by phone or wire and asked to be present to receive the award in person at the ceremony to be held during the Convocation. Awards should not be made "in absentia" unless there is some overpowering reason for the awardee's inability to appear.

The Citations Committee, in co-operation with university officials, should devise an appropriate form for a citation, such as an engraved or engrossed scroll or some other tangible evidence of the honor.

Appropriate citations with a one-minute recitation of the person's accomplishments should be read for each awardee at the time of presentation.

In co-operation with the Publicity Committee for the Convocation, the Committee on Citations should make sure that sufficient publicity is given to the awardees in their hometown newspapers. House organs, trade and professional magazines, etc., are also interested in news of this type and awardees should be asked to furnish a list of the names of such papers which should receive news of their honor. Pictures of the awardees should be supplied with the stories.

It is advisable for the names of members of the Selection Committee to be kept strictly anonymous to avoid any charges of partiality.

> (From Memorandum of Instructions prepared for the Committee on Citations as a guide to selection of outstanding alumni of Brown University and alumnae of Pembroke College)

EXPERIENCE REPORT

VIP Club for Longtime Employees

A testimonial dinner was given recently for longtime staff and board members of Stamford, Conn., Hospital. At a special Recognition Dinner, a new VIP Club was formed to honor persons who had served the hospital for more than 10 years. Those installed in the club included 130 employees, 10 board members, and three from the Medical Board. Their records of service ranged from 10 up to 44 years. Over one hundred persons were on hand at the dinner to receive scrolls "in homage to those who have given a decade, a score, or even more years of faithful service."

> (Courtesy of *Channels*)

7: Convocations Prior to Capital Campaigns

Look in *Webster's Collegiate Dictionary* and you will find at least five definitions of the word *convocation,* one of which under the heading "universities" reads: "In some U.S. and Canadian universities an assembly at which degrees are conferred; commencement."

This chapter deals with the convocation as quite a different kind of special event, planned by colleges and universities for public relations and cultivation purposes in preparation for a capital campaign, and fully adaptable by any organization launching a capital funds campaign.

The concept was developed by Marts & Lundy, Inc., some years ago as an effort to provide an event of significance *preliminary* to a capital campaign. The ultimate importance of the event to a capital campaign is not as a means of capturing an audience for fund-raising purposes. No mention is made at any public session of plans for fund raising.

The convocation as discussed in this chapter is a major public relations event which advertises the university or college, its work and worth to society, to the widest possible audience. It has the indirect effect of making the university's constituency proud of the university's achievements and concerned enough about its future to work and give in the campaign. It may, in fact, involve a *series* of meetings, including the convocation as the final event with an attendance of 6,000 on an invitation basis. This was true in the case study of the *Bucknell University Convocation* reported later in this chapter, when Vice President Humphrey addressed an audience of 6,000 at the final session in a two-day series of stimulating and challenging meetings.

Two Kinds of Kickoff Occasions

There is no set pattern for the series of events leading up to the public launching of a capital campaign. In Chapter 14, two kinds of kickoff occasions are discussed. They are worth identifying at this point.

1. The first occasion is the preliminary "special gifts" event for cultivation of

major gift contributors and prospects, often designated as a Leadership Conference. This is a quiet meeting, or series of meetings, for leaders to inspire dedicated action—the conversion of men and women to a cause. The invitation list should include prospects having the capacity to make substantial gifts in four figures and more. Also it should include those members of the constituency who have taken leadership roles in earlier campaigns, plus representative leaders of the alumni, parents and community. Attendance is thus quite limited. At one small college's Leadership Conference the invitation list included some 200 alumni with spouses, trustees and parents, and resulted in some 70 acceptances. The Leadership Conference sets the tone for the second and major kickoff event which marks *the public* launching of the campaign.

The number, nature and timing of preliminary campaign events must be determined by the Campaign Committee after consideration of many factors. The Leadership Conference, as a *special gifts* and *leadership* meeting, is a must for a campaign of any kind—whether college, university, hospital, church or any other voluntary organization.

2. The convocation can be, and frequently is, decided upon as the public kickoff event which launches the campaign. But, if so, it requires quite a different pattern from the Bucknell Convocation in its planning, organization, theme emphasis, program, speakers, staging, promotion and publicity. Chapter 14 deals with these points. A community organization might conceivably hold a "convocation," as a pre-campaign event leading up to a capital fund drive, on a smaller scale than the Bucknell Convocation but for the same purpose.

A Word on Capital Campaigns

A capital campaign is a big and complex undertaking, often with millions of dollars at stake, sometimes even more than $100 million in these days. Any college, school, or organization such as a hospital, church, health, welfare or recreation center should seek the counsel and services of an experienced and reliable fund-raising firm as the first step in considering plans for a campaign. See Chapter 14 for information about the code of ethics of the American Association of Fund Raising Counsel, Inc., and for a list of other professional organizations which are sources of information regarding fund-raising firms.

CASE STUDY

Bucknell University Convocation

The Bucknell Convocation was conceived as an effort to meet two basic purposes:

1. To attract to the campus those key alumni, parents and friends whose active support and participation in the forthcoming capital campaign was considered to be of importance.

2. To serve as a public relations effort which, by the nature of its magnitude, would attract the attention of the news media and, in so doing, would result in calling to the attention of people across the country the intrinsic worth of the institution.

While the first reason was quite important, the latter was probably of even greater importance. The university had no history of similar efforts. There had been no event or cause to excite the interest of the constituency for at least ten years. The considerable strides made by the university in all areas were unknown to many. Bringing to the campus an outstanding array of national leaders was considered to be the most dramatic way to demonstrate that the university had attained national prominence, stature and importance. In essence, this was to be external evidence of the most compelling nature that our alumni and friends had reason to be proud of Bucknell and to take an active interest in its future growth and progress.

WHAT WAS DONE

The first step, of course, was to obtain support of the board of trustees. This was accomplished and a budget established a year before the event.

A committee made up of faculty, administrators, trustees and other key persons was then established to draw up the general outlines of the event. This was primarily the selection of a theme and compilation of possible speakers. About three to four months was spent on this task. It involved a large number of people (most of them from the faculty) and did much to capture their talents and interest.

An administrative officer of the university was appointed Convocation Director and assumed the major responsibility for organizing and supervising the committees required on campus to stage the event.

It was our good fortune to obtain general agreement very early in the campaign that the major decisions about obtaining speakers, publications, ticket control, and over-all design of the halls to be used would rest with the Vice-President for Planning and Development, the Director of Development, the fund-raising counsel, and the key trustee. They were to consult with the president, trustees, Convocation Director and appropriate committee chairman when it was feasible to do so, but their authority was such that they could make decisions quickly when required. And it was required on many occasions. It was a credit to all involved that it was perceived very early in the planning stages that this was an absolute necessity and that committee plans would often have to give way to considerations known only to the key group. There was remarkably little friction, even though some committee plans were rejected without discussion when it became apparent that other plans would have to be made and there was no time for committee work. This was particularly true in the last three or four weeks before the event.

GETTING A SPEAKER

The task of obtaining speakers was of paramount importance. The scheduled events called for the opening session on Friday evening, four panel discussions on Saturday morning, the main event to be on Saturday afternoon and a musical event Saturday evening.

Due to the university's physical location, relatively isolated in central Pennsylvania, it was considered important to lead off with a well-known speaker; someone who would draw the people we wanted for the entire event. We obtained such a speaker six months before the event and proceeded to build the program around him. Then, eight weeks before he was to appear, he canceled out. While the panel speakers were being lined up without too much difficulty, we found ourselves without our two lead speakers eight weeks before the event.

A trustee, acting decisively on our behalf, obtained Lord Adrian, chancellor of Cambridge University, England, as the Friday evening speaker. Thirteen prominent individuals were contacted for the Saturday afternoon event, but without success. Five weeks before the event we had no speaker for that session. Then, on an impulse, the father of a past graduate was called and he undertook the job of approaching the Vice President of the United States, the Honorable Hubert H. Humphrey. Within forty-eight hours we had the Vice President's agreement to appear. Moral: Don't give up; make certain you cover every possibility for establishing a personal contact with the speaker you want. There is no substitute for the personal approach.

THE AFFAIR

Shortly after the Vice President's acceptance it became apparent that his schedule required a substantial change in our program. The Saturday session must begin at 1:30, an hour earlier than originally planned. The morning session was to end at noon.

Ticket requests quickly mushroomed to a total of 6,000 for Saturday's session. The hall—a gymnasium—seated 3,200. The problem was twofold:

A. How to expeditiously feed those on campus between noon and one o'clock, allowing thirty minutes to enter the gym.

B. What provision was to be made for those who could not be admitted to the gym?

The first problem was met by the erection of several large tents on an adjacent athletic field, with a prepared box lunch placed on chairs, so that there would be no serving lines. It worked extremely well.

A separate luncheon for specially invited persons was held in a large room at the rear of the gym, with direct access to the main floor.

When it became obvious that the response for tickets would exceed the seating capacity of the gym, the alternatives seemed to be to provide only sound or closed circuit TV to those who would be seated in the tents. Without hesitation, the decision of the President was for TV. It was professionally done and we had no complaints from anyone who was unable to obtain admission to the gym. The expense exceeded our budget, but the results proved the decision to have been a wise one.

Professional assistance had been retained for design of a Convocation symbol, the over-all motif on publicity signs and placards. No one would now question the advisability of this decision. It was the best investment we made.

The services provided by the Buildings and Grounds Department of the university were outstanding. Inclusion of its Director at the very earliest stages insured that expenditures for equipment and improvements were, whenever possible, phased into the university's plans for permanent improvements. This saved a substantial amount of money in the long run.

Inclusion of a number of people in the planning paid off handsomely. On numerous occasions we discovered that we had available on-campus experts whose talents could be utilized at great saving in time and money. Their involvement and interest led us to them.

EVALUATION OF RESULTS

Succinctly stated, the results were far more favorable than we had anticipated. The audience reaction was overwhelmingly enthusiastic; the event was reported on all three major TV networks and on radio; favorable newspaper publicity was received across the country and internationally. Letter response was enthusiastic and most complimentary. There were some expressions of concern over a small disturbance and walkout when the Vice President started to speak, but this was generally accepted as a part of the times and did not create a serious problem in later weeks and months.

Perhaps, the best summary comment was made by a professor of over thirty years' tenure who said: "I've waited for years for something like this, something that would be done in style and grace and I have never been so proud of Bucknell."

It was a great event for Bucknell. It set the stage for the campaign in a most effective way.

(Report by Harry Staley, Resident Director)

Organizing a Convocation

To attain the objectives of a convocation, it is necessary to form an adequate organization for carrying it out, to develop a theme which will have popular appeal, to tie the theme into some phase of the university's program, to enlist a roster of speakers whose presence will draw good attendance at all sessions of the convocation and whose speeches can be widely publicized by all forms of communications media.

Basic Organization

The convocation organization is a seedbed for the discovery and development of leadership in the campaign, and an ideal way to secure the active support of prospective donors whose association with the convocation will help to raise their sights for the campaign.

For this reason, the entire organization should be well sprinkled with laymen whose work and support are needed for the university later.

Convocation Chairman. This person should be one of the top leaders in the university's constituency—preferably one who is nationally known; who has a position of great prestige and influence, and whose name alone will draw others into the convocation setup.

Vice-Chairmen. Although these positions are largely honorary, it gives the university an opportunity to select persons of prestige, wealth, etc. for prominent spots in the organization. Their listing as vice-chairmen implies at least

BUCKNELL UNIVERSITY
CONVOCATION

SATURDAY, THE FOURTH OF MAY

NINETEEN HUNDRED AND SIXTY-EIGHT

The Davis Gymnasium

INDIVIDUAL RESPONSIBILITY IN A FREE SOCIETY

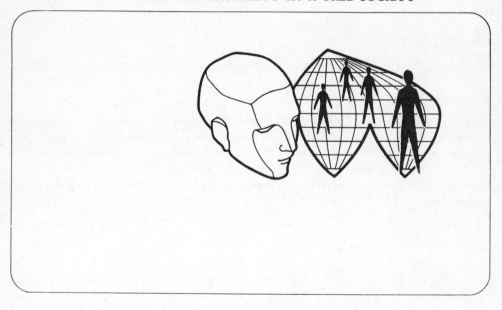

ORDER OF EXERCISES

Presiding

CHARLES H. WATTS II

President of the University

MUSIC

The Bucknell University Symphonic Band
Allen W. Flock, *Director*

*PROCESSIONAL

Fanfare, Flourish, Sennet from "Stratford Suite" .... *Howard Cable*
Crown Imperial .... *William Walton*

*THE NATIONAL ANTHEM

INVOCATION   The Rev. Dr. Clarence W. Cranford, *Minister*
                                                              Calvary Baptist Church, Washington, D. C.

INTRODUCTIONS AND ANNOUNCEMENTS   Dr. Detlev W. Bronk
                                                              President, The Rockefeller University
                                                              Chairman of the Convocation

RECOGNITION OF HONOR STUDENTS   Dr. Mark C. Ebersole
                                                              Provost of the University

ADDRESS   The Honorable Hubert H. Humphrey
                                                              The Vice President of the United States

BENEDICTION   The Rev. Dr. Cranford

*THE ALMA MATER

*RECESSIONAL

Orb and Sceptre .... *William Walton*

The audience standing

Fig. 5.   **Bucknell Convocation Program Cover and Program**

79

tacit approval of the university and its program and indicates to others the type of leadership the university is able to enlist. Furthermore, their own interest is aroused and results oftentimes in more substantial gifts during the campaign. Four or five vice-chairmen seem to be adequate in the ordinary university convocation organization.

Committees. While there may have to be other committees as plans progress, there are several committees which are absolutely necessary to the conduct of any well-organized and well-executed convocation:

- Program Committee
- Invitations Committee
- Attendance Committee
- Publicity Committee
- Arrangements Committee
- Decorations Committee
- Citations Committee
- Registration and Reception Committee

Each of these committees has definite responsibilities which will be elaborated on later.

Liaison

The chief responsibility of the lay members of the convocation committees is to develop the program and policies for the convocation. The execution of most of these broad outlines must necessarily be left to the members of the university's staff who are available day-by-day for this purpose. The practice in some successful convocation organizations has been to appoint a member (or members) of the university staff, including development office personnel, the public relations staff, etc., as liaison officer(s) to carry out the detailed work involved in policy and program procedures outlined by the lay committee.

Convocation Executive Committee

The convocation chairman, the vice-chairmen, the chairmen of the various committees, and the liaison officers of the university should constitute the Executive Committee of the convocation. The Marts and Lundy resident campaign director should be an ex officio, anonymous member of this committee.

Regular meetings of the convocation Executive Committee and of the individual committees operating under it should be held, with increasing frequency, as the time for the convocation approaches.

The functions of the Executive Committee are: to make major plans; to serve temporarily in the capacity of the Program Committee; to co-ordinate the work of the various working committees; to expedite the carrying out of the convocation plans.

Sponsoring Committee

In the absence of a formal development committee or of a campaign organization prior to the convocation, it is generally desirable to enlist a sponsoring committee for the convocation. The purpose of this committee, which is purely honorary, is a further extension of the primary public relations reasons for the convocation. The sponsors list should include alumni, parents, prominent local citizens, leadership and special gift prospects, etc. The number can vary from a hundred or so to several hundred, depending on the size of the university, the size of the city in which it is located, etc.

Program Committee

In general, it can be said that the main functions of this committee are:
1. To help formulate and administer the convocation program.
2. To help select and secure speakers and artists for the convocation.

A detailed listing of the responsibilities of this committee may include:
- Secure some of the speakers, artists, and other participants needed in the convocation events.
- Arrange detailed programs for all events: invocations, introductions, toastmasters, entertainment features, platform seating, etc.
- Arrange for an adequate place for each event.
- Determine menus and provide for catering.
- Provide proper decorations at formal events.
- Determine seating arrangements where needed.
- Provide for public address systems, spotlights, etc.
- Establish minute-by-minute time schedules for each event, and provide participants with cue sheets.

Invitations Committee

This committee should assist in compiling the list of invitees and make suggestions of additional names of those who should be invited. The invitation list should include all alumni, parents and other friends who can be easily identified. The list should be expanded to include local citizens, special groups such as ministers, local and state government officials, corporation officials, etc.

The committee should review these lists and add or delete names as it sees fit.

The committee may also assist in the creation of the formal invitations and approve the final form before they are printed and distributed.

Attendance Committee

This committee may be subdivided into other committees, one for alumni and one for local citizens.

ALUMNI ATTENDANCE COMMITTEE

The principal duty of this committee is to encourage the attendance of alumni at all sessions of the convocation. The committee should devise ways of stimulating attendance and carry out those methods in collaboration with university staff members assigned to this task.

● The national committee should enlist "area attendance" committees in various parts of the country where alumni of Bucknell reside in large numbers. It is probable that the most expeditious way to enlist these committees is through the help of the officers of local alumni clubs. In fact, they may be asked to assume this responsibility.

● If alumni club officers are used as local attendance committees, they may have up-to-date lists of local alumni, which would preclude having to send new lists from the university. In the absence of such lists, they should be provided with a 3 x 5 card file of local alumni addresses from the Alumni Office.

● Area attendance committees should receive suggestions for implementing the attendance campaign from the national committee. Following are suggestions for local committees.

(a) After the invitations for the convocation have been mailed from the university, area attendance committees should follow up local alumni through telephone calls or letters, urging alumni to send in their reservations at once.

(b) Some areas might be willing to conduct a luncheon, dinner, or smoker at which plans for the Convocation are explained.

(c) If possible, local alumni might form car pools, airlift pools, or provide for other group travel reservations to Lewisburg for the Convocation.

(d) Area attendance committees may feel free to employ other means of advertising the convocation and of encouraging attendance, as they see fit.

LOCAL ATTENDANCE COMMITTEE

This committee should devise and execute methods of encouraging attendance of local citizens at all sessions of the convocation. The area surrounding Lewisburg should be effectively canvassed by all means of communications to develop interest in the convocation. The personnel of this committee should include representatives of various community organizations such as clubs, teachers' groups, churches, local alumni associations of other colleges and universities, county and city officials, state officials, etc.

The committee might assign some of its members to a "Speaker's Bureau" which would furnish speakers for brief talks at service club meetings, etc., at which plans for the convocation could be revealed and attendance encouraged. A number of ways of promoting local attendance will occur as committee members begin their work.

Publicity Committee

This committee will have charge of plans for publicizing the convocation and properly interpreting it to the public. It should utilize all the communications media, including wide use of newspapers, magazines, radio, TV and press wires. It should prepare news releases before, during and after the convocation and should assist in the compilation of a brochure setting forth a summary of the proceedings for distribution following the convocation.

The committee is also responsible for arranging radio and TV broadcasts of the convocation events and for arranging for the reception and entertainment of press correspondents and others sent to cover the convocation proceedings.

Arrangements Committee

This committee has responsibility for the physical arrangements for the various convocation events. It is responsible for securing rooms and furniture for the meetings, for providing adequate seating accommodations, for procuring and operating loudspeakers, recording equipment, etc.

The committee should be composed almost entirely of university staff members who have a knowledge of campus accommodations and available equipment. Much of the work of the committee cannot be carefully outlined until plans for the convocation are developed by the Program Committee.

The committee will find it necessary to work in close co-operation with other convocation committees such as those for Decorations, Hospitality, Program, Public Relations, and Reception and Registration.

This committee is also responsible for providing ushers, ticket takers, guides, etc.

Decorations Committee

This committee should plan and carry out a decorating plan for meeting rooms and dinner tables, provide place cards for speakers' table, and in general enhance the atmosphere of the convocation in such manner as the committee members may desire.

Citations Committee

This committee will be charged with the selection of alumni and others who shall be recommended to the administrative officers and members of the board of trustees to be honored with a Bucknell University citation. It is suggested that provision be made for awarding citations in three categories: *(a)* alumni of the university, *(b)* distinguished citizens of the Lewisburg area, and *(c)* other friends of the university.

Using the facilities of the Development Office, a poll of the alumni can be made for the purpose of securing the names of suggested invitees in that category. The committee would be free to determine the extent to which it wishes to be guided by the results of this poll.

Determining the criteria for qualifying, and making the final selection of recommended citees will be the responsibility of the committee.

With the exception of the chairman, the members of the Citation Committee should not be identified.

Registration and Reception Committee

This committee is responsible for receiving and registering guests, for tallying incoming reservations, for distributing tickets, etc.

The Registration and Reception Committee is charged with responsibility for acting as host to special guests at the convocation, as many of the speakers and participants in the Convocation proceedings will be unfamiliar with the campus or with the town.

Members of the committee should arrange to have townspeople and faculty or staff members act as hosts for overnight guests and provide transportation while the guests are in town.

Prominent people taking part in the Convocation and/or their wives might be introduced to others at luncheons, teas, or cocktail parties sponsored by members of the committee.

It is always wise to appoint faculty members or students to act as hosts for the duration of the speaker's stay in town.

The committee should work closely with the Program Committee to discover when and where the guests will arrive or leave and should keep the prospective hosts apprised of this fact with periodic bulletins as the time for the Convocation draws near.

This committee may also be charged with finding and listing lodging places for the benefit of the many hundreds of out-of-town visitors who will attend the convocation.

(Report furnished by Marts & Lundy, Inc., and
Ronald J. Pedrick, Development Director, and
used by permission of Bucknell University)

8:   Open-House Tours

One of the best public relations events for "visibility" and good cultivation of community support is an open-house program, daytime or evening, but preferably the latter. This is true for any organization that has a building in which to stage the event—hospital, museum, library, college, school YMCA, YWCA, YM/YWHA, health and welfare agency, church, or synagogue, to mention only a few out of many.

While open-house events are usually associated with building-centered operations, some organizations may be conducting community-wide programs from small neighborhood centers or units where activities or services are carried on. These offer opportunities, with essentially the same set of problems, on a decentralized basis.

How Success Is Achieved

A successful open-house tour involves handling smoothly large crowds that may number into the thousands. It is essentially an operation that requires careful co-ordination of the tour route at all points, with all the details involved in the setting up and manning of points to be visited, and handling the heavy flow of traffic that is directed into the funnel of the tour route and at possible bottleneck points. This includes reception of guests, hosts and hostesses, guides, exhibits, demonstrations, refreshments, and other arrangements to assure that guests are comfortable, relaxed and at ease so as to enjoy the tour.

All these arrangements call for carefully co-ordinated plans with constant supervision to see that something doesn't bog down—that the flow of guests is handled smoothly so people do not feel herded and can enjoy a reasonably unhurried tour with a chance to stop and ask questions and visit with friends, and an opportunity to get near the punch bowl or other refreshments provided. There are also some hazard situations to be watched; for instance, an overloaded elevator. At such a point a man with a strong will, a strong arm, and good judgment needs to be posted.

These complicated problems can obviously be handled much more successfully in one central building than at a number of outlying points. Adequate equipment for exhibits, for motion pictures, and other audiovisual equipment must be considered. The favorable impressions, enthusiasm, and impact gained by a turnout of large crowds will yield better public relations results with less effort than trying to set up simultaneous programs at a number of points. This is all true if the event is handled smoothly. If extremely large crowds are anticipated, the open house might be held on two successive evenings with best results.

For the organizations with neighborhood service centers a more intimate type of open house can be scheduled on different dates, center by center. This has several advantages for attracting local publics or neighborhood groups near such units.

To underline these points of warning, nothing can be more frustrating and disappointing (and sometimes even hazardous) than bottleneck crowds, overloaded elevators which force many people to plod up and down stairs, or a mob jostling around and spilling punch at the refreshment tables. So Point Number One for the Open-House Committee is to plan with meticulous care, develop a checklist that takes into account every important set of details, and see that there are enough qualified staff members and/or volunteers assigned at strategic points to keep all activities operating smoothly.

An "Inside" Occasion

An open house is a "home base" event operated in familiar surroundings. Most of the people attending will be identified with the organization as active or prospective members, volunteers, parents, contributors.

Staff members of a large organization will have an active part to play, but should be as free as possible to answer questions, visit with guests at an appointed place, or mingle with the crowds.

If an organization is limited to one or two staff members, there will probably be some volunteers who are practically staff members and will be able to serve as chairmen of committees.

In either situation, this is an occasion when volunteers who "know the ropes" can be recruited as active and enthusiastic workers. They will accept their assignments seriously and their participation will be a form of recognition.

Several committees will be required involving trustees, staff (faculty and administrative staff in the case of a school or college), and volunteers. These people will serve as hosts and hostesses at key points; guides to conduct groups; "traffic directors" at elevators and bottleneck points to keep the crowds flowing smoothly; "information" persons stationed at various points to explain exhibits and answer questions about services and activities; checkroom attendants. There should be several teams of attractive females to spell each other in serving refreshments, mingling with the guests, and keeping the flow of traffic moving smoothly in and out of the refreshment area.

All volunteers should wear small identifying badges with *name* and HOSTESS or GUIDE, etc., to identify their function. Needless to say, good judgment is required in selecting people for these posts who will be at once gracious and efficient in carrying out their special assignments. There should be some kind of briefing for all volunteers, and brief mimeographed instructions should be given to all volunteers before they go to their posts as reminders of their specific duties.

A checklist is included in this chapter. It offers many suggestions, but should be considered only as a general over-all guide. Each Open-House Committee should work out its own working checklist tailor-made to fit the organization and the master plan developed as a first step in planning the event.

Other Considerations

For a good many years, large industrial plants and business organizations have been developing various types of plant tours, family nights and open-house programs for employees and their families, the community, stockholders, suppliers, and other general publics. These events are familiar to the multitude of people who have participated. Before planning an open house, it will be helpful to attend one or two such events if possible. This may reveal problems to be dealt with and probably will result in some good ideas. It will be fortunate if someone can be recruited for your Open-House Committee from the public relations staff of an industry or business—a person who has had some firsthand experience in the planning for such an event.

Bear in mind that the open house is a *public relations* event. Its purpose is to acquaint people with your facilities and services. It should not be considered or conducted in any way as a direct fund-raising event. To invite community publics on a hospitality and goodwill basis and then confront them with a raffle, money-raising games or gimmicks, or a pledge blank when they leave, will create resentment instead of goodwill. This admonition may not be necessary, but it is worth the space it takes for emphasis.

For combined public relations impact and general cultivation values, an open house is just about the best possible way to involve people from all of your publics in seeing what your organization does, learning how it contributes to the welfare of the community, and why it deserves support. The resulting favorable impression and knowledge gained will have a positive effect on your guests. So keep in mind the long-range aspects of the open house. It will help build goodwill and approval, leading to generous contributions when campaign time comes around.

How Often?

Should open house be held on an annual basis? This may prove successful in cities with large numbers of people in the membership, contributor, and other community groups. A spacing of two or three years is likely to be better for most organizations. The exception would be for membership or service organizations that have a very active, fast-moving and changing program related to current community needs and problems—enough activities and action to provide varied exhibits, new programs and services that will attract good attendance.

An *annual* open house can build up in popularity and interest values if it is imaginative in what it offers, and is well planned so that it moves people to attend each year—either because they are already involved and anticipate an enjoyable time or because they are interested in finding out more about the organization. By contrast, an open house with a thin trickle of guests will be as depressing as a poorly attended theater benefit party when more than half the seats in the house are empty, implying little interest in the sponsoring organization.

Plan Ahead

A successful open house involves large crowds to be handled and kept moving, with many activities often going on simultaneously that have to be planned carefully and well co-ordinated. This means many details to be checked, and many chances for little things to go wrong that will dull the luster of the event. Much more planning is necessary for a fiftieth anniversary or for a theater benefit, but an open house is just as important in its impressions, public relations values, and direct returns.

No organization's staff or corps of volunteer workers can be infallible. Somebody will always do something wrong, forget to do something, or fail to follow instructions—be it a member of the staff, a volunteer, or a guest. You must hope for the best and follow closely, step by step, your own checklist. Don't rely fully on the general checklist offered with this chapter or on somebody else's checklist. Make up your own. Every open-house event is different in some of its aspects and components.

Open-House Checklist

For your help and guidance, here is a basic checklist enumerating all the many steps that must be taken to make an outstanding success of your open-house tour.

● Form Executive Committee consisting of key staff and volunteer representatives. This committee will be responsible for setting the date and developing the over-all master plan for the open house

● Select chairmen to head the following subcommittees:

1. Arrangements
   Responsibilities: plan tour routes, prepare and set up exhibits, displays, demonstrations, etc.

2. Hosts and Hostesses
   Responsibilities: greet guests, handle registration, mingle with the guests, distribute booklets, annual reports, and other literature as guests leave

3. Tour Guides
   Responsibilities: conduct tours, answer questions, keep groups moving. (Allow one guide per ten people.)

4. Traffic and Safety
   Responsibilities: prepare and post signs as required, set up and maintain checkroom, keep elevators from being overloaded, keep traffic moving smoothly in stairwells, furnish guard or police protection if necessary, enforce fire regulations, oversee parking lot if such a facility is provided

5. Invitations
   Responsibilities: compile a master invitation list, design the printed invitation, prepare letters of invitation for special guests, determine date for mailing invitations

6. Refreshments
   Responsibilities: hostesses will set up buffet and help serve guests

● Organize workers to serve on above committees

• Hold a meeting of the Executive Committee and the heads of subcommittees. Discuss over-all plan, itinerary, and other arrangements

• Schedule a meeting for all members of all subcommittees; explain the purpose of the open house

• Prepare copy for the printed program. This will include information regarding the tour itinerary, brief facts concerning the organization, and the names of the committee members

• Publicity—submit stories to local daily and weekly papers and those in nearby communities; keep up the flow of publicity as follows:

1. First release—general story
2. Second release—program highlights, committee names, and photograph of key person
3. Third release—feature story
4. Fourth release—final plans, day before the event
5. Invite newsmen and photographers from newspapers and radio and television stations to cover the event
6. Have own photographer on hand, in addition to press photographers

• The day before the open house

1. Hold a committee meeting
2. Distribute mimeographed instructions to all members of the committee
3. Be sure that everyone knows what he or she is expected to do
4. Distribute identification badges

• During the open house

1. Set up registration tables; to prevent bottlenecks, arranged according to initial, i.e., A—E, F—J, K—O, P—T, U—Z
2. Distribute programs to arriving guests

• After the open house

1. Thank everyone who helped make the event a success
2. Mail printed program, together with appropriate letter and enclosure, to selected people who did not attend; enclosure might consist of a photo-offset copy of the feature story carried by the local press and some literature concerning the sponsoring organization
3. Evaluate the open house and determine how the next one can be improved

EXPERIENCE REPORTS

Old-Fashioned Open-House Homecoming

The city of Greensburg, Ind., was holding a series of "Old-Fashioned Bargain Days." The YMCA, located within a half block of the city's main business section, followed up with its own "Old-Fashioned Open-House Homecoming." Shoppers were encouraged to leave their children at the YMCA. Folks were invited to relax, rest and recuperate in the midst of their shopping sprees. The Y was suggested as a convenient meeting place. Free movies were shown in the afternoon and evening. Free swims were offered. Teen-agers were provided with a place to dance. Game room and gym facilities were made available. Board and committee members and their wives served as hosts and hostesses.

(Courtesy of Greensburg, Inc., YMCA)

Mardi Gras Theme

The Westerly, R.I., YMCA found a lively open-house theme. Each year the Association is dressed up for the big city-wide Mardi Gras Celebration. The YMCA Mardi Gras presents arts and crafts exhibits, variety show, fashion show, buffet dinner, film program, varsity basketball playoffs, and large book and record sales.

(Courtesy of Westerly, R.I., YMCA)

Free Taxi Service

The Steubenville, Ohio, YMCA really rolled out the welcome mat. Everyone in town was offered *free* taxi service to the Association's open house. Arrangements were made with the Steubenville radio station to accept calls from anyone who needed a lift to the event. The station relayed the pickup information over the air to the "taxi" cars. Volunteers from the Y's Men's Club served as cabbies.

(Courtesy of Steubenville, Ohio, YMCA)

Open Houses Bring Constructive Feedback

The New York League for the Hard of Hearing took an unusual route to tell its story and find out how a variety of influential persons felt about the organization and its program. The league held a series of open houses in the fall for some major contributors—business, political and professional people. Only a handful were invited to each open house, held late in the afternoon, and each guest had as a host or hostess a member of the organization's board of directors.

The guests were encouraged to take part in demonstrations of electronically simulated hearing loss and to sit down at a computer-based teaching machine and try out a few lessons. In addition, video monitors showed taped broadcasts of hearing and speech therapy, and a slide projector illustrated the scope of the league's activities. While the demonstration and exhibits served as points of focus, the prime goal was talk. Wanting to find out what the guests were thinking, the board members asked how they rated the league and its programs and candidly invited comparison to other organizations. Summing up the results, the league's public relations director, Seymour Stark, reported: "Not all comments were congratulatory, but we knew where we stood and how we could better interpret our programs in the future."

(Courtesy of *Channels*)

Open House Shows Hospital in Action

A massive and largely human exhibit was an unforgettable attraction at Memorial Hospital in Sarasota, Fla., when a new Service Building was recently dedicated. The exhibit was designed, reports the Florida Hospital Association, to promote better public understanding of present-day hospital costs. Every department of the hospital was on display, covering an area of 8,000 square feet, and every piece of hospital equipment had a price tag. The exhibit entrance represented a hospital lobby where the history and current expansion plans of the hospital were depicted by scale models. The lobby display also featured the workings of the hospital's administrative organization, as well as the kinds of services donated to the institution by volunteer groups. After leaving the simulated lobby, exhibit visitors were "admitted" to the hospital to witness live demonstrations in the emergency room, laboratory, and other departments. Nurses and technicians were on hand to demonstrate their skills with the most modern equipment, and each department, which had prepared its own display for the huge exhibit, illustrated its services for the visitors.

(Courtesy of *Channels*)

PART III
FUND-RAISING
SPECIAL EVENTS

Introduction

The dinners, the balls, the bazaars, and countless other events sponsored by charitable agencies throughout the country supply the wherewithal which supports an incredible number and variety of programs.

For scores of charities, special events are the chief source of income. This is particularly true of small organizations that receive little or no financial aid from foundations, corporations, or Government agencies. Charities that cannot rely upon those sources for assistance must seek private support. Usually they turn to special events as a means of raising the funds required to maintain their programs. Without the income derived from such events, many voluntary agencies would cease to function, and, as a result, many communities would be deprived of important services.

Special events are not limited to small community organizations. Hundreds of large national agencies sponsor one or more events each year, with the proceeds going to fill many needs that are not covered by other sources of support.

Aside from the financial aspects, there are other benefits that accrue. For instance, an event can serve as a "handle" for creating publicity which focuses attention on the agency's program. Often, the publicity stimulates interest that can be developed into financial support.

In addition, an event may act as a keystone in building a corps of volunteers. Without volunteers no charity can function and the more dedicated workers it can attract and hold, the more likely it is to succeed in its efforts.

To summarize, special events have a threefold purpose: raising money, creating publicity, and attracting volunteers.

9:   Campaign Opening Events

Two kinds of campaigns are discussed in this chapter: (1) capital gifts or endowment campaigns and (2) annual fund-raising drives. Some kind of opening event is needed for each type. The extent of planning will depend upon the nature of the project. The care in planning must be uniformly excellent. A scholarship fund, or some other project, with a goal of a million dollars more or less would call for the kind of special kick-off event involved in a capital gifts campaign or an annual fund drive. In the past ten to fifteen years the goals for capital fund campaigns have soared to astronomical figures—which before long may well be termed stratospherical—with tens of millions or even more than a hundred million dollars at stake. These are usually in the university and college field, or related to some national or civic institution such as a museum, a fine arts center, or a recreation center. Annual fund drive goals for local organizations and institutions likewise now run into the millions.

In any case it is essential to plan successful kickoff events. They serve as springboards for the campaign and play a vital part in determining its success or failure. They set the pace for developing conviction and enthusiasm among the campaign leaders and workers. They help increase both the major gifts needed to reach the campaign goal and the smaller contributions, in both number and amounts.

Two Kinds of Kickoff Events

Actually, two types of events are essential for every campaign with a substantial goal, whether capital gifts or annual fund drive. The first is a preliminary kickoff event. This is held for a limited number of carefully selected and specially invited guests. It is a quiet meeting of leaders to inspire them to dedicated action. It involves the campaign planning committee and other leaders related to the organization; community leaders whose moral support and active participation are desired; and major gift prospects. It is planned to inform these groups about the purpose of the campaign, and to cultivate their understanding—and ultimately generous gifts.

The second, and much larger, kickoff event marks the public launching of the

97

campaign. Among the guests who should be invited are the campaign committee and other leaders of the organization; school, church, civic, business, industrial and professional leaders; and prospects from the general contribution list. Major gift prospects should receive special invitations. There will also be invitations to members, volunteer workers and staff of the organization. Newspaper reporters will be notified, extended personal invitations, and seated at a special press table. There may be coverage by a radio station. Television coverage should be avoided, unless for some very special reason and with a suitable setup, because it is too distracting. This is the big send-off for the campaign. It demands an all-out promotion effort to assure a large and enthusiastic attendance. There must be an outstanding program to match the occasion. These are the ingredients needed to assure good publicity coverage, to win support from those who attend the kickoff, and to encourage public response.

The Importance of Good Campaign Management

At this point an explanatory statement should be made. It is not the function of this handbook, or the intent of the authors, to deal with the planning and organization, problems to be handled, techniques and methods required in the *management* of major fund-raising campaigns. In other chapters it has been suggested that organizations will find it desirable to obtain, if possible, professionals who can assist in any major special event. In large cities arrangements can often be made to engage on a fee basis the services of a professional public relations or fund-raising firm to carry major responsibility for staging the event, working with the organization's staff and volunteers. Most classified directories list public relations and fund-raising firms that can be consulted. Sometimes it may be the public relations division of an advertising agency. Check with a qualified member of your organization, if possible, for recommendation of reliable firms, and discuss with one or more of these how much it will cost for the services needed. Another possibility is to engage, on a package basis for a fee, some individual with professional experience in handling special events.

So much for assistance in staging the event. For capital gifts campaigns, and for annual fund drives with large goals, it is important to have the services of an experienced and reliable fund-raising firm. Many a campaign has failed because of the lack of professional know-how. Some trustees will vigorously oppose "hiring a firm" believing the cost is too high and that the staff and volunteers can and should do the job anyway. Most staff members realize the importance of, and feel the need for, expert advice and help.

All reliable fund-raising firms today operate on a fee basis that is reasonable and moderate—measured against the total funds raised when the organization provides the necessary teamwork. It is wise to investigate what a reliable firm can provide—or may decline to consider if it reaches the conclusion after a preliminary study that the facts do not indicate the organization is ready for a campaign.

Sources of Ethical Professional Assistance

The American Association of Fund Raising Counsel, Inc., 500 Fifth Avenue, New York, N.Y. 10036 has a membership of twenty-nine fund-raising firms throughout the United States and Canada that subscribe to its code of ethics. Information about the AAFRC, its functions, the code of ethics it recommends, and a list of its member organizations will be supplied upon request.

If information is desired regarding local fund-raising or public relations firms —or those in a nearby city—there are other organizations that can be queried for recommendations, such as the following:

American Alumni Council
1 Du Pont Circle, N.W.
Washington, D. C. 20036

American College Public
  Relations Association
1 Du Pont Circle, N.W.
Washington, D.C. 20036

Public Relations Society
  of America
845 Third Avenue
New York, N.Y. 10022

National Public Relations
  Council of Health &
  Welfare Organizations
419 Park Avenue South
New York, N.Y. 10016

National Society of Fund
  Raisers, Inc.
130 East 40th Street
New York, N.Y. 10016

The Preliminary Special Gifts Event

In college and university capital gifts campaigns this kickoff event is often announced as a Leadership Conference. Among community organizations it is usually called by campaign planning committees a Special Gifts event. Whatever it may be called, its purpose is the cultivation of major gift prospects.

Strategically, the preliminary Special Gifts event holds great importance for success of the campaign. The quota formula for a major campaign calls for 80 to 90 per cent of the gifts to be raised from 10 per cent of the contributors. The trustees must spearhead the major gifts, with a quota of 25 to 33 1/3 per cent or more toward the campaign goal.

This cultivation event lays groundwork for later personal solicitation. If one or several very large bellwether contributions can be announced at the event they will help raise the level of other big precampaign special gifts. The total response will in turn provide encouragement and impetus at the campaign public kickoff, or whenever the campaign committee chooses to announce large contributions to give a lift to the drive.

A Leadership Conference is often a weekend of program events, with a convocation type of general meeting, a series of special meetings, tours, a dinner, a luncheon, a cocktail party, or other social gathering. The nature of the campaign, the total time available, and other factors will govern decisions regarding the most effective program.

For community organizations the preliminary Special Gifts event is usually a much smaller, private meeting. Invitations are carefully screened and not sent in letter form but extended on a more intimate person-to-person basis. The Planning Committee may decide on an evening meeting in a home, a dinner or a luncheon—usually in a private club providing an attractive setting and good food. The type of meeting will be governed by the nature of the organization, the purpose of the campaign and its goal, and the people who are to be invited.

The Campaign Public Kickoff

In contrast to a special gifts preliminary event, the public launching of a campaign is quite a different kind of kickoff. It is usually held in a hotel ballroom or some other large banquet room which provides an attractive setting, with opportunities for imaginative decorations and for some striking exhibits if these can be developed.

One objective is to promote the largest possible attendance. Important are: clearly visible table numbers, assistance of ushers to insure smooth handling of seating, and efficient and rapid food service. Many a campaign dinner program has suffered because of slow seating and lagging meal service. The planning, promotion, and arrangement for campaign public kickoff dinners follow in general the pattern outlined in the checklist for dinners. (See Chapter 10.)

If the kickoff is an evening meeting without a dinner, the natural setting is usually a large auditorium. This kind of event involves the same problems in the smooth handling of arrangements and program.

Dinner Meeting Recommended

For many organizations a dinner meeting is most effective. A kickoff dinner followed by a lively, smooth-flowing program provides an enjoyable social occasion for a mixed audience. There is more time for visiting and cultivation at the tables. An attractive setting—music, flowers, decorations—can add atmosphere, warmth and color with favorable effect on the guests. There is ample time—if the total program is kept under control—to tell the story and make the case effectively for the campaign purpose and goal.

A luncheon meeting may be necessary, and can be effective. But then time is limited and the program must be streamlined to a tight schedule. An evening meeting, without a dinner and followed by an informal reception or mixer with refreshments has proved successful for many organizations. An evening meeting kickoff offers opportunities for personal cultivation of specially invited small groups at private dinner parties hosted by trustees, campaign committee members and other organization leaders. Cocktail parties preceding a dinner kickoff offer the same opportunities.

Careful planning and imagination are two major requirements for a successful public kickoff event. Several committees, small and co-ordinated, will be needed for the over-all planning and arrangements. These will include invitations, seating lists, all services for the banquet hall and dinner, or auditorium, program, hospitality, and publicity.

A dinner is a dinner. It can be just that and dull without imaginative touches. A meeting can also be dull and boring, and a handicap to the campaign. Top-flight speakers and top-flight entertainment can make all the difference in the world. To repeat once again: the setting, the atmosphere, the food, the beverages, the service, the music, the flowers, the decorations, the people at the table, and, finally, an efficiently handled checkroom with no lost wraps or hats to ruffle tempers—all will contribute to the flavor and warmth of the occasion, and to the favorable or unfavorable impressions made upon guests. But the program is the most important and conclusive part of the event. It will enhance or weaken the enthusiasm, conviction, and intentions that each guest carries home to ponder in deciding the amount of his or her contribution to support the purpose of the campaign.

CASE STUDIES

Augustana College Campaign Leadership Conference

In conducting a survey for a client, it sometimes happens that although the leading constituents may be in favor of the institution and its proposed plans, they frequently do not have a full appreciation of the service which the institution is rendering. Furthermore, many of them are not tied in closely with the enterprise—that is, they do not have a working interest in the institution. If a capital fund-raising program is to succeed, it is these relatively few prospects, about 10 per cent, who must provide anywhere from 80 to 90 per cent of the money. It is important, then, that the leading prospects gain a fuller appreciation of the value of the institution. A working interest must be engendered in their minds and the need for substantial giving must be carefully put before them.

PURPOSE

The Leadership Conference is designed to help create a positive campaign climate within the leading constituency before the actual organization work and solicitation gets under way. Part of the purpose of the conference is to provide prominent alumni, parents and friends with an opportunity to observe at first-hand the attributes of the institution which make it worthy of support. Those attending should gain a fuller understanding of its goals, its opportunities for service and the needs which must be met for its further advancement.

The conference should show that top leaders are already taking an active role in the planning of the campaign. It should be made clear that additional leadership will be required for success of the program.

Still another purpose of the conference is to make the leading prospects aware of the scale of giving required for success. They should know that they are part of the select 10 per cent group that will have to provide anywhere from 80 to 90 per cent of the money. It is important that these fund-raising facts not be overlooked during the conference. Any conference that does not include them is losing a valuable opportunity for educating the leading prospects in the need for substantial giving.

It should be noted that the Leadership Conference differs from the convocation in several ways. The conference is directed specifically at leadership and special gift prospects, whereas the convocation is pointed at the entire constituency. The convocation is usually broader in scope and may last several days while the leadership conference is pointed and of shorter duration.

The responsibility for developing a creative Leadership Conference rests squarely in the hands of the Resident Director. This responsibility cannot be delegated to a staff person at the institution. *The Leadership Conference is a significant fund-raising event and not a cultural or educational conference.*

KEYNOTE SPEAKER

The first step the Resident Director must take is to discuss the importance of this occasion with the head of the institution. It should be pointed out that a keynote speaker of national prominence is required to focus attention on this event. He should be asked for suggestions as to who might be the most natural person to do this—someone whose participation would elicit a favorable response from the leading prospects. The best speaker is a nationally known person who has had some identification with the institution. To come up with the right keynote speaker is not always easy.

Frequently, college presidents will suggest an educator or a second-line politician. The best person, however, is usually a leading national industrialist who can speak authoritatively about the value of private institutions and the need for strengthening their support.

The head of the institution should be asked to appoint a small committee to work with the Resident Director on the details. The committee should involve key members of the staff, faculty, and campaign leadership. This step needs to be taken three to four months before the event.

The Resident Director plays a critical role in the selection of the keynote speaker. In doing this, he needs the suggestions of not only the president and the committee, but also key trustees and campaign leaders. The persons recommended must be researched by him and an appraisal made of their qualifications along the following lines:

—what is the proposed speaker's prominence?

—is he considered a good speaker?

—by his involvement, would leaders want to attend?

—is his political persuasion in step with the leaders of the institution?

—can he make a substantial gift to the campaign?

The answers to these questions are important in determining who the speaker will be. Here, the creative abilities and professional experience of the director come into play in guiding the client in making this key selection. As suggestions are crystallized it would be well for the Resident Director to review these possibilities with his supervisor.

Many times clients have nationally prominent people in their own constituency whom they have not clearly identified. This was the case at Augustana College. When we sat down to discuss possiblities for the keynote speaker all kinds of suggestions were made—from the President of the United States on down. Most of the persons had little or no identification with the college and were just "big names." It took nearly six weeks of careful study to discover and identify the person who proved to be an excellent choice for Augustana to invite as the keynote speaker for its National Leadership Conference.

Once the top candidate for keynote speaker has been agreed upon, the next two questions to be answered are (a) who invites him to speak, and (b) how is this best accomplished? The person (or persons) who invites the candidate to speak should be someone the candidate would respond to because he knows and respects him, or someone the candidate should respect because of his position in the institution. In most situations the best person is the chairman of the board and/or the president of the institution because of their rank and stature.

The best way to invite the candidate to speak is to arrange for an appointment to see him in person. There is no substitute for a personal call. When the candidate is called upon, he should be presented with a clear picture of the importance of this event in launching the campaign and the need for his participation in the program. He will want to know what he is expected to speak about and for how long. The suggested topic should allow the speaker sufficient breadth to discuss the importance of private institutions in our society and the need for continued support to strengthen and enlarge their areas of service. His address should be about 20 to 25 minutes in length. A tentative program should be presented to him and an offer made to furnish the necessary background information and materials. Most top men will want to write their own speeches and will require only supporting information.

Before the visit is actually made, the Resident Director must meet with the callers to review in detail the whole pattern of the call. He will need to prepare an outline for the callers on the important points to be discussed with the prospective speaker. This briefing session affords the Resident Director a key opportunity to get across the design of the program. The callers must understand the design thoroughly in order to effectively convey this idea to the prospective keynote speaker. An important help is the outline mentioned. With sufficient preparation by the Resident Director and understanding by the callers, an effective presentation will be made and an affirmative response assured.

THE PROGRAM

The Leadership Conference Program should be designed to fit the particular institution and should appeal to the leading constituency you are attempting to reach. The program should allow those persons who are being invited to gain a better appreciation of the institution, the service which it is rendering and the need for its strengthened support.

In developing the program the Resident Director works closely with the Leadership Conference Committee. Members of the committee will look to the director for guidance. In this situation the director must take a leadership role. Faculty and staff people will typically tend to think along the lines of an educational or cultural conference. The director needs to focus their attention on the important elements of a Leadership Conference and to gain their help in developing these elements to show off the institution in the best possible light.

The important elements of the Leadership Conference which should be carefully considered are:

● *The theme*. This is the central idea around which the conference should revolve. It does not have to be a catchy phrase but should simply express the reason for the conference. At the Colby College Leadership Conference the theme was "The Ford Foundation Gift and Its Challenge." A similar theme was used in the Brown University Conference.

● *The calendar*. The Leadership Conference should be a compact event and not a marathon. Top leaders today simply do not have the time or inclination to spend several days at an institution. The conference program should not be overbearing and should allow just enough time to get across the central theme with impact. A good length for the Leadership Conference is one that begins on a late Friday afternoon or early evening and ends on a Saturday afternoon or evening. Try to set it on a date that does not conflict with annual events, such as Homecoming.

● *Areas of service.* Each institution has some particular areas of service which should be highlighted during the Leadership Conference. It takes a great deal of imagination on the part of the conference committee members and the Resident Director to determine these areas and to develop the format of presenting them at the conference. You simply cannot show off every aspect of the institution at the conference, instead you must select for emphasis the areas where the institution is doing an unusually fine job or which are unique.

Some conferences provide guided tours of the campus to see new facilities, visit laboratories in action, and participate in departmental seminars. This aspect of the program has to be handled carefully so that what is being done in the laboratories and seminars will be meaningful to the conference participants.

At Augustana we decided to focus on the student and his experiences at the college. Six outstanding students were selected to present papers on "Living and Learning at Augustana." They developed their own speeches with the guidance of committee members. They covered in depth the values of a small liberal arts college as they saw and experienced these values. Their presentations to an audience of more than 500 leaders at our opening general session set the whole tone for the Augustana National Leadership Conference. The students were so well received we decided to reprint their speeches and mail them to the entire constituency.

● *The needs.* At the heart of the Leadership Conference is an explanation of the needs which must be met to further improve and strengthen the institution's areas of service. Usually the president is the person who can most effectively speak about the needs. Sometimes the chairman of the board can also participate in this aspect of the program.

Visual aids such as a blown-up campus map, artist's renderings, and a listing of estimated costs will help in making this presentation. To add to the effectiveness of the presentation, similar supporting materials should be placed in the portfolios of each conference participant.

● *Meeting the needs (the role of leadership).* Once the needs have been explained, the next aspect of the program should cover how these needs are to be met. The best person to head this part of the program is the national chairman or one of the top campaign leaders. The elements that should be covered are:

—announcing that a fund-raising campaign will be held to meet the needs.

—announcing the persons who have already agreed to serve in leadership roles.

—noting that substantial giving will be required to raise the required funds.

—announcing the scale of gifts required for success, emphasizing that 90 per cent of the money will be raised from 10 per cent of the donors and that less than 1 per cent of the donors will give half the money. A campaign leader should make this presentation.

—an endorsement of the contemplated program by the national chairman and an invitation to join in meeting the objective.

This part of the program must be given careful attention by the Resident Director. By effectively utilizing top leaders, basic fund-raising concepts should be implanted in the minds of the conference participants. The Resident Director should write the remarks and speeches for this section of the program and go over them with the campaign leaders so that they fully understand each element in the presentation.

● *Keynote speaker.* The address of the keynote speaker adds impact to what has already been said and places the institution in a national context. He endorses this kind of an institution and the program it is contemplating. He puts the frosting on the cake.

MATERIALS

● *Hold date letter.* Ample notification to leading prospects of the date of the conference is important. A "hold date letter" explaining the purpose of the conference, and that a formal invitation will follow should be mailed about five to six weeks before the event. This letter should be personally typed on automatic typewriters and signed by the conference chairman, chairman of the board, or the president of the institution.

● *Invitation lists.* The invitation list should comprise prospects having the capacity to give $1,000 or more, those members of the constituency who have taken leadership roles in earlier fund campaigns, and representative leaders of the alumni, parents, and community. The Resident Director needs to spend a great deal of research in developing this important list. If he fails to do so, the invitation list may be comprised of the same old group who are at every event of the institution. In effect, the Resident Director has to dig for leading names and do it thoroughly. An analysis of screening results to date will be helpful in providing much of this list.

● *Formal interviews.* A 5″ x 7″ printed invitation from the president and directors of the institution should be prepared and mailed three to four weeks before the event. The envelope should be hand-addressed and the invitation should contain:

　—the name of the event,

　—the dates,

　—name and title of the keynote speaker,

　—a capsule of the program,

　—a personal message from the head of the institution urging their attendance,

　—a reply card and stamped reply envelop addressed to the head of the institution.

A good technique to assure better attendance is to offer to provide hotel or motel accommodations for those guests who will be coming from outside the area. If this offer is being extended, it should be included in the reply card.

● *Invitations to special reception.* It may be advisable to hold a special occasion for a few of the top prospects and campaign leaders. This event might be a president's reception honoring the keynote speaker. If such an event is contemplated, it would be advisable to hand-address the invitations on the president's personal stationery with reply requested. This lends prestige to the occasion and will let the top prospects know they are in the inner group.

● *Printed program.* A complete program of the conference events should be printed. This program should include date, time, place of all events, and names and titles of participants. It should also include names of the members of the National Campaign Committee and the names of the National Committee of Sponsors for the fund-raising program. The printed program should be included as part of the portfolio materials for each conference participant.

● *Portfolio.* Each conference participant should receive a portfolio which may include the following materials:

—conference program,
—information about lodging and meals,
—list of immediate needs with estimated costs,
—campaign map showing placement of new facilities,
—booklet of renderings and floor plans,
—scale of giving required to raise the necessary funds,
—list of commemorative opportunities, if available.

The portfolio should be distributed at the registration centers spotted around the campus.

● *Visual aids.* It is helpful in making some of the fund-raising presentations to have certain visual aids:

—blown-up campaign map showing placement of facilities,
—architect's sketches of the new facilities,
—large mounted scale of giving,
—slide presentation, carefully worked out.

PERSONNEL

● *Program participants and events.* An itinerary should be prepared by the Resident Director for the keynote speaker and for each principal participant so that they know where they are supposed to be and at what time. A key member of the faculty or Conference Committee should be assigned to act as host for these important persons.

Each event of the conference should be presided over by a campaign leader— a key member of the faculty or the Conference Committee.

A detailed script for each event should be prepared by the Resident Director and reviewed carefully with the person presiding and with the participants. These events should be run off like clockwork and this can only be achieved when all aspects of the event are thought through and carefully put down on paper.

● *Registration.* Guests should be greeted on arrival at registration points clearly identified around the campus. Students can be involved in registering the guests. A member of the Conference Committee should be at each registration point. Portfolios of materials are distributed at the registration points.

● *Faculty.* Department heads and ranking members of the faculty should be invited to all events. Several may participate in the actual program. Another way to utilize the faculty is to have them host a table of guests at each luncheon or dinner. This is an excellent way to make the guests feel that they are being given personal attention by the institution. They will appreciate the opportunity of knowing the faculty better and, more important, the conversation usually revolves around the institution.

● *Conference Committee.* Each member of the committee should have a specific assignment to carry out as his responsibility for the success of the program. If the responsibility is spread around, the Resident Director should be free to oversee each event and make certain that everything is moving along on schedule.

• *Pre-arranged seating.*   At all luncheons and dinners, guests with reservations should be assigned pre-arranged seating. This will enable friends to be seated together and with their tables spotted on the floor according to their prominence. A Multilithed or printed alphabetical seating list should be prepared shortly before the event and distributed when the guests arrive. This will require a great deal of attention by the Resident Director and his staff, but will enhance the program immensely.

• *Miscellaneous.*   It is important that traffic control be maintained around the institution, that police be spotted at critical intersections, attendants be in the parking lots, and sufficient directions posted to help conference guests.

PUBLICITY AND FOLLOW-UP

In every possible way the institution should tell the story of the Leadership Conference. All local news media, TV and radio stations should be invited to the principal events. An advance copy of the keynote speaker's address should be secured and prepared for distribution to the various news media. In the case of a particularly distinguished nationally prominent person, a news conference may be desirable.

If possible, all principal addresses should be recorded on tape. This will be helpful in checking the original text of an address and preparing copy for later publications.

If the institution is a college and has a radio station, the students will probably want to cover the key events and broadcast them live.

A campaign report should be prepared immediately following the Leadership Conference which should contain all the highlights of the program along with full picture coverage. If the addresses at the conference were significant, it would be well to publish them in a small booklet and mail them to the entire constituency.

CONCLUSION

An effective Leadership Conference can set the tone for the entire campaign and can create a great deal of interest in the institution by the leading constituency, whether or not they attend. These persons will develop a fuller appreciation of the values of the institution and its area of service. They will be encouraged to work actively on the fund-raising program through the example of the leaders who have participated in the conference. Those who attend should go away with the feeling that this institution is really on the move and preparing to do great things to enhance its area of service in the future.

The Resident Director is the master architect of the Leadership Conference. Through his imagination, guidance, and careful work the conference will make a lasting impact on persons who can provide the top gifts for a successful fund-raising program.

(Courtesy, Marts and Lundy, Inc.
From report prepared by Howard R. Braren,
Resident Director for the Capital Campaign)

Colby College Campaign Leadership Conference

While there may be nothing new to the general principle that it is a good idea to get alumni leaders back to the campus for campaign indoctrination, the Leadership Conferences held in our recent Ford Foundation challenge campaigns have achieved a twist which is interesting.

Some 200 alumni (with spouses), trustees and parents were invited, with some seventy acceptances. The invitees included special givers and those slated for area chairmanships or similar organization posts. The response was fair. Some real giving power was represented, especially among parents, and for all those who did come, it was powerful cultivation. I only wish more of our special prospects could have had the experience.

In the first planning stage, there was discussion as to whether to hold our Leadership Conference in August (which would doubtless have brought more people) or in September when the students would be there. The latter was the decision and, as it turned out, the wise one.

The local hotel was reserved and the college assumed all expenses of lodging and meals. The program started Friday, late afternoon, and ended Saturday after dinner.

The opening event was a social hour in the president's home, followed by an elegant dinner in a college dining hall. Here, place cards marked HOST, STUDENT, or GUEST insured the desired scattering at each table. Except for a Welcome and announcements, there was no after-dinner program. Instead, the guests were assigned to faculty hosts and went to their homes for the evening. Each home had two faculty couples, about four guests and two or three undergraduates. No line of conversation was pushed, but the talk inevitably revolved around the college, and the visitors couldn't help but size up the faculty and students and come away very much impressed.

On Saturday morning (promptness was stressed) the program consisted of four academic resumes—each in a different building, and each with a faculty spokesman telling of all the laudable and exciting things going on in terms of curriculum changes, faculty strength, and faculty-student research. The four fields were: the sciences, the social sciences, library and humanities, and the fine arts. A coffee break in the faculty lounge gave further chance to meet professors. This morning program was the crux of the whole conference. The writer, who has made it a point to know everything about Colby for forty years, was astounded to learn of academic developments and excellences that he had never heard of before. In short, this was a convincing demonstration of what the Ford Foundation found at this college which was "worth betting on." For many of the visitors, besides the academic impact, this was the first chance to inspect the wonderful facilities in the new buildings.

Saturday's luncheon (Maine lobster!) was held in the Men's Union following which the visitors gathered in the music auditorium for "the commercial." The president outlined the step-by-step story of winning the Ford grant. The executive vice-president gave details as to the proposed buildings, and financial projections to show the necessity for a greater endowment. View Master slides illustrated this talk. Finally, the vice-president for development gave a rousing "how we shall proceed" presentation, including the scale of giving, the coming area campaigns, and the absolute necessity for giving "over our heads."

Another social hour at the President's house and dinner at the Men's Union (steak) completed the day. Here, again, students were interspersed among the guests. The President of the board gave the top speech of the evening—an eloquent and moving appeal for supporting what Colby is endeavoring to do in the American scene.

The writer attended this conference as one of the invited guests, rather than as one of the campaign staff, and can testify to its effectiveness. One of the best things, and this was echoed by all with whom he talked, was the reassuring knowledge that today's students are able, ambitious and attractive youngsters, and this is a convincing reason for holding such a conference while college is in session.

All in all, testing my own reactions, I am sure that such an experience enormously strengthens one's incentive for giving. One gets a firsthand conviction about the worth of one's college that is far more powerful than what can be done through brochure, speeches, a movie, or one of our regular convocations (although these have other special dividends, too). In other words, a Leadership Conference could well be considered in many kinds of campaigns as a device for nourishing the basic motivation for giving—*a deep desire to see the goal attained.*

JOSEPH C. SMITH
(Report furnished by Marts and Lundy, Inc.)

10:   Award Dinners

Award dinners are held by various groups, organizations, and industries to honor individuals who have made important contributions to charitable causes, played major roles in the development of their communities, or performed outstandingly as civil servants.

A dinner can honor a single person or several people simultaneously. It can be a fund-raising event or it can be held for the sole purpose of paying tribute to local citizenry. This chapter deals with the dinner as a fund-raising event.

A fund-raising dinner serves two main purposes: (*a*) it provides a means of honoring a distinguished citizen and (*b*) at the same time serves as a vehicle for raising funds to support the work of a charitable organization.

Usually, the individual to be honored is chosen by a Nominating Committee. The members of this committee are appointed by the trustees and/or board members of the organization conferring the honor. The honoree is presented with a scroll, plaque, statuette, U.S. Savings Bond, or some other tangible means of recognition.

A successful fund-raising dinner requires a dedicated chairman, a committee of 25 to 100 persons depending upon the size and scope of the event, and several months of preparation.

The general chairman is the key person. In selecting a chairman, look for someone with previous experience in dealing with large events. In addition to experience, he must have strong leadership ability, be able to assume responsibility and to cope with details, and have a talent for handling people. Above all, he should be well known and respected within the community so that he will have no difficulty in attracting outstanding people to serve on his committee.

Organizing the Committees

The Dinner Committee should be composed of people from all walks of life—management, labor, the professions, the arts, retailing, civil service, etc. The Dinner Chairman will organize the following subcommittees: Program, Arrangements, and Subscriptions. Appoint a chairman to head each committee. If a souvenir journal is planned, designate a chairman and form a committee. (The souvenir journal is discussed later in this chapter.)

Regular meetings are necessary to keep abreast of progress. The meetings will give the general chairman and the heads of various committees a chance to detect any minor troubles and to correct them before they can develop into major problems.

Honorary Chairmen

The honorary chairmen should be well-known citizens such as the governor, senators, the mayor, the president of the city council, and other individuals who occupy important positions in the community.

Honorary chairmen are for prestige purposes only. They are "name lenders" who perform no actual work, but merely serve as window dressing. The appearance of their names in newspaper publicity, the invitation, the program, and other printed materials signifies their endorsement of the event. Usually, the trustees and/or board members of the sponsoring organization are responsible for obtaining their co-operation.

Budget

Calculate expenses and determine goal for net proceeds. The two sums will provide the information needed to set a realistic ticket price for the event. The price range will vary: in a metropolitan area, tickets often are priced at $75 to $100 a head. This is necessary because costs of facilities, entertainment, etc., are much higher in a large city. A small community might sell tickets at a much lower price and still realize a favorable profit.

Here is a sample budget for a dinner held in a metropolitan area:

SAMPLE BUDGET

Estimated Income

General Subscription	$37,500
(500 at $75 per plate)	
Souvenir Journal	13,000
	50,500

Estimated Expenses

Printing and postage	2,400
Meetings and local travel	300
Orchestra	1,000
Hotel	8,000
Entertainment	1,000
Decorations	250
Miscellaneous	200
Temporary clerical assistance	400
	13,550

Anticipated Net Proceeds	$36,950

TO: Members of the Committee

FROM: Jack Martin, Chairman

Please list below names and addresses of those you wish to invite to the dinner. Return the list as soon as possible to Harold Weiman, Chairman of the Subscription Committee.

NAME	ADDRESS (include zip code)

Fig. 6. Form Used to Solicit Names of Possible Guests

When selecting a place to hold the dinner, consider the physical requirements of the event. If a large, formal affair is planned (music, dancing, professional entertainment, etc.), the ballroom of a hotel will be the logical choice. If, however, a smaller, less elaborate event is planned, it can be adequately handled by a local restaurant or held in a rented hall, a gymnasium, or a church social room and serviced by a good caterer.

Invitation List

Names must be submitted by committee members, the trustees and/or board members, and the guest of honor. If the sponsoring organization is one that regularly conducts fund-raising drives, check the files for names of large donors. Another source is the local newspaper; check it daily and cull names of people frequently involved with civic and social activities.

Type names and addresses on 3″ x 5″ cards which will serve as the master list. File the cards alphabetically to prevent duplication. Names submitted by the committee should be marked regarding origin—that is, if Jack Martin supplied William Morris' name Mr. Martin's name should appear on the master card.

Acceptance List

As acceptances are received, type names and addresses on 3″ x 5″ cards. Place the cards in a secondary file, also arranged alphabetically. The cards will provide up-to-date acceptance information.

Mail tickets as soon as acceptances are processed. Specify on the cards in the secondary file the date tickets were mailed and the ticket numbers.

When all the acceptances have been received, the cards will serve as the basis for preparing the seating chart. (Preparation of the seating chart is discussed later in this chapter.)

Printing

Copy for all materials (invitation/envelope, reservation card/return envelope, tickets, program) should be submitted to the printer well in advance of the date set for the event so he will have ample time to do a good job. Request the printer to submit checking proofs for all printed materials.

Invitations

The invitation should be dignified and in good taste. The front page contains the name of the sponsoring organization, the guest of honor's name, date and time of event, place it will be held, manner of dress, and cost of subscription. On the inside pages, list the names of all people connected with the event—honorary chairmen, general chairman, heads of various committees, and names of committee members. (Note: Publication of their names requires their consent, so be sure that they sign consent cards.)

Mail invitations eight weeks prior to the event. Include a reservation card and a return envelope. (Incidentally, the following statement might be included on the reservation card: "I/we cannot attend the dinner for John Brewster but en-

You are cordially invited to attend the

ANNUAL AWARD DINNER

of

[name of organization]

John Brewster, Guest of Honor

Sunday evening, November sixteenth, nineteen sixty-nine

at eight o'clock

Waldorf-Astoria Hotel, Park Avenue and Fiftieth Street

Subscription $75.00 per plate   Black Tie

Fig. 7.   Invitation for Award Dinner

Please reserve _____ places at the Annual Award Dinner, Sunday evening, November 16, 1969 at the Waldorf-Astoria. Enclosed is my check in the amount of $ _____ ($75.00 per plate).

Name _____

Address _____

_____ zip code _____

☐ I/we cannot attend the dinner for John Brewster but enclose a contribution toward the work of your organization.

(Please indicate on the back of this card the names of the people with whom you wish to be seated.)

Fig. 8.   Reservation Card for Award Dinner

close a contribution toward the work of your organization." This is a fund-raising gimmick; it's aimed at reaching people who are not interested in attending such events. Frequently they will send a donation because they feel it gets them "off the hook.")

Hand-addressing is not necessary; neat typing is acceptable and stamps present a nicer appearance than a postage meter.

The two-week period immediately following the mailing of invitations will serve as a barometer. A very light response will indicate the need for the committee to contact friends and associates, either personally or by telephone, and urge them to attend the dinner.

Program for the Award

Designate someone to present the award to the recipient. The presenter can be the president or some other officer of the organization's governing board or a personal friend of the recipient. Instruct the recipient of the award to keep his acceptance speech brief.

Inform the guest speaker how much time has been allotted for his speech so he can prepare it accordingly.

Entertainment

The extent of the entertainment will be determined by the size of the budget. The entertainment can include a comedian, folk singer, barbershop quartet, etc. A combo or an orchestra will be needed to provide music for dancing.

We have reserved a place for

[name of guest]

at our

ANNUAL AWARD DINNER

Sunday evening, November 16, 1969, at the

Waldorf-Astoria, Park Avenue and 50th Street

Reception and Cocktails   *Please hand this card*
promptly at seven   *to your waiter*

Fig. 9. Sample Ticket for Award Dinner

PROGRAM

NATIONAL ANTHEM   *performed by William B. Miller*

INVOCATION   *Rt. Rev. Msgr. Peter Frost*

INTRODUCTION OF DAIS GUESTS   *Charlie Monaco*

DINNER

GREETINGS   *John S. Potter*

PRESENTATION OF AWARD
  John Brewster   *presented by Dr. Harry Galin*

GUEST SPEAKER   *Stanley Saunders*

ENTERTAINMENT   *Charlie Monaco*

DANCING   *Paul Barnes' Orchestra*

Fig. 10. Program for Award Dinner

An experienced master of ceremonies is necessary to keep the program moving smoothly. If funds are available, hire a professional emcee; if not, the job can be filled by someone from the sponsoring organization who has a quick wit and a gift of gab.

The General Seating Plan

Follow the instructions contained in Chapter 17 on Charity Balls with the exception that the chairman's assistance will not be required. Staff people will be able to handle the seating plan because the guests attending the dinner will represent such a cross section of the community that it will be impossible to know who are friends and who are not.

Preparation of the seating plan can be simplified if the reservation card carries the following statement: "Please indicate on the back of this card the names of your guests or the names of the people with whom you wish to be seated."

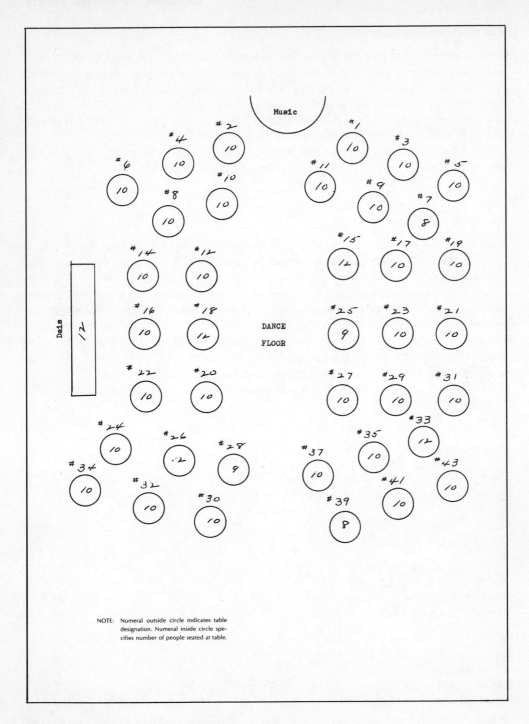

Fig. 11. Seating Chart for Award Dinner

117

The Dais Seating Plan

Seat the master of ceremonies in the center of the dais (or head table as it is sometimes called) with the guest of honor and guest speaker sitting on either side of him. The master of ceremonies will introduce each person at the dais, reserving introduction of the guest of honor until last.

No one is seated at the dais until the guest of honor arrives and takes his place, although guests at the other tables may be seated before then.

Use place cards at the dais and arrange for flowers, a lectern, and a microphone. Be sure to test the mike before the program begins.

Pre-dinner Reception

Plan a pre-dinner reception for the dais guests, honorary chairmen, the committee and their wives, and other important people. Hold it in a small room near the dining room.

For other guests, drinks can be served in an area adjacent to the dining room. If the cocktails are free, remember that a crowd of heavy drinkers can affect the net proceeds. So control the amount of liquor consumed by limiting the drinking time. For example, if the reception is scheduled for seven and the dinner is at eight, signal guests to begin entering the dining room promptly at 7:45. By eight everyone will be seated and the dinner program can get under way.

If the drinks are not on the house, set up two cash bars on opposite sides of the room.

The Dinner

Post a copy of the seating list outside the dining room where it can easily be seen. The seating list can be made up similarly to the following sample list:

NAME	TABLE NO.
A	
Mr. & Mrs. Arthur Abrams	14
Mr. & Mrs. Thomas Alloway	2
Mr. & Mrs. George Ammison	10
Mr. & Mrs. David Axelrod	16
B	
Mr. & Mrs. Gerald Barnett	9
Mr. & Mrs. Saul Bienstock	9
Mr. Norton Blum & Guest	2
Mr. & Mrs. John Brewster	Dais
C	
Mr. & Mrs. John Carlini	10
Dr. & Mrs. Andrew Carson	Dais
Mr. Philip Carter & Guest	11
Mr. & Mrs. Lawrence Cohn	2

D

Mr. & Mrs. Charles Damian	7
Mr. & Mrs. Henry Delman	7
Mr. & Mrs. George De Witt	12
Dr. & Mrs. Dominick Du Pasquier	2

and so on

Station people at the door to greet guests and distribute seating lists and programs. Be prepared for those guests who have forgotten to bring their tickets. Have a supply of tickets stamped DUPLICATE.

Work closely with the caterer or banquet manager of the hotel. He must know several days in advance how many guests will attend, the time to serve, and whether entertainers and press representatives will be fed. Instruct him how to handle the service of beverages. If the menu includes wine, one glass may be placed at each setting; a second glass can be served on request.

If liquor is served at the table at the guest's request, establish a rule regarding payment. Otherwise, the cost of the drinks will be added to the caterer's bill.

Determine in advance if tickets will be collected at the door or picked up by waiters at time of service.

Souvenir Journal

A journal can be a money-maker but it requires a chairman who can provide strong leadership and line up a committee of supersalesmen to sell ads. They must have numerous business contacts and cannot be shy about approaching these contacts regarding the purchase of space. (*Note:* The Journal Committee is basically responsible for selling space; however, to insure the journal's success, everyone connected with the event should lend a hand.)

Ad blanks are necessary. The contracts can be professionally designed and printed if funds are available; if not, mimeographed forms can be used. The blanks will list the cost of advertising space, contain space for writing ad copy, and state the deadline for submitting copy. Be realistic regarding cost of space. Don't exceed what the traffic will bear.

The wisest procedure to follow in selling space is to obtain payment when the advertising contract is signed. If this is not done, it will be necessary to prepare and mail statements; not only is this time-consuming, but payment may never be made. Establish a card file for advertisers; record the following information on 3" x 5" cards: name and address of advertiser, cost of ad, name of solicitor, and date of payment.

Someone with journalistic experience will be needed to plan and organize the journal and to work with the printer in co-ordinating production details.

The journal should include a statement by the organization's president, a write-up about the guest of honor, together with a photograph, a story concerning the sponsoring organization and its work, the names of the honorary chairmen, general chairman, chairmen of various committees, members of the committee, and the officers and trustees of the agency.

Distribute the journal to the guests at the dinner.

Mail a copy of the journal, together with a note of thanks, to each advertiser.

Selling space is hard work and those who have been successful certainly deserve an expression of gratitude. A small plaque or some other means of recognition might be given to those who achieve a fixed goal.

Publicity

Request the guest of honor and the guest speaker to furnish biographical data and photographs for publicity purposes.

Submit releases to local daily and weekly papers and to those in nearby communities. Local papers are usually willing to provide coverage for community events, although the amount of coverage depends on the importance of the people involved.

Stories should be paced to keep up the flow of publicity. Release stories as follows:

1. Initial story announcing name of the general chairman, date of dinner, where it will be held.

2. Story, with photograph, about the guest of honor.

3. Story, with photograph, about participating celebrities, if any.

4. Report of anticipated attendance, availability of tickets, names and photographs of principal program participants.

5. A few days before the dinner, an "all is in readiness, still time to get tickets" story.

6. Immediately following the dinner, a story which reports the success of the event.

The guest of honor and the guest speaker may be members of various professional and/or civic organizations; if so, submit releases to the editors of publications of these organizations.

Request the guest of honor and guest speaker to provide copies of their speeches. Mimeograph the speeches and make them available to the press.

Arrange a pre-dinner news and picture conference, featuring the main speakers and celebrities.

Invite newsmen and photographers from newspapers and radio and television stations to cover the dinner. Set up a press table and assign a responsible person to assist the press representatives by supplying names, answering questions, and so on.

Post-dinner "Musts"

Everyone likes to be thanked, so don't forget to express gratitude to those who helped to make the event a success.

Thank-you notes should go to committee people, honorary and otherwise, the guest speaker, and all others (including press and other media people) who helped in any way. Have the president of the organization sign the notes. The chairman should write short thank-you notes to the members of his committee.

If merchandise was donated (liquor, flowers, etc.), issue receipts (with your thanks) to the donors. Furnish each journal advertiser with a receipt and a copy of the journal—and add your thanks to him, too.

● Pay bills promptly.

Sample Timetable

1. Enlist general chairman by July 1.
2. Enlist other chairmen by July 10.
3. Select guest of honor by Aug. 1.
4. Obtain guest speaker and entertainment by Aug. 15.
5. Enlist committees by Sept. 1.
6. Publicity, press, radio, etc.   Sept. 15-Nov. 18.
7. Invitations printed and mailed to master list by Sept. 15.
8. General subscription campaign—Sept. 15-Nov. 16.
9. Complete program arrangements by Oct. 1.
10. Dinner on Nov. 16.

Suggested Organization Chart

Honorary Chairmen

General Chairman

Chairmen for Program Committee, Subscription Committee,
and Arrangements Committee

A. Program Committee responsible for—
   (1) obtaining guest speaker
   (2) arranging for entertainment
       (a.) master of ceremonies
       (b) comedian
       (c) orchestra
       (d) other
   (3) obtaining clergymen to deliver invocation and benediction
   (4) assisting master of ceremonies in preparing his notes
   (5) arranging order of events of the program

B. Arrangements Committee responsible for—
   (1) arranging committee meetings
   (2) selecting a place to hold the dinner
   (3) selecting the menu
   (4) arranging for flowers, decorations, lectern, and microphone
   (5) reserving hotel rooms for out-of-town guests, if necessary
   (6) reserving dressing rooms for entertainers
   (7) selecting guests to be seated at head table
   (8) assigning places at head table
   (9) preparing place cards for head table guests
   (10) arranging for reception

C. Subscription Committee responsible for—
   (1) compiling a master invitation list
   (2) printed invitations
   (3) personal and telephone follow-up to achieve maximum patronage

Checklist for Award Dinner

1. Set date.
2. Select chairman.
3. Name heads of various committees:
   A. Program.
   B. Subscription.
   C. Arrangements.
4. Organize workers—furnish heads of committees with names, addresses, and telephone numbers (office and residence) of the members of their respective committees.
5. Line up guest speaker.
6. Select place to hold dinner.
7. Determine seating capacity of place.
8. Invitations and tickets:
   A. Determine price of tickets.
   B. Make up invitation list.
   C. Submit copy to printer for invitation/envelope, reservation card/return envelope, and admission ticket.
   D. Invitation with reservation card and return envelope mailed.
   E. Tickets sent as acceptances are received.
9. Seating and decorations:
   A. Arrange dais, seats, tables, etc., and make chart of the arrangement.
   B. Prepare seating list and have it mimeographed and collated.
   C. Arrange for space for press representatives.
   D. Get decorations and see that they are put up.
   E. Arrange for lectern, microphone, and special lighting, if necessary.
10. Music:
    A. Arrange for combo or orchestra.
    B. Arrange musical program with orchestra leader.
11. Speakers and entertainers:
    A. Arrange for emcee, person to present award to recipient, clergymen, entertainers, and someone to sing the national anthem.
    B. See that everyone is fully instructed—offer assistance in preparing speeches, if necessary.
    C. Arrange for transportation for speakers, distinguished guests and entertainers, if necessary.
    D. Arrange for dressing rooms for entertainers.
12. Dinners:
    A. Make arrangements with banquet manager (or caterer) for dinners, selection of menu, and number of dinners necessary.
    B. Advise banquet manager regarding time of service.
    C. Arrange for overflow in case of unexpected crowd.
    D. Arrange for reception for special and general guests.
    E. Arrange for dinners for entertainers and press representatives.
    F. Submit floor plan and seating list to banquet manager.
    G. Arrange with banquet manager to put identifying numbers on tables.

13. Incidentals:
    A. Arrange for cloakroom and attendants.
    B. Arrange for tipping waiters, attendants, etc.
14. Program—arrange for order of events, etc.
15. Souvenir journal:
    A. Appoint chairman and organize committee.
    B. Determine price of space and have ad blanks printed.
    C. Contact reliable printers to obtain firm written bids for production of the journal.
    D. Compile list of potential advertisers, including names submitted by the committee, friends of the organization, and the guest of honor; prepare material for a general mailing—including letter, ad blank, dinner reservation card.
    E. Arrange for journal committee to contact all potential advertisers within three days of the mailing. Contact the company general manager, rather than the advertising manager.
    F. Send ad copy to printer on a daily basis.
    G. Be prepared to fill parts of pages on which no ad appears with copy concerning the sponsoring agency, its aims and achievements.
    H. Four working days before ad deadline, hold a "home-stretch" meeting with the journal committee in order to get in all funds and ad copy before the finish.
    I. Work closely with the printer in the closing days. Visit his plant to make certain the job is progressing satisfactorily.
    J. See that all advertisers receive copies of the journal, together with appropriate thanks.
16. Publicity:
    A. Get biographical data and photographs from honoree and guest speaker.
    B. Advance stories to press.
    C. Send invitations and tickets to press.
    D. Arrange for space for reporters.
    E. Arrange for press photographers.
    F. Advance copies of speeches for press.
    G. Bulletin the affair, if in hotel.
    H. Have own photographer on hand, in addition to press photographers.

DURING THE AFFAIR

1. Distribute program and seating list at door.
2. Put a journal at each person's place.
3. Have duplicate tickets available.
4. See that speakers and entertainers are on hand and know what they are to do and where they are to go.
5. Assign people to take care of distinguished guests, speakers, or entertainers from arrival to departure.
6. Have one person in charge of press room or table to take care of reporters and photographers.

AFTER THE DINNER

1. Check number of dinners served with banquet manager.
2. See that the decorations are taken down and returned.
3. If carpentry work is done, see that it is taken down.
4. Prepare and mail statements to journal advertisers who have not paid for space.
5. Write thank-you notes.
6. Pay bills.
7. Preserve the invitation list for use in other special events.

SUMMARY

1. Add up income and expenses and determine net proceeds.
2. Evaluate the event and determine how to improve the next one.

11:   Charity Balls

During the social season, charity balls attract thousands of affluent people. Many of them pay as much as $175 a head for an evening of fun and games. Some of them attend because they are honestly interested in the work of the sponsoring organization; others are there merely to see and to be seen. Their reasons, however, are inconsequential. What *is* important is that they provide revenue which contributes to the support of many worthy causes.

With skillful leadership and proper management, a ball can produce thousands of dollars for a charity. In addition to raising funds, a ball acts as a vehicle for getting publicity. This is especially true if the chairman and the committee people are socially important. Then the society press will be more than willing to co-operate and the ball will be well covered in stories concerning the charity and with photographs of the committee chairmen.

Any charitable organization can sponsor a ball. By adhering to the following formula, it can be socially and financially successful: 1) a top-notch chairman, 2) a hard-working committee, 3) ample time for preparation (ten to twelve months), 4) the financial assistance of underwriters and patrons, 5) expenses kept to a minimum through the donation of services and merchandise, and 6) a great deal of thoughtful planning.

Because the chairman is required to perform much of the actual work involved in running the ball, she (usually the chairman is a woman) must be a self-starter and a dedicated worker. Also, she must be of such social standing that she will have no difficulty in lining up a host of society figures to serve on the committee for the ball. More often than not, women are lured to a committee far more by the chairman than by the appeal of the charity. Consequently, a popular chairman with a good following can, in most cases, practically guarantee the success of a ball.

A chairman can be chosen from the board of trustees or perhaps recruited by a board member with good social connections. But regardless of how the chairman is acquired, be absolutely certain she's the best person available.

125

The Charity Ball Committee

Co-chairmen and heads of the ball's various subcommittees are appointed by the chairman. They will assist her in finding people to serve on the committee (25 to 100 depending on the size and scope of the event), determining the date of the ball, selecting the place to hold it, deciding on a theme, planning the menu, and choosing an orchestra and entertainers.

They will also help in working out contracts with the hotel and orchestra. If they are active in charitable work and frequently serve on social committees, the hotel may offer a reasonable price in the hope of getting future business. This may also apply to the orchestra, which is looking ahead to other balls as well as possible debutante party bookings.

The journal chairman and her workers are responsible for selling ads; however, everyone on the general committee should lend a hand. The sources will be furriers, jewelers, beauty salons, department stores, boutiques, florists, restaurants, and so on.

The committee should take advantage of any contacts they may have. For example, a professional decorator who will do the decor either without charge or perhaps at cost. He will have access to dealers and manufacturers who will donate, or provide at cost, the materials needed to create a spectacular setting for the ball.

A connection with a florist or two can be a big help. It can mean that the flowers will be donated or offered at a reduced price.

An artist can be particularly helpful. He can design the printed materials which are used in connection with the ball and plan the layout of the souvenir journal so it will have a slick, professional appearance.

Junior Committee

The chief responsibility of the "under-thirty" group is to interest the young crowd in attending the ball. Tickets are usually offered at reduced rates as a come-on to the juniors; they get into the ball for half price.

Budget

Expenses must be carefully calculated in advance. The estimated expenditures, plus the goal established for net proceeds, will determine the cost of tickets. A survey of charity-ball-oriented organizations in New York City disclosed a wide price range, with the cost of tickets starting at $35 a head and escalating all the way up to $175.

An underwriter will offset the expense involved in running a ball. It may be difficult, however, to find someone who is willing to take on the burden of solo sponsorship. In that case, several individuals or corporations can team up to sponsor the affair. Usually, the trustees of the sponsoring agency assume the responsibility for securing these benefactors.

Patrons are another source of revenue. They are contributors to a fund which is established to take care of expenses that arise before ticket money starts to come in. A proficient chairman, with the help of some persuasive committee people, can raise the funds which are needed to finance pre-ball parties for publicity purposes and to pay for temporary clerical assistance, postage, telephone, and other expenses connected with the ball.

All About Invitations

A carefully compiled invitation list is essential. Most of the names will come from the committee, with each member submitting 50 to 100 names. But don't overlook large donors to the organization's annual fund appeal and people who have attended other events sponsored by the organization. Another source of names is the *Social Register*.

Type all names and addresses on 3″ x 5″ cards; file the cards alphabetically to prevent duplication. Indicate the source on each card, i.e., committee, contributor, etc. Names submitted by the committee should be marked regarding origin. For instance, if Mrs. Roger Moore requested that an invitation be sent to Mr. and Mrs. Timothy Evans, Mrs. Moore's name should appear on the master card.

As acceptances are received, type names and addresses on 3″ x 5″ cards. Place these cards in a secondary file, also arranged alphabetically. Mail tickets as soon as acceptances have been processed. Specify on the file cards the date the tickets were forwarded.

When all acceptances have been received, the cards will serve as the basis for preparing the seating chart.

A ball requires a formal invitation. This invitation must contain the name of the sponsoring organization, date and time of event, place it will be held, manner of dress, and price of subscription. The invitation lists the names of all people connected with the ball: patrons, general chairman, co-chairmen, chairmen of various committees, and the committee members. (Note: Publication of their names requires their consent so be sure that they sign consent cards.)

Send invitations on a 1 to 5 ration, i.e., if an attendance of 1,000 is desired, 5,000 invitations must be mailed.

Mail invitations six weeks prior to the date of the ball. Include a reservation card and return envelope. Invitations should be hand-addressed, preferably by the committee. Affix stamps; *never* use a postage meter.

Printing

Copy for all printed materials (invitations/envelopes, reservation cards/return envelopes, tickets, advertising contracts, souvenir journal) must be submitted to the printer in time to insure a comfortable margin for production.

Request the printer to furnish proofs for all printed materials. Check proofs for typographical and other errors. Double-check for correct spelling and omission of names. To take care of possible omissions, which can occur despite careful proofreading, add "list incomplete" at the end of the committee roster.

Casino

A gambling casino will provide entertainment as well as additional revenue. Since it is illegal to use cash for prizes in charity games, a large assortment of

Bal Rouge et Noir

Irvington House invites you to the Bal Rouge et Noir, Wednesday, April 21, 1971, Trianon Suite, New York Hilton Hotel

Cocktails from 7:30 to 8:30

Casino, Buffet and Dancing 8:30 on

Music by Lester Lanin and his orchestra

RSVP   BLACK TIE

Fig. 12.   Inside Page from Charity Ball Invitation

Bal Rouge et Noir

for the benefit of Irvington House
Trianon Room, New York Hilton Hotel
Avenue of the Americas at 54th Street
Wednesday, April 21, 1971.

Cocktails 7:30 o'clock, Casino, Buffet and Dancing 8:30 o'clock

ADMIT ONE

Fig. 13.   Ticket for Charity Ball

IRVINGTON HOUSE, 566 FIRST AVENUE, NEW YORK, N.Y. 10016

Please make a reservation for me at the BAL ROUGE ET NOIR to be held at the New York Hilton, on Wednesday, April 21, 1971.

Please send me:

☐ Tickets at $50 each for Buffet and Dancing (includes cocktails and wine).

☐ I enclose my check for $
    It will greatly facilitate seating arrangements if you will give on the following page, a list of your guests for the evening, or with whom you wish to be seated.

☐ I cannot attend but am enclosing a contribution.

NAME_____

ADDRESS_____

_____

_____

Please make check payable to Irvington House. The deductible contribution on each ticket is $35.

Closing date for reservations: April 8th, 1971.

Fig. 14. Inside of Folded Reservation Card

merchandise will be needed. The entire committee, including the juniors, should solicit merchandise.

Prizes could include any or all of the following items:

HOME

Bars, stack tables

Bathroom accessories, baskets, soap dishes, etc.

Blankets, blanket covers

Bridge table and chairs, bridge table covers

Clocks

Posters, graphics

Housewares, electrical appliances, coffee makers, hair dryers, etc.

Fancy foods

Fancy candles

Flower arrangements

Linens, sheets, place mats, towels, etc.

Radios, television sets, tape recorders

PERSONAL

Cameras, binoculars, etc.

Cars

Children's clothes, large stuffed animals, toys

Costume jewelry, fine jewelry, watches (men's and women's)

Gloves

Luggage, wallets, small leather goods

Men's robes

Nightgowns, negligees, small furs

Perfume, soaps, cosmetics, etc.

Pipes, tobacco pouches

Records (good)

Sports shirts (men's)

Sports equipment, golf clubs, golf balls, fishing rods, tennis rackets, skis, etc.

Sweaters

Umbrellas (men's and women's)

Wigs, hairpieces, hair ornaments, wig cases

Men's electric shavers

MISCELLANEOUS

Fancy dog collars and other equipment for pets

Fine books

Games, such as chess sets, Mah Jongg, playing cards

Liquor

Several reliable cashiers will be needed to sell scrip ("play money") for use in playing games of chance. Consult the Yellow Pages for sources regarding the rental of roulette wheels, blackjack tables, and equipment for other games.

Display the prizes that are available for the winners but don't forget to provide adequate security. Unguarded merchandise has been known to disappear.

Gifts for the Ladies

Gift boxes containing sample merchandise such as perfume, cologne, cosmetics, liquor, gourmet items, and other articles are presented to the ladies at the ball.

Seating Chart

Preparation of the seating chart is most easily handled by three people: the chairman and two staff members. The chairman's participation is vitally important because she usually knows who is not on good terms with whom in the social set. Her assistance will prevent placing unfriendly people at the same table.

The following statement on the reservation card will also help: "It will greatly facilitate seating arrangements if you will give on the following page a list of your guests for the evening, or with whom you wish to be seated."

Ten people are usually seated at a table, but a table can accommodate as few as six or as many as twelve.

Hotels provide floor plans (See Fig. 11, page 117) for use in connection with the preparation of the seating chart. If there is space to spare, strike out tables which are located in undesirable spots, i.e., too close to the orchestra, directly in front of doors leading to and from the kitchen, near an exit which is likely to be drafty, too close to an air-conditioning unit, etc.

Mimeograph the seating list (see Chapter 10) and make copies available to those attending the ball. Submit several copies to the banquet manager, together with a properly marked floor plan, the day before the ball. This will give him sufficient time to study the plan and discuss it with the head waiter.

Pre-dinner Reception

Plan a cocktail reception to precede the dinner; hold it in an area adjacent to the ballroom.

At the Door

Post the seating list outside the ballroom where it can easily be seen. Station people at the door to greet guests and direct them to their tables.

Be prepared for those guests who have forgotten to bring their tickets. Have a supply of tickets stamped DUPLICATE.

Publicity

Begin to publicize the ball at least four months in advance. In the initial news story, announce the selection of the general chairman, date of ball, where it will be held. After that, publicize all events which are held in connection with the ball: meetings, of various committees, promotional parties to which leading socialites are invited, meetings of the junior committee, and so on.

Invite the society press to attend the get-togethers and be sure to have a photographer on hand.

Don't overlook the women's editor as a possible publicity outlet. She may be interested in doing a feature on the chairman.

Society gossip columns are another publicity source; plant items about people who are involved in arranging the ball. And, of course, invite the society press to attend the ball. Provide complimentary tickets.

A day or so after the ball, release a story to the press reporting the social and financial success of the event.

Winding Up Details

Don't forget to thank everyone who helped run the ball. Thank-you notes must go to underwriters, patrons, committee members, and all the other people who contributed in any way, such as donors of merchandise and service, journal advertisers, etc. Issue receipts to underwriters, patrons, donors of merchandise, and journal advertisers. Be sure to send a copy of the souvenir journal to each advertiser.

Most important of all: *Pay bills promptly.* It will insure happy relations between the charity, hotel, orchestra, entertainers, and anyone else who provided service and they will be pleased to transact future business with your organization.

Checklist for Charity Ball

PRELIMINARY ARRANGEMENTS

1. Select chairman.
2. Select co-chairmen.
3. Name heads of various committees:
   A. Sponsors.
   B. Patrons.
   C. Juniors.
   D. Souvenir Journal.
   E. Entertainment.
   F. Casino.
   G. Prizes.
   H. Gifts.
4. Organize workers—furnish heads of committees with names, addresses; and telephone numbers of members of their respective committees.
5. Select date.
6. Select place to hold ball.
7. Decide on theme.
8. Line up underwriters and patrons.
9. Invitations and tickets:
   A. Determine price of tickets.
   B. Make up invitation list.
   C. Submit copy to printer for invitation/envelope, reservation card/return envelope, and admission ticket.
   D. Invitation with reservation card/return envelope mailed.
   E. Tickets sent as acceptances are received and processed.
10. Arrange for decorations.
11. Select orchestra and entertainment.
12. Souvenir Journal:
    A. Appoint chairman and organize committee.
    B. Determine price of space and have contracts printed.
    C. Contact reliable printers to obtain firm written bids for production of the journal.
    D. Establish a card file for advertisers; record the following information: name and address of advertiser, cost of ad, name of solicitor, and date of payment.
    E. Designate someone to plan and organize the journal and work with printer in coordinating production details.
    F. Send ad copy to printer on daily basis.
    G. Include in the journal a brief statement by the organization's president, the names of the general chairman, chairmen of various commit-

tees, members of the committee, and the officers and trustees of the agency.

    H. See that all advertisers receive copies of the journal.

13. Casino:

    A. Solicit prizes.

    B. Keep a file on donors.

    C. Rent equipment for games of chance.

    D. Arrange for croupiers and cashiers.

    E. Establish checking system for handling money and scrip.

    F. Arrange for reliable people to handle the distribution of prizes.

14. Gift Boxes:

    A. Solicit manufacturers for merchandise.

    B. Assemble merchandise for boxes.

15. Hotel:

    A. Make arrangements with banquet manager for dinners, selection of menu, and number of dinners required.

    B. Advise banquet manager regarding time of service.

    C. Arrange for cocktail reception.

    D. Reserve dressing rooms for entertainers, if necessary.

    E. Arrange to have gambling equipment set up.

    F. Arrange for committee to set up display of prizes on the day of the ball.

    G. Provide proper security for prizes.

    H. Check amplifying equipment.

16. Prepare seating list and chart.

17. Publicity:

    A. Advance stories to press regarding all pre-ball activities.

    B. Send invitations and complimentary tickets to society press.

    C. Arrange for press photographers.

    D. Have own photographer on hand in addition to press photographers.

DURING THE AFFAIR

1. Post seating list.
2. Distribute seating list at door.
3. Put journal at each person's place.
4. Have duplicate tickets available.
5. Assign someone to take care of press people.
6. Distribute gift boxes.

AFTER THE BALL

1. Check number of dinners served with banquet manager.
2. See that decorations are taken down and returned.
3. If carpentry work has been done, see that it is taken down.
4. Prepare and mail statements to advertisers who have not paid for space.

5. Write thank-you notes.
6. Pay bills.
7. Preserve the invitation list for use in connection with future events.

SUMMARY

1. Add up income and expenses and determine net proceeds.
2. Evaluate the ball and determine how to improve next one.

12: Fashion Shows

Fashion shows rank high in popularity. Whether held in big cities or small towns, they are always well attended. And as long as women have an active interest in clothes and are curious about what's going on in the fashion world, these events will continue to flourish and endure.

The manner in which fashion shows are conducted may vary with respect to geographic location. For example, in urban communities, shows are frequently planned, organized, and produced by professional co-ordinators. For a fee, these experts will perform most of the work involved in running the show. They will handle such details as creating a theme, selecting clothing and accessories, engaging models, preparing and delivering the commentary, arranging the entertainment, and planning the musical program.

There's no doubt that professional help eases the job of running a fashion show; lack of such assistance, however, need not prevent a show from being successful. With good leadership, thoughtful planning, and sufficient time for preparation, a fashion show staged by volunteers can enjoy total success.

Organizing the Show

As in all special events, the general chairman is the key figure, so she must be chosen with care.

Chairmen will be needed to head the following committees: clothes and accessories, cleanup, decorations and equipment, entertainment, invitations, luncheon, models, prizes, program, and publicity. The chairmen can choose their own committee members.

After the committees have been organized, the next step is to set the date. Fashion shows should be held two or three months before the season; for instance, model winter clothes in the fall, summer outfits in the spring, etc.

Contact a local department store and/or specialty shop to arrange for clothes, accessories, and jewelry. Consider the audience when determining the price range and type of clothing to be modeled. Don't concentrate solely on the young, slim set; be sure to include a few items for the older (and not so slim) women in the audience.

135

A collection of Spring Fashions by the following designers:

Fashion Show Coordinator
MARY ALICE RICE

Scene 1   *On the Avenue*
           Kasper for Joan Leslie

Scene 2   *Town or Country*
           Vera Maxwell

Scene 3   *Come Fly With Me*
           Cisa of Italy Knits

Scene 4   *Party Time*
           Wilson Folmar

Scene 5   *Romantic Evenings*
           Malcolm Starr
           designed by Elinor Simmons

A group of ASPCA dogs for adoption will be presented

During Luncheon in the Terrace Room

THE PLAZA

Thursday, March 12th, 1970 — 12:30 p.m.

Please bring a salable gift to be resold

at "The Ark" for the benefit of the

ASPCA's ADOPTION SERVICE
(No clothing, books or records)

Door Prizes for Gift Donors

FOR RESERVATIONS:
PLaza 9-7010. Banquet Dept.
Prix Fixe Luncheon — $6.00

For further information call:
ASPCA Special Activities Office
30 East 60th Street ·PLaza 5-1650

Fig. 15.   Invitation to Fashion Show Planned by Professional Co-ordinator

THE THRIFT SHOP

of

THE SOCIETY OF MEMORIAL SLOAN-KETTERING
CANCER CENTER

invites you to attend

The Annual Luncheon-Fashion Show

BONWIT TELLER

presents

THE BEST OF BOUTIQUE FASHIONS

Grand Ballroom • Waldorf-Astoria

Thursday, February 5, 1970 at 12:30

Cocktails a la carte from 12 noon

Fig. 16.   Invitation to Fashion Show Presented by Department Store

Models

At least six models will be needed. The store that provides the clothes will also supply the models, but more interest in the show is created if some of the models are local people. Furthermore, the use of nonprofessionals will be an important factor in keeping expenses down. The fee for a professional can run as high as $50 an hour, plus a 10 per cent agency commission.

In metropolitan areas it may be possible to find celebrities from the social, theatrical, and sports worlds who are willing to serve as models. Their participation will enhance the event and encourage attendance.

Selecting a Place

Fashion shows are usually held in connection with a luncheon. Therefore, space in a hotel, restaurant, or hall should be reserved in advance. In selecting a place to hold the event, look for the following: a room large enough to accommodate the number of people who are expected to attend; sufficient space to set up a runway; adequate electrical outlets to handle microphones, spotlights, and other electrical equipment which may be needed; a large dressing room which will permit the models to change quickly and easily and with enough space for racks to hold their personal clothing along with the outfits they will display.

Theme

Develop a theme which can be carried through on the invitation, program, and decorations. For example, the theme might be keyed to travel, art, flower power, signs of the Zodiac, the moon shot, historical events, hit songs, Broadway shows, etc.

Invitation List

The invitation list will be composed of names submitted by the committee, donors to the agency's annual fund appeals, and guests who have attended other events sponsored by the agency.

Establishing and Maintaining the List.
    See All About Invitations, Chapter 11.
Handling Acceptances.
    See All About Invitations, Chapter 11.

Invitations

The front page of the invitation should contain the following information: name of sponsoring agency, when and where the show will be held, and the cost of admission.

On the inside pages list the names of the chairman and the committee. If the commentator and the models are celebrities, list their names. The names of the stores that supplied the clothes and accessories should also appear.

Mail invitations six weeks before the event. Include a reservation card and a return envelope. Hand-addressing is not necessary; neat typing is acceptable.

Printing

Printed materials for a fashion show will include invitations and mailing envelopes, reservation cards and return envelopes, admission tickets, programs, and raffle books.

Copy for all materials must be submitted to the printer well in advance of the date set for the show so he will have plenty of time to do a good job. Request the printer to submit checking proofs for all printed materials.

Programs

Programs can be produced inexpensively by using preprinted menu covers. Several major airline and steamship companies provide these beautifully designed covers free of charge. The menu, program, names of committee people, and the list of prizes and donors can be printed on the inside and back pages which are blank.

Organizations that are interested in taking advantage of this service should consult the Yellow Pages for names and addresses of leading airline and steamship companies. Contact them by letter; address communication to Manager, Advertising and Sales Department.

If funds are not available to print the programs, mimeograph them. This is an easy, inexpensive method and a skillful typist with an eye for design can produce good results.

I shall be pleased to attend the Fashion Show and Luncheon on Thursday, March 12, 1970, at 12:30.

I enclose $ _____ for _____ luncheon reservations at $6.00 per person.

I cannot attend, but enclose a contribution of $ _____.

Name _____

Address _____

_____

(Please indicate on the back of this card the names of the people with whom you wish to be seated.)

Fig. 17. Reservation Card for Fashion Show

PROGRAM

National Anthem _____

Invocation _____

LUNCHEON

Chilled Melon
Served on Ice in Silver Supremes

Breast of Chicken Chasseur
with Mushrooms
Roasted Potatoes   *Glazed Baby Carrots*

Frozen Baked Alaska
Brandied Cherries

Petits Fours
Coffee

Welcome _____

Greetings _____

FASHION SHOW

Drawing of Prizes _____

Music by _____

Fig. 18. Program for Fashion Show

Raffles and Prizes

A raffle will increase the show's proceeds. A large assortment of prizes will be needed—theater tickets, gift certificates from department stores, restaurants, boutiques, and beauty salons, household appliances, liquor, perfume, cosmetics, etc. Everyone on the committee must solicit prizes and sell chances to insure the success of the raffle.

Print raffle books and distribute them to the committee a few months before the show.

Door prizes are another source of revenue. Sell chances at the show and offer at least five very attractive prizes for the winners. List all prizes in the program, together with the names of the donors. Mention the donors' names when the winners are announced.

Make arrangements to have the goods picked up from the donors.

Keep a file on merchants and their contributions. Record the following information on 3" x 5" cards: name and address of donor, name of solicitor, the type of merchandise donated and its retail value.

To take advantage of the free publicity, local merchants and businesses may be willing to donate table favors such as ballpoint pens, mending kits, cosmetics, perfume, trading stamps, book matches, calendars, etc.

Entertainment

Engage a combo, string trio, accordionist, or pianist to provide appropriate background music during the show. Other entertainment, i.e., comedian, vocalist, etc., is optional.

Co-ordinating Models and Clothes

Two weeks before the show, select clothes and check out models for size, fit, and color. Then plan the sequence of appearance of the models.

Commentary

In preparing the commentary, allow approximately 45 minutes for the show, including the introduction and closing remarks. Devote about 1½ minutes to each model's appearance. Models can appear singly, in couples, or in groups of three or four. Allow enough time between appearances to permit models to change costumes.

Keep the commentary brisk, direct attention toward smart styling details and be brief regarding retail prices.

The script for the commentary must be easy to read. Use large type, wide margins, short lines, and triple spacing. Do not divide a word at the end of a line and do not break a sentence at the bottom of a page. Number pages consecutively. Use good quality bond paper; flimsy paper is too difficult to handle.

See that the commentator has a copy of the script a few days before the show so she will have a chance to study it and practice her delivery.

The cue mistress will need a copy of the script, too.

Commentator

A good commentator is very important to the show's success. A poised, self-assured person is required, someone who can follow a script with ease and ad lib if necessary.

Try to find a celebrity who will donate her (or his) services. If this is impossible, a local disk jockey may be willing to handle the job.

Seating Plan

Determine the location of the dais (head table—see Fig. 11), then place the other tables around the room and prepare a chart of the arrangement. Each table usually seats ten people, but a table can accommodate as few as six or as many as twelve.

Preparation of the seating plan can be simplified by including the following statement on the reservation card: "Please indicate on the back of this card the names of the people with whom you wish to be seated."

Mimeograph the seating list (see Chapter 10) and make copies available to those attending the show. Supply the banquet manager and/or caterer with the list and seating chart a day or two before the show.

Backstage

A competent cue mistress is needed. She will be responsible for giving the models their walk-on cue and noting and correcting errors in models' walk.

Several wardrobe mistresses will be required. They will see that the outfits are lined up on racks in order of appearance and that each outfit is correctly tagged with the name of the model who will wear it. They will check make-up and hair-dos, assist models in changing costumes, and place final stamp of approval on the over-all appearance. They will also be ready with needle and thread to handle minor repairs.

At the Door

Assign people to sell admission tickets and hand out programs and seating lists.

Have people on hand to sell chances for raffle and door prizes.

Be prepared for the guests who have forgotten to bring their tickets; have a supply of tickets stamped DUPLICATE.

Post the seating list outside the dining room.

Publicity

A month before the show release a story announcing the names of the chairman and members of the committee, date of event, where it will be held, and other pertinent details. Send the story to local daily and weekly papers and to those in nearby communities.

Send stories to local industries that publish house organs for their employees. Also send stories to churches, women's clubs and organizations, professional associations and other groups that print and distribute bulletins and/or newsletters to their membership.

Send announcements concerning the show to churches, local colleges, banks, factories, and other businesses; request them to post the announcements on their bulletin boards.

List the show in the Calendar of Events section of the local paper. Specify what the event is, when and where it will be held, the price of tickets, and where they can be obtained.

Request radio stations to publicize the show with public service spot announcements. Supply stations with the necessary information three weeks ahead of the show date so they will have time to include it in their broadcast copy.

If the budget permits, design and print posters. Display them in department stores, banks, beauty salons, and other places of business.

After the Show

Write thank-you notes to everyone who helped put on the show—committee people, donors of merchandise, the store that supplied the clothes, and all the people who contributed in any way, including those who helped to publicize the event.

Provide donors of merchandise with receipts.

Checklist for a Fashion Show

PRELIMINARY ARRANGEMENTS

1. Select chairman.
2. Name heads of various committees:
    A. Clothes, accessories, etc.
    B. Cleanup.
    C. Decorations and equipment.
    D. Entertainment.
    E. Invitations.
    F. Luncheon.
    G. Models.
    H. Prizes.
    I. Program.
    J. Publicity.
3. Organize workers.
4. Set date.
5. Arrange for clothes, accessories, jewelry, and, if possible, free hairstyling.
6. Select place to hold show.
7. Appoint commentator.
8. Obtain models.
9. Engage orchestra and line up entertainment.
10. Invitations and tickets:
    A. Determine price of tickets.
    B. Make up invitation list.
    C. Submit copy to printer for invitation/envelope, reservation card/return envelope, and admission ticket.
    D. Invitations with reservation card and return envelope mailed.
    E. Tickets sent after acceptances received and processed.
11. Solicit prizes and table favors.
12. Determine price of chances for raffle and door prizes.
13. Print and distribute raffle books.
14. Seating, equipment, and decorations:
    A. Arrange dais, tables, etc., and make chart of placement and number all tables.
    B. Rent or borrow runway and spotlights.

    C. Arrange for microphone and lectern for head table and for commentator.

    D. Get decorations and see that they are put up.

    E. Get flowers and place cards for head table.

    F. Assemble equipment for dressing room—
- (a) clothing racks,
- (b) full-length mirrors,
- (c) makeup and hairspray,
- (d) combs
- (e) facial tissues,
- (f) sewing equipment,
- (g) iron and ironing board,
- (h) safety pins,
- (i) disposable dress shields.

15. Appoint cue mistress and wardrobe mistresses.
16. Lunches:

    A. Make arrangements with banquet manager (or caterer) for lunches, select menu, and advise him regarding number of lunches required.

    B. Advise banquet manager regarding time of service.

    C. Arrange for waiters to pick up tickets when lunches are served.

    D. Prepare for overflow in case of unexpected crowd.

    E. Submit floor plan and seating list to banquet manager.

    F. Arrange to have an identifying number placed on each table.

17. Publicity:

    A. Submit advance stories to press.

    B. Prepare and distribute announcements.

    C. Prepare spots and submit to radio stations.

    D. Arrange to have posters printed and distributed.

    E. Bulletin affair if held in hotel.

18. Program:

    A. Arrange program, order of events, etc.

    B. Submit program copy to printer.

    C. Prepare commentary, type and submit to commentator.

    D. Plan musical program with orchestra leader; key the program to the commentary so the selections will be appropriate.

19. Incidentals:

    A. Mimeograph and collate seating list.

    B. Arrange for cloakroom and attendants.

    C. Arrange for tipping waiters, attendants, etc.

    D. Appoint someone to draw winning tickets for raffle and door prizes.

DURING THE SHOW

1. Test microphone before show begins.
2. Adjust spotlights to focus properly on runway.
3. Arrange for sale of tickets at door.
4. Distribute seating lists and programs at door.
5. Arrange for sale of chances for raffle and door prizes.

6. Have receptacles ready to receive stubs for raffle and door prizes.
7. Establish checking system for tickets and chances sold and money received.

AFTER THE SHOW

1. Check number of lunches served with caterer.
2. See that all borrowed or rented equipment is returned.
3. See that decorations are taken down and returned.
4. If carpentry work is done, see that it is taken down.
5. Write thank-you notes.
6. Pay bills.
7. Preserve the invitation list for use in future special events.

SUMMARY

1. Add up income and expenses and determine net proceeds.
2. Evaluate the show and determine how the next one can be improved.

13:   Art Exhibits

During the last few years art exhibits have become increasingly popular as fund-raising vehicles. The amount of money raised by these events usually depends on whether or not a formal opening is held, the size and scope of the affair, and the price range and number of works sold. Some art exhibits feature only the works of "name" artists while others display good original art by young artists who are not yet widely recognized.

The exhibit materials can be supplied by a gallery or by several individual artists. Names of the latter may be found by contacting local art associations, art supply dealers, and private collectors. All artwork is taken on a consignment basis.

Exhibits are more interesting and effective if the artwork is varied; graphics, sculpture, wood carvings, drawings, oil paintings, and watercolors can be included in the collection.

Artists set their own prices and the sponsoring agency adds a commission to the artists' fees to determine the final selling price. The commission is usually 10 to 20 per cent of the selling price, but if a gallery is involved, the commission is split. Prices for exhibited works can range from $10 to $150 and more.

Exhibits can be staged in galleries, community centers, showrooms, building lobbies, hotel ballrooms, and even in private homes. But regardless of where a show is held or whose work is exhibited, the requirements for success are essentially the same: the right chairman, a good ticket-selling committee, careful budgeting, sufficient time for preparation of the event, and an effective publicity campaign.

CHAIRMAN

Choosing the chairman requires careful consideration because the person who heads an Exhibit Committee must play a dual role. In addition to handling the normal duties of organizing the committee and overseeing and co-ordinating its activities, she or he will be responsible for selecting and assembling the

146

```
THE VOLUNTEERS

FOR

PREVENTIVE MEDICINE INSTITUTE

STRANG CLINIC

Present

ÉKLEKTRA '70


AN EXHIBITION AND SALE

OF

CONTEMPORARY ART
```

Fig. 19.   Invitation to Art Exhibit and Sale

works to be exhibited. This calls for someone with a thorough knowledge of art and an understanding of the community's artistic awareness and preferences. The latter is particularly important because it will serve as a guide in determining the type of art to be displayed. If the collection does not coincide with local tastes, the exhibit is bound to result in financial failure—people simply will not buy what they don't like.

COMMITTEE

The chief function of the committee is to sell tickets for the exhibit's opening. Therefore, only those with excellent ticket-selling potential should be invited to serve on the committee. Each member of the committee should assume responsibility for selling at least ten tickets. The size of the committee will depend upon how many tickets you plan to sell.

HONORARY CHAIRMEN

Chapter 10 has full details on honorary chairmen and their function.

BUDGET

Expenses should be carefully calculated in advance. To be included are printing, postage, promotion costs, supplies for mounting paintings, refreshments served at the opening, and the cost of the exhibit space if it is not rent free. The assistance of underwriters will lower the cost of running an exhibit. Usually, the trustees and/or board members of the sponsoring agency assume responsibility for securing these benefactors.

PRINTING

Printed materials for an art exhibit include invitation/envelope, reservation card/return envelope, catalogue, and advertising contract if a souvenir journal is planned. *(Note:* Refer to Chapter 10, for instructions regarding souvenir journals.)

Copy for all printed materials must be submitted to the printer in time to insure a comfortable margin for production. Request the printer to provide proofs for all materials. Check proofs for typographical and other errors; double-check for correct spelling and omission of names.

INVITATIONS

A carefully compiled invitation list is essential. Most of the names will come from the committee; other prospects are donors to the organization's annual fund appeals and people who have attended previous events sponsored by the organization. Type all names and addresses on 3″ x 5″ cards; file the cards alphabetically to avoid duplication.

Names submitted by the committee should be marked regarding origin. For example, if Mrs. Thomas Deegan submitted the name of Mrs. Donald Hayes, Mrs. Deegan's name should appear on the master card.

The invitation for an exhibit opening can be formal or informal, depending on the event. If the opening is a black tie and champagne affair, naturally a formal invitation is necessary.

The invitation contains the name of the sponsoring agency, date and time of event, place it will be held, manner of dress, and price of subscription. It lists the names of all people connected with the exhibit: honorary chairmen, general chairman, co-chairmen, and the members of the committee.

The reservation card lists subscription prices and carries the following statement: "I am unable to attend but enclose a contribution."

Each committee member should hand-address and hand-stamp the invitations which are sent to the people on her list.

Mail invitations six weeks before the event.

The Acquavella Galleries

have the honour to invite you to attend

the Gala Opening of an exhibition

of Odilon Redon

for the benefit of

The Lenox Hill Hospital

on Wednesday, the twenty-first of October

nineteen hundred and seventy

Eighteen East Seventy-ninth Street

6:00 p.m. to midnight
Black Tie   Champagne

Fig. 20.   Invitation to Hospital's Art Exhibit

The Odilon Redon Exhibition
Gala Opening, October 21, 1970

☐ I am enclosing my cheque for $_____for_____tickets.
($25.00 per ticket)

☐ I am unable to attend but enclose a contribution.

Name _____

Address _____

(Make cheques payable to Lenox Hill Hospital.
All contributions are tax deductible.)

Fig. 21. Reply Card Enclosed with Invitation

As acceptances are received, type names and addresses on 3″ x 5″ cards. Place these cards in a secondary file, also arranged alphabetically. As soon as acceptances have been processed, mail tickets; include a receipt and a thank-you note.

The acceptance file will serve as the basis for preparing the guest list.

AT THE OPENING

Assign hostesses to greet and mingle with the guests and handle the sale of art work. Instruct them to place an adhesive-backed star on each piece as it is sold.

Appoint one reliable person to handle money and/or checks received for the sale of art work.

Assign hostesses to serve food and drink.

Assign two or three people to take care of those guests who have forgotten to bring their tickets. Furnish them with guest lists.

Station two people at the door to distribute souvenir journals and/or catalogues.

AFTER THE EVENT

Thank-you notes should go to committee people, honorary and otherwise, those who publicize the event, and anyone else who helped run the event.

If merchandise was donated—champagne or other refreshments—issue receipts and appropriate thanks to the donors.

If a journal was published, furnish each advertiser with a receipt, a thank-you note, and a copy of the publication.

Pay bills promptly.

Publicity

No event sells itself; a well-planned, well-co-ordinated publicity campaign is needed to handle the selling of almost any affair. And to be effective, the campaign must be aimed at the proper audience. This is especially true of an event which has specialized, rather than widespread, appeal. All publicity efforts must be channeled into the most productive areas.

An art exhibit, like many other cultural events, will appeal to a particular segment of the community. Therefore, the publicity campaign must be designed to reach those people.

An exhibit campaign may include the following:

1. *Press.* Release all stories to local daily and weekly papers as well as those in nearby communities.

> A. Release initial story to society editors two months prior to the event. Announce the names of honorary chairmen, general chairman, and co-chairmen.
>
> B. Release the second story to society editors one month prior to the event. Announce the names of participating artists; include a photograph of the chairman and one or two of the artists.
>
> C. Contact women's page editors regarding feature stories concerning the chairman.
>
> D. Contact art editors regarding stories concerning the participating artists.
>
> E. Throughout the campaign, feed material to society gossip columnists; plant items concerning people who are involved in arranging the exhibit.
>
> F. Notify all papers to list the exhibit opening in the Calendar of Events section. Specify when and where the exhibit will be held, the price of tickets, and where tickets can be obtained.
>
> G. Place a paid advertisement in the art section of the local paper.
>
> H. Two or three days after the opening, release a story reporting the social and financial success of the event.

2. *Radio*

> A. A month before the opening, arrange interviews on women's programs for the chairman and one or two of the participating artists.
>
> B. On-the-spot coverage at the opening.

3. *Television*

> A. Interviews with the chairman and one or two of the participating artists.
>
> B. On-the-spot coverage at the opening.

EXPERIENCE REPORTS

Loan Exhibit for a Hospital

The event held by the Lenox Hill Hospital, New York City, was a loan exhibition. Paintings were contributed by private art collectors and were not for sale. Following the gala opening, the exhibit was open to the public for five weeks. The admission fee was $1.50.

Art Exhibit Benefits a Clinic

At the event sponsored by the Preventive Medicine Institute—Strang Clinic all works were offered for sale, with the Clinic receiving a percentage of the proceeds. Following the preview and reception, the exhibit was open to the public for one week. Admission was free.

A souvenir journal produced in connection with the exhibit provided additional income.

14:   Bazaars

Everyone loves a bargain, which no doubt accounts for the enduring popularity of bazaars. Most bazaars are chock-full of useful, attractive items usually priced far below retail value. They have been around for years and have been sponsored by organizations everywhere. The proceeds provide support for a variety of causes—scholarship programs, medical research, hospitals, rehabilitation centers, orphanages, churches, homes for the aged, and animal shelters, to mention just a few.

Often an entire community will join forces and sponsor a bazaar to help raise funds to fulfill a particular need—an ambulance, a fire engine, a school bus, uniforms for a Little League baseball team, and so on.

Bazaars have been held in community centers, school gymnasiums, armories, churches, and sometimes even in hotel ballrooms.

It takes a lot of know-how, imagination, time, intelligent planning, and hard work to organize a bazaar and bring it to a successful conclusion.

Planning

A good general chairman is required; she will be responsible for supervising and overseeing all the committees and co-ordinating their activities.

Chairmen will be needed to head the following committees: booths, cleanup, decorations, equipment, handmade articles, pricing, and publicity.

The chairmen can choose their committee members.

When to Hold

The best time to stage a bazaar is during the months of November and December when shoppers are on the lookout for holiday gifts.

Merchandise

Most of the shoppers look for articles that are useful and reasonable. The following items will be popular: kitchen accessories and gadgets, soaps and detergents, cooking utensils, linens, silver, glassware, china, wearing apparel and accessories, costume jewelry, cosmetics, perfume, toys, sporting goods, automotive supplies such as waxes, polishes, oil and gasoline additives, windshield defrosters and antifreeze, garden supplies and equipment, pet supplies and accessories, comic books and other paperbacks, record albums, cameras and related equipment, gift wrappings and other paper products, sewing equipment, and carpenter tools.

Handmade articles, which are usually made and donated by members of the sponsoring organization, are good sellers. These can include place mats, pot holders, aprons, laundry bags, stuffed toys, needlepoint, embroidery, and knitted or crocheted items such as afghans, mufflers, gloves, mittens, and baby clothes. Homemade candies, preserves, and baked goods also sell easily.

Don't forget the rummage corner. It can be stocked with secondhand wearing apparel which has been cleaned and pressed, discarded Boy Scout uniforms, outgrown bikes and baby carriages, and toys that are still in good condition.

About eight or ten months are needed to accumulate enough merchandise. The job requires the full co-operation of all members of the committee regardless of their other duties. Begin by compiling a list of potential donors. The list will include names submitted by the committee members and names of previous donors. Canvass potential donors by letter; one week after the letters have been mailed, contact the prospective donors personally or by telephone. For handmade and secondhand articles, friends, relatives, and neighbors should be contacted personally. Make arrangements to have the goods picked up from the donors. Here is a sample letter with reply coupon soliciting merchandise for the bazaar.

Dear _____:

Our annual bazaar will be held on _____.

This year our goal is to exceed the net proceeds of last year's bazaar which totaled $_____. However, to accomplish this, we will need the help of our loyal friends.

We hope that you will join us in this endeavor by donating merchandise to be sold at the bazaar. If you wish to contribute, please complete the form below and return it to our office. A representative of the organization will pick up the merchandise at your convenience.

Hoping for a favorable reply,

Sincerely yours,
Florence Greenberg
For the Bazaar Committee

- -

Date _____

We will donate the following merchandise for use in connection with your forthcoming bazaar:

The retail value of this merchandise is $ _____. Please pick up the mermerchandise on_____.
                                    (date)

                      Name _____
Solicitor: F. Greenberg   .   Address_____

A place will be needed to store the merchandise until the event is held. The owner of a local warehouse might be persuaded to donate storage space or perhaps someone on the committee may have an unused attic, basement, or garage in which you may store the articles.

As merchandise is received, establish a file on the donors. Record the following information on 3" x 5" cards: name and address of donor, type of merchandise donated and its retail value, and the name of the person responsible for obtaining the donation. Here is a sample notification form to send to the people responsible for obtaining the donations:

Date _____

Dear Mrs. Greenberg:

During the past week we have been advised by the following people that they will donate merchandise for the bazaar. These people were solicited by you.

Name & Address	Merchandise	Date of Pickup

When the merchandise is delivered, we will forward a receipt and a thank-you note to each donor.

Hopefully, all the merchandise required will be donated by local stores, businesses, and individuals. If these sources fail to yield a sufficient quantity, however, contact manufacturers and wholesalers who may be willing to offer merchandise at cost or on consignment.

Bazaar Preparations

Booths or large tables will be needed to display merchandise. In arranging the tables and/or booths, leave enough space for wide aisles so shoppers can move about easily and browse. As a convenience for shoppers, provide shopping bags. These can be donated by local department stores.

A clever decorating committee can turn an ordinary room into a colorful marketplace. Used imaginatively, such decorating aids as gaily striped bunting, contact paper in floral patterns, and bright-colored streamers, mobiles, and balloons will create a carnival atmosphere which will contribute to the spirit of the bazaar.

The main reason people shop at bazaars is to pick up bargains, so be realistic and fair in setting prices.

A door prize will increase the profits of a bazaar. Sell chances before and during the bazaar. Offer a very attractive prize for the winner. This might be an electric mixer, blender, or percolator.

To help prevent shoplifting, assign several people to patrol the area and oversee the merchandise. As an aid in preparing publicity, see Chapter 12 on Fashion Shows.

After the Bazaar

Write thank-you notes to everyone who helped run the bazaar—committee people, donors of merchandise, and all others who contributed in any way including those who helped to publicize the event.

Provide each donor of merchandise with a receipt specifying the retail value of the contribution.

Checklist for a Bazaar

PRELIMINARY ARRANGEMENTS

1. Set date.
2. Locate place to hold bazaar.
3. Select chairman.
4. Name heads of various committees:
    A. Booths.
    B. Cleanup.
    C. Decorations.
    D. Equipment.
    E. Handmade and secondhand articles.
    F. Pricing.
    G. Publicity.
5. Organize workers.
6. Compile list of potential donors.
7. Contact potential donors by letter.
8. Arrange for committee to follow up potential donors—either personally or by telephone—five days after letters have been mailed.
9. Conduct personal solicitation in the community regarding handmade articles and secondhand items.
10. As notices are received regarding donations:
    A. Send notification forms on a weekly basis to committee members responsible for the donations
    B. When merchandise is delivered, forward receipt and thank-you note to each donor
11. Set price for door prize chances.
12. Equipment and docorations:
    A. Rent tables and booths.
    B. Get decorations.
    C. Have signs made (if necessary).
    D. Get shopping bags.

13. Publicity:
    A. Submit advance stories to press.
    B. Prepare and distribute announcements.
    C. Prepare spots and submit to radio stations.
    D. Arrange to have posters printed and distributed.

THE DAY BEFORE THE BAZAAR

1. Price merchandise—use adhesive-backed stickers.
2. Set up booths and tables.
3. Arrange merchandise.
4. Put up decorations.
5. Be sure that all booths will be adequately manned.

DURING THE BAZAAR

1. Establish an accounting system for monies received at booths and for chances sold for door prize.
2. Supply booth attendants with cashboxes for handling money.
3. Arrange to sell door prize chances—set up two tables at entrance.
4. Have receptacles ready to receive stubs for door prize.
5. Appoint someone to draw winning ticket for door prize.

AFTER THE BAZAAR

1. See that all borrowed or rented equipment is returned.
2. See that decorations are taken down.
3. If carpenter work is done, see that it is taken down.
4. Arrange to dispose of unsold merchandise.
5. Write thank-you notes.
6. Pay bills.
7. Preserve the donor file for use in future bazaars.

SUMMARY

1. Add up income and expenses and determine net proceeds.
2. Evaluate the bazaar and determine how the next one can be improved.

15:   Fairs

As special events go, fairs are the oldest of the lot. These events originated in Greece thousands of years ago when warring tribes would declare a
temporary truce and come together at certain spots to exchange goods. They re-
garded the fairground as a holy place and believed that God would punish anyone who fought or cheated there. Apparently, once the peaceful exchange had
taken place, the feeling of trust and good fellowship vanished and the tribesmen
returned to the battleground where they continued to fight their wars.

It wasn't until 1810 that a fair was held in this country. The event took place
in Pittsfield, Mass. A gentleman by the name of Elkanah Watson conceived the
idea and called his brainchild the "Berkshire Cattle Show." The fair's activities
consisted mainly of cattle showing and judging, with prizes being awarded for
the best of various breeds. History records the event as highly successful and
well attended. Even the women of the community participated; at Mr. Watson's
invitation, they prepared and contributed foodstuffs.

Fairs have come a long way since this early exhibition. Today, fairs are often
sophisticated events that raise thousands of dollars for various charities. As
proof of this, a group of New Jersey women sponsored a fair for the benefit of
their local hospital and netted more than $50,000. The fair featured an auction,
games and entertainment for children, a boutique, a midway, garden section,
food booths, and a rock marathon in which local rock bands competed for prizes.

Planning and Budgeting

To be an effective fund-raising vehicle, a fair must be carefully planned and
budgeted. This means that all expenses must be carefully calculated in advance;
to be included are rental fees for equipment, the cost of merchandise, food, entertainment, decorations, promotion materials, and rent for the fairground, if the
space is not free.

The people involved in planning and organizing a fair must cut financial cor-
ners whenever possible. At all times, when seeking merchandise and other materials, their slogan should be "Get It for Nothing." If that is impossible, they
should try to get it for cost or, at the very least, at wholesale rates.

The assistance of an underwriter will improve the fair's financial status, although it may be difficult to locate one person who is willing to foot the entire bill. In that case, perhaps several individuals can be persuaded to join forces and provide financial backing. Usually, the trustees and/or board members of the sponsoring organization assume responsibility for securing these benefactors.

Organization

Whether a fair is large or small, the fundamentals of running it remain the same: *a)* a competent chairman, *b)* an industrious committee, *c)* ample time for preparation (nine to ten months), *d)* expenses kept to a minimum through the donation of services and merchandise, *e)* thoughtful planning, and *f)* an extensive publicity campaign.

The initial step, of course, is to find the right chairman. A fair calls for a master co-ordinator with imagination and plenty of clever ideas. She will need a hard-working committee—people with sufficient energy and resourcefulness to translate ideas into reality. The number of workers needed will depend on the size and scope of the event. A large fair, such as the one produced by the New Jersey group, requires forty to fifty people.

The committee should be divided into small groups as follows: booths, cleanup, decorations, entertainment, equipment, food and drink, games, merchandise, prizes, and publicity. Subchairmen must be appointed to head the various groups of workers.

When and Where

Most fairs are held on Saturday to insure maximum patronage. Where the fair is held will depend on two factors: its size and scope and the facilities offered by the community. The New Jersey group stages its annual fair at a local athletic field. Other successful fairs have been staged in parking lots, playgrounds, and on the grounds of private estates. Street fairs have been held in public thoroughfares which are roped off for the duration of the event.

Before a final decision is reached regarding a site, however, be sure that local zoning laws do not prohibit the holding of an outdoor event at that particular location. The county clerk can provide information with respect to zoning and the local police will issue a permit, if necessary.

No matter where a fair is held, there must be sufficient space to accommodate all the booths and stands and still leave enough room for a free flow of traffic.

Weather

Since fairs are generally held out of doors, a rainy day can spell disaster. However, there are two solutions to be considered: *(a)* an alternate date, or *(b)* house the fair in tents.

Merchandise

The sale of merchandise will account for a large part of the fair's income. Therefore, well-stocked booths are essential. The following list contains suggestions regarding "sure-sale" merchandise. The list is not comprehensive, of course, but it will help the Merchandise Committee to get started.

BOUTIQUE

Household items: ashtrays, brandy snifters, candy dishes, canister sets, chafing dishes, closet accessories, coasters, coffee mugs, condiment dishes, cookie jars, cooking thermometers, cordial glasses, cream and sugar sets, decanters, demitasse, fancy candles, fondue sets, kitchen gadgets, paper products (napkins, towels, etc.), pepper mills, salad bowls, salt and pepper shakers, serving pieces, spice racks, steak knives, trays, vases.

Personal items: brushes, cigarette cases, combs, cosmetics, costume jewelry, fancy soap, hair ornaments, key chains and cases, mufflers, neckties, perfume, scarves, shower caps, sunglasses, travel clocks, wallets and other small leather goods.

Miscellaneous items: games, gift wrappings, greeting cards, pet accessories, playing cards, stationery, toys.

FLEA MARKET

Almost anything old will be acceptable: jewelry, such as brooches, rings, lockets, hat and tie pins, art nouveau objects, bric-a-brac, glass paperweights, beer steins, and other pottery pieces. Clean and polish all articles and make repairs, if necessary.

BOOK STALL

All types of books: new and used, hard cover and paperback, children's and adults'.

FLOWER MART

Real and artificial flowers, flower arrangements (centerpieces, etc.), plants, seedlings.

HOMEMADE FOODSTUFFS

Cakes, pies, cookies, jams, jellies, candies, puddings, potato salad, coleslaw, baked beans, and other casserole dishes.

HANDCRAFTS

Place mats, pot holders, aprons, laundry bags, stuffed toys, needlepoint, embroidery, and knitted and crocheted items such as afghans, mufflers, gloves, mittens, and baby clothes.

Display works of professional artists only. Take the paintings and other art on a consignment basis. Charge the artists a commission for all works sold.

Entertainers

Whenever possible, use local talent. There are two excellent reasons for doing this: *(a)* usually it's free, and *(b)* more interest in the event is created if the performers are local citizens.

Some ideas for income, as well as fun: *For adults*—a fortune-teller, a caricaturist, a handwriting analyst, a palmist, and an astrologist. *For children*—a puppet show, a story lady, a magic show, and clowns.

Games and Contests

People of all ages will enjoy penny throwing, bingo, beanbag toss, ring toss, test-your-strength, dart throwing, and guessing the number of beans in the jar. The winners can choose between a prize or a free ticket which entitles them to participate in the drawing for door prizes.

Youngsters will enjoy an "instant art" contest. The only requirements are paper and children's finger paints, which can be obtained from a local art shop, and a supply of Wash 'n' Dri Towelettes for cleanup purposes. Offer prizes for the three best paintings.

An old-fashioned pie-eating contest can be fun. The requirements are minimal—just pies and hungry kids. (And, possibly, Pepto-Bismol.)

Raffle

A raffle will increase the fair's proceeds. The prizes can be glamorous, practical, unusual, edible, and liquid. A few gag prizes can be included just for kicks.

Use balloons for raffle chances—print prizes on slips of paper and insert the slips into the balloons before inflating. (Of course, not every balloon will contain a winning slip; some will contain blanks.)

If clowns are part of the entertainment program, use a couple of them to circulate among the guests and sell balloon raffles.

Door Prizes

Door prizes provide another source of revenue. Offer a couple of very special prizes for the winners, but keep the nature of the prizes secret until the drawing takes place. Mystery never fails to pique curiosity.

Getting the Merchandise

Obviously, a great deal of merchandise will be needed to stock booths and satisfy winners of prizes. Refer to Chapter 14 for instructions regarding the soliciting and handling of merchandise.

Other Preparations

REFRESHMENTS

Refreshments can range from punch and cookies to hot dogs, hamburgers, hero sandwiches, and gourmet items. Again, remember the slogan: "Get It for Nothing." Appeal to local food distributors for donations.

DECORATIONS

An ingenious Decorations Committee can work wonders with paper flowers, colored contact paper, flashy bunting and streamers, and balloons in assorted sizes and colors.

Provide the following equipment for the decorators: staple gun, claw hammer, carpet tacks, thumbtacks, one-coat rubber cement, double-face vinyl tape, double-face cellophane tape, and heavy-duty string.

SECURITY

To help prevent shoplifting, several volunteers will be needed to patrol the area and oversee the merchandise.

EQUIPMENT

The following equipment will be required for a fair: portable heating and refrigerating gear for food, cooking and serving utensils, paper plates, cups for hot and cold beverages, plastic eating utensils, paper napkins, booths, tables, chairs, trash receptacles, and tents.

Publicity

Well-planned publicity is one of the major keys to a successful event. Therefore, all available outlets must be utilized to achieve maximum visibility for the fair.

1. *Press.* Stories should be paced to keep up the flow of publicity. Release stories to local daily and weekly papers as well as those in nearby communities:

    A. Four weeks before the event—a story announcing the names of the general chairman and members of the committee, date of fair, where it will be held, and other pertinent details.

    B. Three weeks before the event—a story with photograph, concerning well-known local citizens who will provide entertainment by acting as barkers, clowns, fortune-teller, caricaturist, magician, etc.

    C. Two weeks before the event—a story regarding the fair's attractions, i.e., boutique, bookstall, flower mart, entertainment for children, balloon raffle, games of skill, mystery door prizes, etc.

    D. The week of the event—final "all is in readiness" story urging everyone to attend and enjoy a day of fun and excitement.

    E. List the fair in the Calendar of Events section of the local paper; specify what the event is and when and where it will be held.

F. After the fair, release a story reporting the success of the event.

2. Send stories to local industries that publish house organs for their employees. Also send stories to churches, women's clubs and organizations, professional associations and other groups that print and distribute bulletins and/or newsletters to their membership.

3. Send neatly typed notices regarding the fair to churches, local schools and colleges, factories, and other businesses; request them to post the notices on their bulletin boards.

4. Contact managers of local companies regarding the use of "statement stuffers" to publicize the fair. Prospects are department stores, banks, and telephone, power, and other companies that mail monthly statements. If permission is granted, print (or mimeograph) notices. The notices must be folded and ready for insertion when delivered to the various companies.

5. If the budget permits, design and print posters advertising the fair's attractions—balloon raffle with fabulous prizes, mystery door prizes, chic botique, fascinating fortune-teller, clever caricaturist, trash and treasure flea market, entertainment for children. Place the posters in department stores, banks, beauty salons, barbershops, and other places of business.

6. Again, if the budget permits, print and distribute bumper stickers and handbills.

7. *Radio*

A. Interviews with committee chairmen and the fair's entertainers, i.e., fortune-teller, magician, clowns, etc.

B. Public service spot announcements. Supply stations with information at least three weeks ahead of the fair so they will have sufficient time to include it in their broadcast copy.

8. *Television*

A. Interviews with committee chairmen and some of the fair's entertainers.

B. On-the-spot news coverage, including preparations on the day preceding the fair and while the fair is in progress.

After the Fair

Write thank-you notes to everyone who helped run the event: committee people, donors of merchandise, and all other people who contributed in any way, including those who helped to publicize the fair.

Issue receipts to donors of merchandise.

Checklist for a Fair

PRELIMINARY ARRANGEMENTS

1. Select a chairman.
2. Name heads of various committees.
   A. Booths
   B. Cleanup.
   C. Decorations.

    D. Entertainment.

    E. Equipment.

    F. Food and Drink.

    G. Games.

    H. Merchandise.

    I. Prizes.

    J. Publicity.

3. Organize workers.

4. Set date. Clear and list with community calendar.

5. Select place. Clear with respect to zoning laws and obtain police permit if necessary.

6. Compile list of potential donors of merchandise.

7. Contact potential donors by letter.

8. Arrange for committee to follow up potential donors, either personally or by telephone, five days after letters have been mailed.

9. As notices are received regarding donations:

    A. Send notification forms on a weekly basis to committee members responsible for the donations.

    B. When merchandise is delivered, forward receipt and thank-you note to each donor.

10. Canvass women of the community for donations of handmade articles and homemade foodstuffs.

11. Establish prices for:

    A. Merchandise.

    B. Food and drink.

    C. Games.

    D. Entertainment.

    E. Door prize chances.

    F. Raffle chances.

12. Arrange for entertainment. Rent costumes for performers, if necessary.

13. Rent equipment (heating and refrigerating gear, cooking and serving utensils, booths, tables, chairs, trash receptacles, tents).

14. Purchase (or solicit) paper plates, cups for hot and cold beverages, plastic eating utensils, paper napkins.

15. Arrange for food and drink.

16. Have signs made.

17. Get decorations.

18. Publicity:

    A. Submit advance stories to press.

    B. Contact radio and TV stations regarding coverage.

    C. Prepare and distribute announcements to schools, churches, etc.

    D. Prepare spots and submit to radio stations.

    E. Arrange to have posters, handbills, and bumper stickers printed and distributed.

    F. Arrange to have "statement stuffers" printed.

19. Provide first-aid facilities.

20. Provide rest room facilities.

21. Arrange for Lost and Found facilities.

22. Prepare a plan of the fairground showing location of booths, equipment.

THE DAY BEFORE THE FAIR

1. Set up booths and equipment according to plan (22 above).
2. Put up decorations.
3. Price merchandise; use adhesive-backed stickers.
4. Arrange merchandise.
5. Inflate balloons for raffle.
6. Be sure that all booths will be adequately manned.
7. Brief all entertainers and make sure they know what's expected of them.
8. Arrange for guards to patrol grounds until the fair officially opens.

DURING THE FAIR

1. Establish an accounting system for monies received at booths and for chances sold.
2. Supply booths with cashboxes for handling money.
3. Arrange to sell door prize and raffle tickets.
4. Have receptacles ready to receive stubs for door prizes.

AFTER THE FAIR

1. See that all borrowed or rented equipment is returned.
2. See that decorations are taken down.
3. Arrange to dispose of unsold merchandise.
4. Write thank-you notes.
5. Pay bills.
6. Preserve the donor file for use in future events.

SUMMARY

1. Add up income and expenses and determine net proceeds.
2. Evaluate the fair and determine how the next one can be improved.

16:   House Tours

Maybe it's a love of art or maybe it's a desire to get a firsthand look at how the rich live. Whatever the reason, there's no doubt that people enjoy house tours. During the tour season, which runs from April to June, thousands of people gladly pay for the privilege of visiting well-decorated homes. As a result, thousands of dollars are raised for the benefit of various charitable causes.

To hold or not to hold a tour depends on two factors: *a)* the availability of appropriate houses and/or apartments and *b)* the willingness of the owners to show them. In most metropolitan areas, as well as in many suburban communities, there are people who own distinguished collections of paintings, sculpture, and decorative art. Only a few of them, however, will be willing to open their doors to the general public. The trick is to determine which ones are agreeable and then find a way to obtain their consent. Usually, this can be accomplished through the trustees and/or board members of the charity that is interested in sponsoring a tour.

An average tour includes four to six houses which are on view from 1 to 5 P.M. The price of tickets varies according to the community.

Chairman and Committee

The chairman and members of the committee should be selected according to their ability to sell tickets. The number of people needed will depend on the number of tickets that the sponsoring agency hopes to sell. Each member of the committee should assume responsibility for selling (or purchasing) at least ten tickets. By operating on this 10 to 1 ratio, a committee of twenty should dispose of a minimum of 200 tickets.

Invitations

The invitation list consists of names submitted by the committee and trustees, donors to the agency's annual fund appeals, and guests who have attended other events sponsored by the charity. Type the names and addresses on 3" x 5" cards which will serve as the master list. File the cards alphabetically.

Cornellians At Home

✿ ✿ ✿

CORNELLIANS WHO WILL OPEN THEIR DOORS FOR A VISIT TO THEIR HOMES AND COLLECTIONS

✿ ✿ ✿

SATURDAY — APRIL 15, 1961
1 - 5 P.M.

For the Benefit of

The Federation of Cornell Women's Clubs Scholarship Endowment Fund and the Georgia L. White Memorial Fund (student emergency aid fund).

CONTRIBUTION $7.50
TAX DEDUCTIBLE

CORNELL WOMEN'S CLUB OF NEW YORK SCHOLARSHIP BENEFIT

☐ I enclose my check for.............tickets at $7.50 each.

☐ I shall not be able to attend, but enclose my check for.............as my contribution to the SCHOLARSHIP FUND.

NAME _____

ADDRESS _____

Please make checks payable to The Cornell Women's Club of New York and mail to: Mrs. Monroe S. Goulding, 136 West 55th St., New York 19, N. Y. Tel JU 6-6743. (Tickets will be limited. Reservations should be made at once.)

CORNELL PARENTS – of undergraduate Michael D. Abrams '62

Mr. and Mrs. Harry N. Abrams
33 East 70th Street

The Abrams art collection, one of the finest in the city, consists mainly of 20th century French and American paintings. Included are works of Picasso, Chagall, Pascin, Soutine, and Rouault. Among the Americans are artists such as Burliuk, Soyer, Maurer, Lebduska, and Eilshemius.

A CORNELL FINANCIER

Mr. Harold L. Bache '16
812 Park Avenue
and Mrs. Bache

The gracious, homelike quality of the Bache apartment is enhanced by the many beautiful objects which, in the course of their travels, they have brought back from the far places of the world—primitive sculpture, masks, and artifacts from Asia, Africa, and the South Pacific. There are other treasures from Europe and America.

A CORNELL TELEVISION COMMENTATOR AND DESIGNER

Mr. Richard S. Stark '34
125 East 72nd Street
and Mrs. Stark

The Stark home, decorated with great flair by Mr. Stark himself, provides an attractive setting for an individual and intimate contemporary art collection. With but two exceptions, all artists represented are personal friends of the Starks. Particularly intriguing is the room designed as a Japanese teahouse and ornamented with old Japanese woodcuts.

A CORNELL BUILDER

Mr. Harold D. Uris '25 and
941 Park Avenue
and Mrs. Uris

Complementing the simple lines of this tastefully decorated, spacious duplex are many varied and valuable works of art. Particularly notable are a Chinese screen from the Ching dynasty, some excellent sculpture, and a large group of post-impressionist graphics among which twelve vibrant lithographs by Chagall figure importantly.

Fig. 22. **Program for Cornell Women's Club House Tour**

Names submitted by the committee and trustees should be marked as to origin. For instance, if Mrs. Thomas Beale requested that an invitation be sent to Mrs. William Arnold, Mrs. Beale's name should appear on the card.

As acceptances are received, type names and addresses on 3″ x 5″ cards. Place these cards in a secondary file, also arranged alphabetically. Mail tickets as soon as acceptances have been processed. Specify on the file cards the date the tickets were forwarded.

When all the acceptances have been received, the cards will provide the information needed to prepare the guest list.

The invitation should contain the following: address and brief description of each house featured in the tour, time of showing, cost of subscription, and names of the chairman, members of the committee, and patrons. Mail invitations six weeks before the event. Include a reservation form.

Preserve the invitation list for use in future special events.

Printing

Printed materials for a house tour include invitations and mailing envelopes, reservation forms, and admission tickets.

Copy for all materials must be submitted to the printer in time to insure a comfortable margin for production. Request the printer to provide checking proofs.

During the Tour

A copy of the guest list should be available at each house to facilitate handling of guests who have forgotten their tickets. Chances are that these people will be "legitimate" and duplicate tickets can be provided for them. On the other hand, some of them could be "crashers." In either event, a glance at the guest list will determine their status.

Two people will be needed at each house to sell tickets to guests who arrive without reservations.

Three or four hostesses should be assigned to each house to greet the guests, prevent them from straying into restricted areas, and to keep the traffic flowing smoothly.

The following rainy-day equipment should be provided for each house in the tour: coat rack, umbrella stand, and plastic runners to protect rugs and floors. Consult the Yellow Pages regarding rental of these items.

Publicity

See Chapter 12 on how to handle publicity for this event.

After the Tour

Write thank-you notes to the people who provided the houses for the tour, the committee, and those who helped to publicize the event.

17: Theater Benefits

Basically, a theater benefit involves buying and selling tickets. And since the tickets are usually sold at prices which are considerably higher than the original cost, a theater benefit can produce substantial profit for the sponsoring agency.

Ticket selling alone, however, cannot insure the success of the venture. This depends on several factors—ample time for preparation (6 to 8 months), the type of benefit, proper timing, good judgment in determining the number of tickets to be purchased, and, above all, a good committee headed by a strong chairman, and a carefully-planned publicity campaign. By adhering to this formula, any agency can successfully sponsor a theater benefit.

What

So far as theater benefits are concerned, *what* generally depends on *where*. For instance, in New York, there are three main choices with general appeal—Broadway plays or musicals (previews and regular showings) and movie premieres. Other choices include concerts, operas, modern dance recitals, and ballet performances. These events, however, have limited appeal.

In Boston, Philadelphia, Washington, and a few other large cities, there are Broadway tryouts, hit shows performed by touring companies, and movie premieres. Smaller communities can choose among stock company productions, musical tent shows, and previews of first-run movies.

A final decision regarding the choice should never be made until the potential market has been determined. What it boils down to is, "Does the production have sufficient appeal to attract a great many people who are willing to pay benefit prices?" If the answer to this question is No, then other possibilities must be considered.

How

This differs with respect to location. In metropolitan areas there are agencies that specialize in providing theater benefit service. These agencies offer expert help and advice regarding both the selection of productions and the planning of benefits. Consult the Yellow Pages concerning the whereabouts of these people; they're listed under "Theatre Parties Arranged." In other areas, where these agencies do not exist, arrangements must be made directly with theater managers.

When

This depends mainly on location. In urban areas, a week night is usually the best choice. In smaller communities, a weekend is preferable. Before setting the date, however, the sponsoring agency should consult the Community Calendar. Failure to do this may result in a conflict with another event and the ensuing competition might seriously affect ticket sales. When the date for the benefit has been finalized, place it on the Calendar so other community groups will be aware of the event.

Usually, the Community Calendar is maintained by a community agency such as the chamber of commerce. In some areas the local newspaper keeps a listing of coming events. But wherever the Calendar is kept, find it. The right timing can mean the difference between success or failure of the benefit.

Tickets: How Many and How Much?

Some organizations take the "whole house." This means buying all the seats in the theater. However, filling thousands of seats at benefit prices is a major undertaking and unless the agency is backed by strong volunteer support, taking the whole house is not advisable. No agency should bite off more than it can chew. It's better to buy a few hundred tickets, with an option to take more later, than to be oversupplied with a quantity of seats that cannot be sold.

The estimated expenditures and the goal established for net proceeds are the primary factors to be considered when determining ticket prices, although geographic location must also be taken into account. Prices in metropolitan areas are traditionally higher than those in smaller communities.

Ticket prices should be high enough to provide a substantial profit for the sponsoring agency but low enough to attract a large segment of the community. The best way to achieve this balance is to establish *three* price categories. In a large city the scale might be $100, $50, and $25. Naturally, subscribers to the most expensive tickets will be seated in what is considered the best section of the house. In addition, the top price usually entitles them to attend an associated function such as dinner before, supper after, a pre-theater champagne party, or some other type of social gathering.

Subscribers to $50 tickets get good seats and $25 ticket holders are assigned to fair seats, but neither category is permitted to attend the associated function.

Honorary Chairmen

Refer to Chapter 10 on Award Dinners for information regarding honorary chairmen and their function.

Chairman

The chairman should be selected according to her (or his) ability to organize an effective ticket-selling committee.

Committee

The chief function of the committee is to sell tickets. Therefore, only those persons with good ticket-selling potential should be invited to serve on the committee.

The number of people required depends on the number of tickets the agency wishes to sell. To reach a determination, use a 10 to 1 formula, i.e., 10 tickets per each committee member. For example, for 500 tickets a committee of 50 will be needed.

The objective is to sell *all* the tickets at benefit prices. If this goal is not achieved, however, the unsold tickets can be disposed of by box-office personnel at regular prices.

Associated Function

If an associated function is planned, a small committee should be established to organize and arrange it.

Souvenir Journal

If a souvenir journal is planned, a chairman and a committee will be needed. Refer to the Chapter 10 on Award Dinners regarding instructions for producing a journal.

Underwriters

The assistance of underwriters will lower the cost of running a benefit. Usually, the trustees and/or board members of the sponsoring agency assume responsibility for securing these benefactors.

Invitation List

The invitation list consists of names submitted by the committee, guests who have attended other events sponsored by the agency, and large donors to the agency's annual fund appeals.

Establishing the Master File

Type all names and addresses on 3″ x 5″ cards; file the cards alphabetically to avoid duplication. The names submitted by the committee should be marked regarding origin.

Sometimes the same name will be submitted by more than one committee member. Whenever that happens, determine which person is likely to have the most influence with the individual and assign the name accordingly.

As indicated in the sample card below, Mrs. Marks' name was assigned to Mrs. Mullen. However, if Mrs. Marks fails to respond to Mrs. Mullen's invitation, Mrs. Rankin will have a try when the next benefit is held.

```
Mrs. Joseph Marks                               Mullen—6/69
117 E. 65th St.                                 Rankin
New York, N.Y.    10021
```

After the names have been carded and placed in the master file, make up an individual invitation list for each member of the committee. This list will contain all her prospects. As they respond, record the information.

Printing

Printed materials for a theater benefit include invitation/envelope, reservation card/return envelope, and resolicitation card. Advertising contracts will be required if a souvenir journal is planned.

Copy for all printed materials must be submitted to the printer in time to insure a comfortable margin for production. Request the printer to provide proofs of all materials. Check proofs for typographical and other errors; double check for correct spelling and omission of names.

Invitation

An informal invitation is permissible for a theater benefit. It should contain the following information: name of sponsoring agency, date and time of event, manner of dress (black tie optional), and where the event will be held.

The invitation should also contain information concerning the associated function along with the names of the honorary chairmen, general chairman, and committee members. (*Note:* At the end of the committee roster, add "list incomplete". This is advisable because the invitation copy often goes to press while the committee is still in formation.)

The reservation card lists subscription prices and carries the following statement: "I cannot attend but enclose a contribution."

Each committee member should hand address and handstamp the invitations which are sent to the people on her list. A handwritten message on each invitation will add a personal touch.

Mail invitations to committee prospects four months before the benefit. Mail invitations to all other prospects three months ahead of the event. Enclose a reservation card and a return envelope with each invitation.

The Second Mailing

It would be gratifying to dispose of all the tickets with one mailing; unfortunately, it never happens. Therefore, a second (and sometimes even a third) mailing is necessary.

The second mailing should go out two months after the first. It is addressed to those committee prospects who failed to respond to the initial mailing. It is identical to the first mailing with one exception—this time a resolicitation card is enclosed. The resolicitation card should be "personalized" by the committee member, as illustrated below:

Hope you plan to be with us on December 11 for the benefit performance of "COCO." It's a great opportunity to enjoy Katharine Hepburn's return to Broadway and, at the same time, help a wonderful cause.

Jane Mullen

The second mailing does not require hand addressing; neat typing will suffice.

Handling Acceptances

As reservations are received, stamp each card with the arrival date, note on the card the name of the committee member who sent the invitation, post the return in the master file, and issue a receipt which will be accompanied by a note of thanks.

The reservation cards will be used to establish the *benefit file. Do not file these cards alphabetically.* Separate the cards according to the various price categories, then file the cards within each category according to the date received.

Be on the lookout for cards that contain special requests regarding seating; "flag" these cards to facilitate seating the house.

Seating the House

As mentioned before, holders of the most expensive tickets get the best seats. However, "best" varies with respect to the type of theater benefit.

If it's a play, the best location is up front, starting with the first row. For a musical, it's the center of the house beyond the fifth row. And for a movie, the middle of the house toward the rear is the most desirable section.

Before attempting to seat the guests, however, take a look at the theater and prepare a house plan.

Begin seating the house by removing the reservation cards in the most expensive category from the benefit file; extract the cards with flags. Seat these guests first and mark off the seats on the house plan.

Next, fill the remaining seats in the "best" section. This will be done on a first-come, first-served basis with seats assigned according to the arrival date on the reservation cards. Mark off the seats on the house plan as assignments are made.

Follow the identical procedure in handling other price categories.

Post seat locations on the reservation cards.

After all seat locations have been posted, mail the tickets. Then reorganize the benefit file *alphabetically*. Use the file to prepare a guest list. The list will be used at the theater to facilitate handling of guests who have forgotten, or lost, their tickets.

Mailing Tickets

Mail tickets two weeks before the benefit. Use an opaque envelope to conceal the contents. Or wrap the tickets in one of the agency's promotional folders before inserting in the envelope. Either way will help insure safe arrival of the tickets.

Be sure the envelopes are correctly addressed, including zip codes.

Publicity

When it comes to special events, publicity and success are closely related. Almost without exception, an event that enjoys success is one that is backed by an extensive, well-planned publicity campaign.

In the case of theater benefits, effective use of all media is particularly important. Frequently people are asked to spend as much as $100 for something that normally costs $15. So why not pass up the benefit and save $85.

That's where publicity comes in—properly planned and managed, it creates a desire to participate. A good publicity campaign includes the following:

1. *Press.* Stories should be paced to keep up the flow of publicity. Release stories to local daily and weekly newspapers as well as to those newspapers in nearby communities.

    A. Release initial story four months prior to the benefit. Announce the names of honorary chairmen, general chairman, title of the play, musical, or film, and where and when it will take place. Include a photograph of the chairman and two or three committee members.

    B. Release the second story two months prior to the benefit. This story concerns celebrities who are participating in the event. (Obtaining the co-operation of celebrities is discussed later in the chapter.)

    C. Six weeks prior to the event, approach women's editors regarding feature stories on the chairman.

    D. Three weeks prior to the benefit, notify all papers to list the benefit in the Calendar of Events section. Specify what the benefit is, when and where it will be held, the price of tickets, and where tickets can be obtained.

    E. A few days before the event, an "all is in readiness, still time to get tickets" story.

    F. Throughout the campaign, feed material to gossip columnists; plant items about people who are involved in arranging the benefit.

    G. Two or three days after the benefit, release a story reporting the social and financial success of the event.

2. *Radio.*

    A. Two months prior to the benefit, arrange interviews on women's programs for the chairman and one or two members of the committee.

    B. Request radio stations to publicize the benefit with public service spot announcements. Supply stations with the necessary information three weeks prior to the benefit so there will be sufficient time to include it in the broadcast copy.

    C. On-the-spot coverage at time of event.

3. *Television.*

    A. Interviews with the chairman and one or two members of the committee.

    B. On-the-spot coverage at time of event.

4. Other publicity outlets depend on the size and type of the community, i.e., handbills, window displays, and posters; these may be effective in small communities but would be of little value in a large city.

    ● If possible, arrange to have a celebrity participate in the event. In a metropolitan area, the star of the production may be willing to appear briefly at an associated function. However, this usually depends on "somebody who knows somebody else who knows the star's manager."

    ● A movie premiere is something else. Film distributors are ever anxious for a film's success and having stars on hand at premieres is one way to help achieve it. Their presence insures good coverage by press and other news media. A small community may encounter difficulty in getting a star to attend a movie benefit. However, there's surely no harm in trying to get one. This can be accomplished by writing the company that distributes the movie. The letter should include information concerning the sponsoring agency and an outline of the proposed publicity campaign. The more extensive the campaign, the better the chances for getting the distributor's co-operation. If the movie was recently issued and the star is on a promotion tour, the company may be willing to include the benefit in the star's itinerary.

● If there are no stars available, do something else to stir interest. For instance, conduct a "look-alike contest" to find local citizens who closely resemble the stars of the film. Naturally, the winners would be the guests of honor at the benefit.

There are any number of gimmicks that can be used to arouse community interest—all it takes is a little imagination.

During the Benefit

Assign two or three people to take care of those guests who have forgotten to bring their tickets. Furnish them with guest lists.

Distribute the souvenir journals. If the benefit is a "whole house" affair, obviously everyone will receive a journal. However, if the agency has purchased only a portion of the house, place a journal on each seat. For a gratuity, theater personnel will handle the job; make arrangements beforehand with the management.

If an associated function is held, assign hosts and hostesses to greet and mingle with the guests.

After the Benefit

Everyone likes to be thanked, so don't forget to express gratitude to those who helped to make the event a success.

Thank-you notes should go to committee people, honorary and otherwise. Have the president of the organization sign the notes.

The chairman should write short thank-you notes to the members of her committee.

Thank those who publicized the benefit; also thank celebrities who participated.

If merchandise was donated—champagne or other refreshments for the associated function—issue receipts and appropriate thanks to the donors.

Furnish each journal advertiser with a receipt, a thank-you note, and a copy of the journal.

Pay bills promptly.

Checklist for a Theater Benefit

I. PRELIMINARY ARRANGEMENTS

1. Determine type of event
2. Set date—clear and list with Community Calendar.

3. Make arrangements to reserve tickets for event (in metropolitan areas, professional "theater party arrangers"; in small communities, the manager of theater).

4. Select a chairman.

5. Organize committee.

6. Make decision regarding an associated function; if affirmative, appoint chairman and organize committee.

7. Invitations and tickets:

    A. Determine price of tickets.

    B. Compile invitation list.

    C. Submit copy to printer for invitation/envelope, and reservation card/ return envelope.

8. Arrange for second mailing; have resolicitation cards printed.

9. Souvenir journal:

    A. Appoint chairman and organize committee.

    B. Determine price of space and have ad blanks printed.

    C. Contact reliable printers to obtain firm written bids for production of the journal.

    D. Compile list of potential advertisers, including names submitted by the committee and friends of the organization; prepare material for a general mailing—letter, ad blank, invitation/reservation card/return envelope.

    E. Arrange for journal committee to contact all potential advertisers within three days of the mailing (see D above) — contact the company manager rather than the advertising manager.

    F. Send ad copy to printer on a daily basis.

    G. Be prepared to fill parts of pages on which no ad appears with copy concerning the sponsoring agency, its aims and achievements.

    H. Four working days before ad deadline, hold a "home-stretch" meeting with the journal committee to get in all funds and ad copy before the finish.

    I. Work closely with the printer in the closing days; visit his plant to make certain the job is progressing satisfactorily.

    J. See that all advertisers receive copies of the journal, together with appropriate thanks.

10. Publicity:

    A. Advance stories to press.

    B. Contact TV and radio stations regarding interviews.

    C. Prepare and send spot announcements to radio stations.

    D. Have photographer on hand at the benefit and associated function.

II. DURING THE AFFAIR

1. Distribute souvenir journal.

2. Assign people to take care of guests who have forgotten to bring their tickets; have guest lists available.

3. Assign hostesses to greet guests at the theater.

4. Assign hostesses to greet and mingle with guests at associated function.

1. Write thank-you notes.
2. Prepare and mail statements to those who have not paid for tickets.
3. Prepare and mail statements to journal advertisers who have not paid for space.
4. Pay bills.
5. Preserve the invitation list for use in connection with future special events.

IV. SUMMARY

1. Add up income and expenses and determine net proceeds.
2. Evaluate the event and determine how to improve the next one.

Sample Materials

The following materials are necessary in the planning and organizing of a theater benefit.

1. Letter sent by the chairman to prospective committee members. See Fig. 23.

2. Acceptance card enclosed with the chairman's letter. See Fig. 24. The affirmative responses will be filed alphabetically to establish the committee file.

3. Memorandum from the chairman to those who agreed to serve on the committee but could not attend the meeting. See Fig. 25.

4. Consent card enclosed. See Fig. 26.

5. Memorandum from the chairman to those members who attended the meeting. See Fig. 27.

6. Invitation to theater benefit. See Fig. 28. The committee member sending the invitation has provided a personal touch by writing a message on the invitation.

7. Reservation card to be enclosed with Invitation. See Fig. 29.

8. Letter acknowledging receipt of ticket order. See Fig. 30.

9. Letter sent by chairman to committee members explaining the need for a second mailing. See Fig. 31.

10. Individual invitation list showing response to initial solicitation. See Fig. 32.

11. Notification card advising committee member of invitee's response. See Fig. 33.

12. Reservation card (see Fig. 34) which indicates:
   A. special request flag,
   B. number of tickets ordered,
   C. seats assigned,
   D. committee member responsible for order,
   E. date order was received.

The invitation shown illustrates points to be kept in mind in determining what kind of a benefit event will be held, and where it will be held.

Dear _____:

I have accepted the chairmanship of the theater benefit. This year's presentation is a preview performance of Coco, starring Katharine Hepburn.

I invite you to serve with us on the Benefit Committee. If you accept, please sign the enclosed card and return it promptly.

A meeting of the committee will be held on June 18 at 2:30 P.M. in our office. Since it will be the only committee meeting, we will appreciate it if you will make every effort to attend.

Last year's benefit raised $_____. This year we hope to exceed that amount and with your help I am sure we can do it.

Hoping for a favorable reply and anticipating your enthusiastic support,

Cordially,

Chairman
Benefit Committee

Enc.

Fig. 23. Letter for Prospective Committee Member

I (will) (will not) serve on the committee for the theater benefit.

I (can) (cannot) attend the meeting on June 18.

Signature _____

Address _____

Telephone _____

Fig. 24. Reply Card Enclosed with Letter

179

TO: Members of the Benefit Committee

FROM: _____, Chairman

DATE:

    We're sorry you were unable to attend the recent meeting of the Benefit Committee.
    However, to bring you up to date regarding plans for the forth-coming benefit, we enclose a copy of the minutes of the meeting.
    We are asking each committee member to help us compile the invitation list and will appreciate it if you will send us the names of your invitees as soon as possible.
    Please sign the enclosed card and return it to us.
    Thank you.

Fig. 25. **Memorandum from Chairman to Absent Committee Member**

You are authorized to list my name in the benefit printed materials.

Signed _____

Address _____

Telephone _____

Fig. 26. **Consent Card Enclosed with Memorandum**

TO: Members of the Benefit Committee

FROM: _____, Chairman

DATE:

    Thanks so much for attending the recent meeting of the Benefit Committee.
    So many constructive suggestions were offered and the response of those present was so enthusiastic that I'm sure our event will be a rousing success.
    A copy of the minutes of the meeting is enclosed.

Fig. 27. **Memorandum from Chairman to Members Who Attended Meeting**

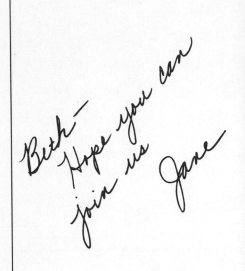

Beth —
Hope you can
join us
Jane

Recording for the Blind, Inc.
invites you to
a preview performance of
Katherine Hepburn

in

COCO

at

The Mark Hellinger Theatre
237 West 51st Street
8:30, Thursday, December 11th
Tickets: $50 ($32 tax deductible)

Pre-theatre cocktails in
Gallagher's Trophy Room
228 West 52nd Street
7:00—8:15

Fig. 28. Theater Benefit Invitation with Handwritten Note

COCOCOCOCOCOCOCOCOCOCOCOCOCOCOCOCOCOCOCOCO

Please send me_____tickets at $50 each for **COCO**
December 11th. My check for $_____is enclosed.
I will_____come for cocktails at Gallagher's.
I cannot attend but enclose a contribution_____
(Please make checks payable to Recording for the Blind, Inc.)

Name_____

Address_____

_____

COCOCOCOCOCOCOCOCOCOCOCOCOCOCOCOCOCOCOCOCO

Fig. 29. Reservation Card Enclosed with Invitation

Dear _____:

Many thanks for your ticket order for our forthcoming theater benefit. For your records, we attach our official receipt.

Your tickets will be mailed to you two weeks before the event, so be on the lookout for them.

With sincere appreciation for your interest and support,

Cordially,

Fig. 30. Letter Acknowledging Receipt of Ticket Order

Dear _____:

On the whole, the response to the initial solicitation for our forthcoming theater benefit has been rather good. However, we still have a long way to go if we are to equal or, hopefully, exceed the amount raised last year.

We enclose a copy of your invitation list and have indicated which of your invitees have responded so far.

We plan to resolicit those who have not yet responded. To help us do this, we ask that you sign the enclosed cards and return them to our office.

With thanks,

Cordially,

Chairman
Benefit Committee

Fig. 31. Letter to Committee Members Announcing Resolicitation

Mrs. William Mullen   Invitation List
164 East 71st Street
New York, New York 10021

Mr. and Mrs. George F. Adams   2 @ $50 $100
155 East 38th Street
New York, New York 10016

Mr. and Mrs. Thomas Andreas
117 East 65th Street
New York, New York 10021

Mrs. Roland Barker   2 @ $50 $100
150 East 72nd Street
New York, New York 10021

Mrs. Joseph Marks   4 @ $50 $200
117 East 65th Street
New York, New York 10021

Mr. and Mrs. John B. Norris   2 @ $50 $100
164 East 71st Street
New York, New York 10021

Mr. and Mrs. David O'Brien
720 Park Avenue
New York, New York 10021

Mr. and Mrs. James Percy
605 Park Avenue
New York, New York 10021

Mr. and Mrs. Alfred K. Peterson   2 @ $50 $100
605 Park Avenue
New York, New York 10021

Mrs. Ralph J. Pillsbury   3 @ $50 $150
170 East 69th Street
New York, New York 10021

Dr. and Mrs. Philip E. Raphael   2 @ $50 $100
1045 Fifth Avenue
New York, New York 10021

                    10 names submitted
                    7 responses to date
                    Total amt. rec'd. $850

Fig. 32.   Individual Invitation List Showing Response

Dear Mrs. Mullen:

We have received an order for four tickets from Mrs. Joseph Marks.
This order has been acknowledged.

However, you may wish to forward a personal thank-you note to her.

Fig. 33.   Information Card for Committee Member

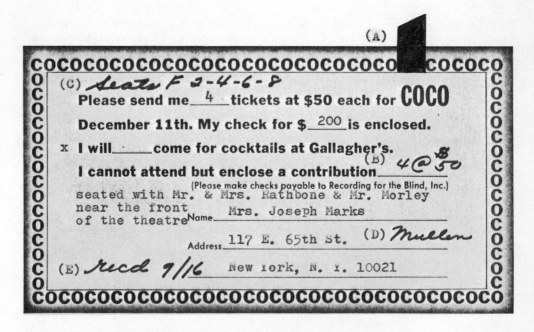

Fig. 34.   Returned Reservation Card Showing Entries which indicate:

A. Special request flag	D. Committee member re-
B. Number of tickets ordered	sponsible for order
C. Seats assigned	E. Date order was received.

184

EXPERIENCE REPORTS

The Benny Goodman Concert

This concert, at Philharmonic Hall, was Mr. Goodman's only New York appearance for the season. Macy's department store held half the concert tickets for its theater club members; Mills College of Education booked one-fourth of the tickets, leaving only one-fourth of the tickets available through the box office. These three factors helped to assure the sale of all Mills' tickets: a popular artist, an "only appearance for the season," and popular demand for a limited number of available seats.

Theater Party Under the "Big Tent"

Summer theatergoers thronged to the "big tent" of the Oakdale Musical Theater when the New Haven, Conn., branch of the American Cancer Society held a benefit night for the fund drive. Star of the theater-in-the-round was comedian Shelley Berman—singing, dancing, and clowning his way through *Where's Charley?*

The idea was born during a coffee break after some strenuous house-to-house campaigning. The New Haven volunteers decided to go ahead and they sold tickets in every way imaginable—by phone, direct mail, contacts with merchants, and a heap of doorbell ringing. Newspaper and radio publicity gave the event a large play. The local paper ran an editorial encouraging attendance, and the mayor gave his official support to the project. An interesting audio aid—a tape made by Shelley Berman—urged public support. Patrons bought tickets at higher prices and met the stars at a post-play reception. As well as the $1,000 netted for the fund drive, the volunteers succeeded in giving widespread promotion to the fund drive. Advertising of the benefit by the theater gave an additional boost.

(Courtesy of AMERICAN CANCER SOCIETY)

Dixieland Jazz Concert

The Ramsey County Unit of the American Cancer Society, Minnesota Division, for the third consecutive year held a benefit Dixieland Jazz Concert, on a Sunday during the month of April. The entire activity was handled by the Special Events Chairman of the unit in co-operation with the members of the St. Paul Musicians' Union. There were no other American Cancer Society volunteers involved in this phase of the event. Materials used were: special posters and educational materials distributed at the event by Society volunteers. Net proceeds have been between $400 and $500 each year. Expenses have been minimal, including janitor service, police service, posters and tickets.

(Courtesy of AMERICAN CANCER SOCIETY)

"Grand Opening" Theater Party

The premiere of the film *Ugly Dachshund* was scheduled by the Ventura County Calif., branch, Oxnard Unit, of the American Cancer Society for the grand opening of a new theater. Tickets were sold at $15 (general admission) and $50 (re-

MILLS COLLEGE OF EDUCATION

Cordially Invites You to Its

SCHOLARSHIP FUND BENEFIT

BENNY GOODMAN

and his orchestra
in their only New York concert this season

"The Worlds of Benny Goodman"
Classical - Popular Program

TUESDAY EVENING, NOVEMBER 5th

8:30 o'clock
Philharmonic Hall, Lincoln Center

"The Worlds of BENNY GOODMAN"
Benefit Concert

Tuesday Evening, November 5, 1963

You may ☐ may not ☐ use my name in connection with this benefit.

Name...Phone...................................

Address...

Enclosed is my check for $..........................for...........................tickets.

No. of Tickets	Location	Box Office Incl. Tax	*Contri-bution	Total
....	Orchestra	$6.00	$11.50	$17.50
....	Orchestra	5.00	10.00	15.00
....	Loges	6.00	11.50	17.50
....	Loges	5.00	10.00	15.00
....	First Terrace	4.00	8.50	12.50
....	First Terrace	4.00	6.00	10.00
....	Second Terrace	3.00	4.50	7.50
....	Second Terrace	3.00	2.00	5.00

☐ I cannot attend, but enclose contribution of $.................................

* Contributions are deductible for income tax purposes. Admission may be had on payment of box office price plus tax. However, the work of the college will benefit only when the total suggested price is paid.

Please make checks payable to Mills College of Education and mail to 66 Fifth Avenue, New York 11, New York. Phone ORegon 5-0162.

Fig. 35.   Front and Back—Mills College of Education Concert Announcement

served). Celebrity support was lined up at the theater and for a post-theater buffet supper. Seven hundred invitations were mailed, using club mailing lists. Ticket sales were promoted through Society volunteers, clubs, local shops and restaurants. The net to ACS was approximately $5,000.

(Courtesy of AMERICAN CANCER SOCIETY)

Theater Party Movie Premiere

The offer to the Fresno County Calif., branch of the American Cancer Society to undertake the *My Fair Lady* opening came from the theater manager, with a 24-hour period in which to accept or reject, and with approximately two weeks to mount the benefit. Since acceptance meant buying the house (933 seats, scaled at $1.50 and $2) an advance to cover expenses was borrowed from the branch budget account with approval of the ACS Division. From the sum paid to the theater costs were borne by the theater for tax, advertising, searchlight, expenses of a guest star, and for printing of tickets.

Expenses paid by the branch were printing of promotional posters, and accommodations for another guest celebrity to enhance the event. Tickets were sold by the Special Events Committee and branch board members, priced at $5 (for the $1.50 section) and $10 (for the $2 loge section). Purchasers of loge tickets were also entertained with a champagne reception to meet the celebrities. Facilities of the theater were suitably restricted to contain the special loge party without encroachment by those who had paid less, and champagne was donated. The *My Fair Lady* venture netted $2,057 for ACS. This sum includes some special gifts in lieu of tickets.

(Courtesy of AMERICAN CANCER SOCIETY)

Broadway Comes to Town

Broadway came to Norwalk when volunteers presented the nationwide premiere of a much-heralded movie *The Hoodlum Priest*. United Artists, who released the film, donated it to the drive prior to a New York opening. In true first-nighter tradition, the theater was sold out. *The Hoodlum Priest* tells the story of Rev. Charles Dismas Clark, the dedicated St. Louis priest who devoted his life to rehabilitating ex-convicts.

Publicity was the secret of its success. A ticket committee was organized well in advance. Several conveniently located centers were selected for selling tickets, and radio and newspaper publicity emphasized this. Also, releases summarizing the plot of the film and calling attention to its high quality were sent out. Patrons and patronesses were chosen, and their names given to the press.

The movie premiere was not only a festive Broadway-style event, but it netted $1,900 for the American Cancer Society fund drive. Three factors contributed to the event's success: *(1)* Well-planned publicity was important, *(2)* the selection of the movie was excellent, as it had a wide appeal, *(3)* the mood of the evening was festive, with a flower-laden lobby adding a first-nighter touch to the occasion.

(Courtesy of AMERICAN CANCER SOCIETY)

Some People Give NOT to Go to Benefit

We don't know how widespread it is, but we periodically hear reports of the staging of non-events to raise some funds for a worthwhile cause. What happens is that people are invited to buy tickets for a fictitious event of some kind. Our latest hearsay on the subject comes from *PR Doctor*, a publication of the American Medical Association. It describes a non-art show run by the Women's Auxiliary of the Alameda-Contra Costa, Calif., Medical Association for their husbands. The ladies actually put on and went to their art show, but their husbands were invited to buy $5 tickets *not* to attend.

(Courtesy of *Channels*)

Community Sponsors Pops Concert

The Boston Pops Orchestra, under the direction of Arthur Fiedler, was the attraction in Providence, R.I., at Rhodes-on-the-Pawtuxet, for a concert to benefit the Emma Pendleton Bradley Hospital. The Women's Auxiliary arranged and promoted the event which netted $32,469, largest amount raised during the ten-year period a series of ten such Hi Neighbor concerts was sponsored by the Narragansett Brewing Company.

Rhodes-on-the-Pawtuxet was transformed into a "beer garden" atmosphere with 112 tables seating 10 to 12 guests, and decked with red and white cloth covers, at which beer was served. A beer cart with horses, that had enhanced the World's Fair in New York, was placed outside the entrance to introduce the beer garden theme. A journal provided underwriting to supplement ticket receipts from patrons and other guests. A supper party immediately following the performance honored the conductor, and a plaque was awarded to the Narragansett Brewing Company on behalf of six other hospitals in Rhode Island which had received welcome financial assistance from the series of concerts cosponsored by women's auxiliary groups.

(Courtesy of EMMA PENDLETON BRADLEY HOSPITAL)

18: Promoting and Publicizing Special Events

Although publicity alone cannot guarantee the ultimate success of an event, it does play a major role and its importance cannot be overemphasized. A well-planned, well-executed publicity campaign which implements the efforts of the committee is a must, without it an event may fail to achieve its anticipated goal.

There are many ways of attracting attention and creating interest. However, to be most effective the publicity should be keyed to the type of event and to the life style of the community. It's the publicity chairman's responsibility to size up the situation and then determine which means seem best suited to the particular event and most likely to produce favorable results.

Of the communications outlets—and these include such visual materials as posters, handbills, and flyers, paid advertising, newspapers, radio, and television—the last three are the most important, the most widely used, and the least expensive.

Gaining the co-operation of the news media is relatively simple—the only requirements are well-written news releases and a few telephone calls.

Press Relations

In dealing with the press, the publicity chairman must realize that the average newspaper editor is extremely busy. Rarely, if ever, does he have time to sit down and discuss the details of forthcoming community events. Therefore, the way to reach him is through a news release. The release should be addressed to him by name. If his name is unknown to the publicity chairman, this information can be obtained by telephoning the newspaper office.

A news release must be clear and concise and provide accurate information concerning who, what, when, where, and why. All names must be correctly spelled. The sender's name, address, and telephone number should appear on the release, together with the date it was prepared.

THE RUTH GOTTSCHO KIDNEY FOUNDATION
916 Ridgewood Road
Millburn, New Jersey 07041

FOR FURTHER INFORMATION: FOR IMMEDIATE RELEASE
Mrs. Eva Gottscho
201 762-7657

The Ruth Gottscho Kidney Foundation of Millburn, N.J., will hold
a dinner dance June 19 at Temple B'Nai Jeshurun, Short Hills.
Mrs. Alex Aidekman, Short Hills, and Mrs. Charles Corge, Spring-
field, are co-chairmen of the event.

(Listing of committee members goes here)

Proceeds from the dinner dance will be used to carry on the work
of The Ruth Gottscho Kidney Foundation. The organization was
established in 1960 by Ira and Eva Gottscho in memory of their
daughter, Ruth, who died of kidney failure. In the intervening years
the statewide, nonsectarian foundation has aided hospitals and clin-
ics and has donated for home use 70 dialysis machines. The organization has no payroll or operating expenses. It is staffed and run
entirely by volunteers.
Tickets for the event are $100 a pair and are available from the
foundation, Ridgewood Road, Millburn, New Jersey.

May 19, 1971

Fig. 36.   Sample Press Release

Radio and Television

Local radio and television stations offer good possibilities for exposure via
"talk" shows.

If a cause is particularly worthy, the host of a talk show may be interested in
interviewing an individual connected with the charity. To take advantage of this
type of publicity, the publicity chairman should contact either the show's pro-
ducer or host by letter. The letter should state the reasons why a representative
of the charity should be interviewed and include literature describing the organization's work.

The
Ruth Gottscho
Kidney
Foundation

AN I.R.S. TAX EXEMPT FOUNDATION

916 RIDGEWOOD ROAD   MILLBURN, NEW JERSEY 07041   PHONES: (201) 688-2400 & (201) 762-7657

April 15, 1971

Arthur Sacks-Wilner, M. D.
c/o "Medical Mike"
Station WTTM
333 West State Street
Trenton, New Jersey

Dear Mr. Sacks-Wilner:

I am writing to request that you consider Mrs. Ira Gottscho
as a candidate for a guest appearance on "Medical Mike".
Mrs. Gottscho is the president and co-founder of The Ruth
Gottscho Kidney Foundation.

As you know, kidney diseases are the nation's fourth-ranking
cause of death. Many of the deaths occur simply because
dialysis machines are unavailable. Because the need for
these machines far exceeds the availability, "who shall live
and who shall die" is a well-publicized real-life drama.
What is not well known or as well publicized is that "more
shall live and less shall die" due to the efforts of The
Ruth Gottscho Kidney Foundation.

For proof of this, I ask that you look at the attached case
histories. While these individuals represent different age
groups and occupations, they have two things in common: they
suffer with chronic kidney disease and they are financially
unable to purchase their own dialysis machines.

Without the Foundation's help, it is doubtful that they
could have survived. However, because of the service provided by the Foundation, they are leading active, productive
lives.

If Mrs. Gottscho were given an opportunity to tell your
listeners about the Foundation's work, I'm sure it would inspire many of them to join us in our efforts to help those
who suffer with chronic kidney disease and for whom there is
no hope without dialysis.

Looking forward to hearing from you,

Sincerely,

Shirley Aidekman

Mrs. Alex Aidekman

Enc.

DEDICATED TO THE THIRD KIDNEY AND THE LIFE IT SAVES

Fig. 37.   Letter to Radio Station Asking for Guest Interview

As a result of the letter addressed to Dr. Sacks-Wilner, Mrs. Gottscho was invited to appear as a guest on his hour-long show. The interview not only provided an opportunity for Mrs. Gottscho to acquaint the public with the Foundation's program, it gave her a chance to plug the organization's forthcoming dinner dance.

The evening news broadcast offers another means of promoting an event, although preference is usually given to events that involve widespread community interest and participation. Inform the station of the affair by addressing a news release to the news editor.

Most radio stations are willing to broadcast public service spot announcements concerning community events. Usually about twenty seconds of air time are allotted to spots; therefore, in order to fit into this time schedule, the announcement must be brief. A mini-version of the press release will do the trick—state the facts regarding who, what, where, when, and the price of admission. (See Fig. 38.) Address the spot announcement to the individual in charge of the Community Events Calendar. His name can be obtained by telephoning the radio station. Submit the announcement to the station approximately three weeks prior to the event.

Just about everyone, including news media people, enjoys an expression of gratitude. So when the event is over, the publicity chairman should send thank-you notes to the media people whose coverage contributed to its success. The gesture will create a good relationship between the organization and the news media and insure future co-operation.

TO: Community Events Calendar
      Radio Station WPAT

   The Ruth Gottscho Kidney Foundation will hold a dinner dance on June 19 at Temple B'Nai Jeshurun, Short Hills, New Jersey. Tickets at $100 a couple can be obtained from the foundation, Ridgewood Road, Millburn, New Jersey.

Fig. 38.   Spot News Announcement for Community Events Calendar

PART IV
IDEAS FOR
SPECIAL EVENTS

19: Brainstorming Ideas

The definition of "Brainstorm" in *Webster's New Collegiate Dictionary* stirs a smile. It reads: "Popularly, any transitory agitation or confusion of mind." This describes poignantly the predicament and state of mind that a Planning Committee sometimes reaches in its effort to come up with a good idea for a special event! The *right* idea is often not easy to come by!

The *Random House Dictionary of the English Language*, unabridged edition, is kindlier. It reads: "A sudden inspiration, idea, etc. (Brain + storm)."

Take either definition, and think of the Experience Reports in this section as an array of ideas for a brainstorming session which may revive the spirit and hopes of your weary Planning Committee.

How to Use These Reports

Over 100 Experience Reports and Case Studies appearing here and elsewhere in the book have been gathered from a wide variety of organizations from coast to coast. They represent *successful* experiences in finding and adapting good ideas to meet the essential requirements for a great variety of special events. This means, of course, relating an idea to the purpose and nature of the occasion and the results desired.

Experience Reports included at the end of various chapters throughout the book are keyed to major *public relations and cultivation events* such as anniversary observances, dedications of buildings, citations and awards, convocations. The chapters dealing with *fund-raising special events* are followed by Experience Reports in great variety—for art exhibits and auctions, campaign opening events, fairs, theater benefits, and many others.

In this Brainstorming Ideas section the Experience Reports cannot be classified so neatly. They offer, however, a stimulating assortment of ideas for special public relations events to promote program activities and projects, or to interpret and cultivate support for dealing with community problems. And ideas for many kinds of fund-raising special events are also reported.

In some cases the *idea* is the lure, important because it will stimulate interest and attract attendance. A good many of the ideas can be used for a variety of events. For instance, a wine-tasting party can be the drawing card for a college alumnae reunion to lure husbands, or for a fund-raising benefit. A cooking demonstration, frog jumping contest, family fair, or an educational show by and for teen-agers, can attract interest for a fund-raising benefit or cultivation event to promote a health program or project, an educational activity, or to interpret a community service or problem.

This section is, therefore, dedicated to Planning Committees! May these Experience Reports (which have been contributed by many organizations) serve to stimulate "a sudden inspiration, idea, etc." for that special event which is driving your committee to its combined wits' end in the search for a good idea!

Experience Reports (Public Relations Events)

Plays for Living

Plays for Living was organized in 1959 as an outgrowth of a similar World War II project. Since then it has developed a repertory of 51 half-hour plays based on realistic treatment of common human problems. The plays have been commissioned by sponsoring organizations which underwrite development of the plays—42 by voluntary agencies, 9 by Government agencies.

Plays for Living has played to audiences totaling 2.5 million persons. These audiences have included church, civic and school groups, PTA's, police forces, colleges and private schools, women's clubs, service clubs, Government groups, unions, national volunteer agencies, annual meetings of various groups, settlement houses, schools of social work, municipal groups and business concerns.

Corporations will find the plays useful in connection with employee and community relations. For instance, Atlantic Richfield Company has used a recent play, *The Man Nobody Saw*, dealing with the problem of civil disorder, for showing to more than 1,000 managerial, professional and technical people. Also, many health, youth, social, medical, adult education, conservation and recreation organizations have used the plays. There are Plays for Living activities in 400 communities, and organized committees in 140 cities.

CAPSULE DESCRIPTION

Who—four or five players. *What*—presenting half-hour plays without scenery or props. *When*—at public meetings, annual meetings, PTA's, schools and colleges, service clubs, community and church forums. *Where*—in hotel ballrooms, community recreation halls, classrooms, schools, churches, public auditoriums. *Why* —to reach the hearts and minds of citizens, students, community leaders, parents, educators, business and professional groups, government and labor groups. *Purpose*—understanding and action.

About the Plays. The plays give dramatic emphasis to situations in the community which need recognition, greater understanding, discussion and, at times, action. They are written by professional playwrights, in conference with authorities in the various fields under consideration, so they are both effective as drama and sound in content.

PLAYS FOR LIVING

A Division of
Family Service Association
of America

10th ANNIVERSARY ISSUE

HISTORY

PLAYS for LIVING was organized in 1959 (as an outgrowth of a similar World War II project). Since then it has developed a repertory of 47 half-hour plays based on realistic treatments of common human problems. Each play is accompanied by a discussion guide. The plays are written by professionals in consultation with experts from the field involved in the play. They are commissioned by sponsoring organizations which underwrite play development and production costs. The Plays are then available for bookings at a small service charge.

Nationally over 2 million people have seen the plays. Sixty-seven schools of social work in the United States and Canada have used the plays. In 1961 PLAYS for LIVING launched a "Go National" program. Since that date 110 localities throughout the nation have organized PLAYS for LIVING programs. Fully a third of all Family Service agencies have PLAYS for LIVING committees.

"THE PLAY'S THE THING . . .

WHEREIN I'LL CATCH THE CONSCIENCE OF THE KING."

Margaret Mead, Consultant to PLAYS for LIVING, says: "The plays are intended to evoke ideas rather than to blueprint solutions. I consider PLAYS for LIVING a unique invention in communication."

The Reverend Paul V. Hostetter says: "I am more than pleased to say a good word for THE HOUSE THAT JACK BUILT, having witnessed performances before many varied groups and in a great variety of settings. This play is doing what we hoped it would do—evoking powerful and personal feelings concerning its very important theme. People are very quickly caught up in the unfolding dramatic action and respond in ways which show how deeply they are moved. Time and again, someone has said to me after a performance, 'That is just like what happened to my neighbor', or 'I wish my neighbor could have seen that', or (most significant of all), 'That said something to me'."

Rabbi David H. Wice—Congregation Rodeph Shalom in Philadelphia—after presenting THE MAN NOBODY SAW as a sermon-in-drama said: "The experience was a confrontation forcing people to be emotionally moved and intellectually stirred by the problems of disadvantaged blacks in our society. Following the presentation, the head of our Fellowship Commission, a human rights organization, was the discussant. He evoked audience participation and deepened their understanding of the problem. At the conclusion of the evening, I summarized in a few sentences, and in the name of religion challenged some commitment and action on the part of the congregation towards the alleviation of this social problem."

PL

Fig. 39.   Cover and Inside Page from "Plays for Living"

197

The Discussion Period Afterwards. In any community there are many points of view. The plays are not an end in themselves, but are intended to stimulate discussion following the performance. This offers opportunity for exploring divergent points of view and leads both to clarification and to new comprehension of the problem presented.

CURRENT PLAYS

The Man Nobody Saw, a stark, moving and powerful play suggested by the report of the President's National Advisory Commission on Civil Disorders.

How Was the Trip? A new play based on drug abuse, written with the idea in mind that the drug problem is everyone's problem.

Tomorrow Is Now. A new play that vividly deals with disturbing questions related to students and campus unrest.

A Shirt a Size Too Small. A play about crime and delinquency, to stir public awareness of improvements needed throughout the U.S.A.

The Well of the World, treating one of the century's foremost survival challenges—the problem of water pollution—in human terms.

You Never Told Me. A dramatic and touching play about VD.

Leave It to Laurie. A play concerned with smoking, for teen-agers.

Lady on the Rocks. A play about the problem of alcoholism.

The Underground Bird. A play on drug abuses, for college students.

Ever Since April. A play on retirement and aging.

Present Pleasure. A play about foster parents.

The Green Blackboard. Showing the effect of too much pressure on little children to perform beyond their capacities.

Eye of the Hurricane. On family counseling.

The Uprooted. A play about the problems of families on the move.

Night of Reckoning. About the dilemma of an overcrowded hospital.

Person to Person Call. To dramatize the volunteer and his or her special place in America.

PUTTING ON A PERFORMANCE

Plays for Living professional casts, already rehearsed, are available to organizations within a 50-mile radius of New York City at a special fee. Beyond the 50-mile radius of New York, performances by local professional or amateur players are encouraged. The first step in getting local players is to get in touch with the Family Service Agency in the community, if there is one, to see if there is already a Plays for Living committee. If there is no committee in your community, the following steps will apply. Almost every community has a little theater, or college drama department, or a drama club which may be interested in putting on plays for organizations. In addition, community centers, Y's, churches, junior leagues and other organizations have acting groups for whom the plays will have a special appeal. The purchase of a script is required if a local performance is to be given. Each script contains complete casting and acting directions, as well as a full discussion guide for leaders. The usual cost is $12 for a set of six scripts; single perusal copy $2.

A booklet is available, listing and describing the 50 plays available. Information about Plays for Living, organizing Plays for Living committees, and communities where Plays for Living activities are now organized will be supplied upon request. Write Plays for Living, Family Service Association of America, 44 East 23rd Street, New York, N.Y. 10010.

The Generation Mix

The following summary was excerpted from a report describing the design and plan, and the results of the intergenerational institute sponsored by the Jewish Family Service of Los Angeles, December 2 and 3, 1968. Organizations interested in planning a Generation Mix conference in their communities may obtain a copy of the full report by writing to Mr. Theodore R. Isenstadt, Executive Director, Jewish Family Service of Los Angeles, 590 No. Vermont, Los Angeles, Calif. 90004.

The Generation Mix

The Andrew Norman Foundation presented a grant to the Jewish Family Service of Los Angeles in 1968, providing for a study of the problems of the aging. As the committee, which was dedicated from its inception to being open and innovative in both attitude and action, planned and discussed this conference, it pondered over the question of the aging. As the committee began to look at the problems of the aging, it was found necessary to look at the problems of the younger and middle-aged persons also in order to understand what was happening to families and within families—indeed, to take a new look at the relationships among the generations. So it was that the idea for the Generation Mix, an institute involving all age groups, was born.

Then the committee looked again, this time at the world today, and the concept of the Generation Mix grew and blossomed into an event involving all the ethnic groups in the total community. The decision of the Committee on the Aging of the Jewish Family Service was that all human problems are the problems of every human being, and that a bright and articulate meeting of many minds from all of the human family is a credible, delightful, and complete logical conference topic.

The name of this unique event—the Generation Mix—came naturally. Just as naturally, in order to be a success, the Generation Mix had to transcend all barriers of race, religion, economics and environment and involve the entire community in representation. This was, incidentally, the first time in the 114-year history of the Jewish Family Service of Los Angeles that the agency made such an all-encompassing community effort.

In a soft age of slick television and super-fun spectacles and entertainment tailored for escapism, some people will attend an unusual event "just to see what's going on," like trying a peanut burger. The Generation Mix staff, consultants and volunteers decided to eliminate the possibility of deadweight, uninvolved and casual onlookers taking up precious communication room. Consequently The Generation Mix was wide open to the representatives of every phase and age of society in the community, but by invitation only.

One thousand letters were written to community leaders in every stratum of the Los Angeles scene, asking for lists of persons whom they would recommend as good ambassadors for their own "special interests." These people were asked to specify the age and ethnic group and agency represented by these envoys in order to make sure that a proper balance was maintained. Winding up with an all-Jewish, all-black or all-white affair would have been a disaster!

THE ROUND-TABLE CONCEPT

In devising the concept of the Round Tables, in which a consultant and a recorder were stationed at each table along with the dozen guests, the committee knew that they would be exposing each group at each table to what was probably the first encounter of its kind for the individual members. Insulated as we are today in our cars and cubicles, it is remarkable to note that the "unaverage person," which every person is, has very little contact with any but his own peer group, outside his immediate family. We stay in cliques and our theories, philosophies, ideas and ideals are pretty much those of our chosen companions. And they think as we do. Therefore, expounding our own "thing" to "one of our own kind" is almost like talking to ourselves. The committee wanted to make very sure that no one at the Generation Mix was talking to himself.

The distinctive Generation Mix symbol made its debut on the invitation mailed to the recommended guests. It was very carefully stressed within the invitation itself that the Generation Mix was not to be a spectator sport, that the participants had been very carefully chosen as being most significantly representative and that accepting the invitation and attending would imply a 100 per cent willingness "to get in the act" and advance the spirit of the event, the exchange of ideas. The process was extremely effective. By requiring a written acceptance and by furnishing tickets and registration cards, the committee had the 600 actively participating guests it wanted at the meeting. Scholarships were given to those participants to whom the two-day all-inclusive $15 fee might have been a hardship.

GROUP CONSULTANTS

The vital leadership role of the group consultants at each Round Table had to be expertly played. For this reason, community leaders with demonstrated skill in group discussion were recruited through personal letters. The tremendous enthusiasm and unstinting support of the consultants when they learned the design of the Generation Mix helped create even more momentum. A half-day orientation and training session for the consultants prior to the big meeting focused on each leader's role and function.

SPEAKERS

Noted people, representing a wide divergence of opinion, were asked to be speakers and panelists. All of these persons were invited personally (through letter or by phone) by someone on the committee who knew them. The unusual format of the Generation Mix was carefully explained to each speaker and panelist so that they could come prepared to help ignite group discussions at the Round Tables.

SUMMING UP

For action which must be individual and very private, we think of what one young fellow said during the conference. Turning to the staid Mr. Businessman at his table, and with a rather smiling defiance, he said: "Okay. What are we supposed to rap about? I don't know you—but I don't know me, either." We must know ourselves so that we can listen and work and grow with everyone in our human family.

(Courtesy of JEWISH FAMILY SERVICE, Los Angeles, Calif.)

Board Members' Bus Tour

A bus tour for board members this year through twenty-three New York City neighborhoods was the first such tour run by the United Neighborhood Houses, a federation of fifty-two settlement centers. It won't be the last, however, according to the UNH. The six-hour tour, including dinner and an outdoor concert, was enthusiastically received by the policy-making volunteers. In addition to a first-hand look at neighborhood conditions the fifty-three board members on the tour heard reports of settlement activities, urban renewal projects, etc.

(Courtesy of *Channels*)

Wagon Train Dramatizes Problems

A wagon train with parents of retarded children as passengers will spend a week crossing the state of Massachusetts to spotlight the problems of the mentally retarded. Those taking the trip pioneer style are members of the Massachusetts Association for Retarded Children. Twelve wagons are expected to make the tour, with some eighty men and women aboard. Sleeping quarters will be the hard ground in the various cities and towns along the way. Dressed in the colorful garb of those who crossed the country in wagon trains a century ago, the "pioneers" will prepare all their meals at the traditional campfire. Square dances and barbecues will enliven the evenings.

(Courtesy of *Channels*)

Let People See for Themselves

A tour of volunteers to a home for unwed mothers was an eye-opener for at least one person, according to the Volunteers of America, in its bulletin *The Volunteer*. The tour was made to a maternity home of the New Orleans, La., Volunteers of America by seventeen young executives being trained for United Fund campaign posts. One of the young executives reported that although jokes were being made about the maternity home on the way over, "I wasn't joking when I left. I met the dedicated people who care for these girls. They explained the tremendous emotional problems, the bitterness, regret, shame, frustration that these girls experience, as well as the problems of adjustment. I learned, too, that they aren't Bourbon Street entertainers or B-girls, but only average young women who happen to have made a mistake."

(Courtesy of *Channels*)

Wine-Tasting Parties

A problem faced by alumnae associations of women's colleges is how to interest husbands in allotting a fair share of the family contribution budget to the wives' colleges in relation to the amounts they contribute to their own alma maters. Something unusual and attractive is needed to bring husbands out for women's college events. Alumnae of Mills College of Education, in New York City, found enthusiastic response in a wine-tasting party. It was successful enough to warrant a repeat party the following year. In addition to the warm and mellow atmosphere created during the rounds in tasting delicious wines, the parties were a marked social success. They brought together alumnae, with their husbands, who had not seen one another for years. And unmarried alumnae were provided with an unusual occasion for invitations to their escorts.

The mechanics of staging and costs for such a party include a private club if possible (often available through a husband or wife member) or some facility on or off campus with adequate space and service available. The only special props are wine glasses—as many as a thousand, two thousand, or more depending upon the number of guests and variety of wines to be sampled. Glasses can be rented at a nominal cost, however, and a contribution from a generous husband may cover that expense. The sources for wines and entertainment are the distributors for domestic and/or imported wines. Representatives of several popular brands of domestic and imported wines are able to furnish as part of their public relations and promotion efforts a selection of their best wines, plus entertainment consisting of a brief talk by a representative (usually female) who presents interesting facts about wines. A booklet or envelope packet of recipes and information about wines is usually available for distribution to guests as they leave. The first step in making arrangements is to approach a wine distributor (preferably in a metropolitan area where more are to be found) and one who is known well by the alumna or board member. Plans may need to be made well in advance, for party schedules are often booked up for as long as a year ahead.

(Courtesy of MILLS COLLEGE OF EDUCATION ALUMNAE ASSOCIATION)

Participation Brings New Audiences

Organizations in increasing numbers are inviting clients and other consumers of service to take part in their conferences. More than 1,000 residents of Birmingham, Ala., took part in "A Forum to Observe the Challenge of Urban Society." Co-sponsored by the Junior League and the Volunteer Bureau of the Community Service Council and applauded editorially by the local press, the two-day conference featured such nationally known speakers as the late Whitney Young, Jr., of the National Urban League, Presidential advisor Daniel P. Moynihan, and Lyman Ford of the United Funds and Councils of America.

(Courtesy of *Channels*)

Youth Project

The Chicago Boys Club organized a program that would inspire teenage boys to expand their horizons and goals by giving them an opportunity to meet and exchange ideas with business, civic and professional leaders, and thus find out what these men considered important to become successful in their chosen fields. The project was planned and carried out through the efforts of a Youth Steering Committee (26 boys, fourteen to eighteen years old, representing thirteen Boys Clubs); and a Program Committee of the Board of Directors made up of twelve board members who had major responsibility for recruiting the 180 civic, business and professional leaders.

The program took place in the ballroom of a Chicago hotel, and was attended by 720 teenage members of the Chicago Boys Clubs and 180 laymen. All boys invited underwent a briefing session on the purpose. Two laymen and eight boys were assigned to each table for dinner. Trained youth table chairmen were placed at each table to assist in introductions, dinner conversation and discussion sessions. The civic, business and professional leaders were brought together for a reception and briefing an hour before the dinner.

The meal and after-dinner program were co-chaired by the chairman of the Youth Steering Committee and the chairman of the Program Committee. The president of the Chicago Boys Club in an opening address challenged the teenagers to learn from the laymen seated at their tables to expand their life goals and broaden their horizons. The youth table chairmen became discussion leaders for a 45-minute period, followed by a closing address by the Chairman of the Board of Boys Clubs of America.

(Courtesy of Chicago Boys Clubs)

Educational Show by and for Teenagers

Staff and volunteers of the San Mateo County, Cal., branch of the American Cancer Society feel they are "communicating constructively" with high-school teenagers. The teenagers, in turn, are engaged in presenting community-service messages to their fellow students. *No Smoking Please* was the title of a particularly ambitious presentation developed by students from six high schools under the supervision of the society in the form of a light and sound show. The purpose was to persuade children in elementary and intermediate schools either not to start smoking cigarettes or to kick the habit. Prior to developing the presentation, the students spent several weeks visiting hospital laboratories, talking with pathologists and reading to acquire knowledge regarding the relationship between cigarette smoking and cancer and other diseases.

(Courtesy of *Channels*)

"Good Old Days" Contest

A "Tom Sawyer" contest staged by the Knoxville, Tenn., Boys Club provided a unique and highly successful event. The program was one of action. The boys climbed greased poles, whitewashed fences, walked rails, raced on stilts, in sacks and wheelbarrows, and spat watermelon seeds better, faster and farther than anyone since Mark Twain's fictional hero. The event won wide attention throughout the state. Prizes were awarded to the "last survivors" of the contests.

(Courtesy of KNOXVILLE BOYS CLUB)

Cancer Story by Movie Bus

Bringing messages and services to neighborhood centers where people congregate is a growing trend in health and welfare activities. Movie mobiles are the latest effort being used by the California Division of the American Cancer Society to reach all kinds of audiences. The self-contained outdoor theaters are taken to centers of "hard-to-reach" populations, such as Mexican-American migratory farmworkers, as well as to middle-class residential sections. All that the movie mobile requires is space for fifteen chairs to be set up and an electrical outlet close by.

The moving classrooms have also been stationed at fairs, shopping centers, playgrounds, industrial plants, carnivals, banks, churches, downtown parking areas, etc. Driven and staffed by volunteers, the units also occasionally have a physician present to answer questions. The success of the educational activity, according to the California agency, "depends entirely on the degree of planning and volunteer recruitment and orientation that takes place before the unit is scheduled."

(Courtesy of *Channels*)

Mobile A/V Unit Goes Into Neighborhoods

A new program with a great deal of public relations potential has been launched by the New York City YWCA. The YWCA has in effect gone on the road with a mobile unit to serve teen-agers and young women literally "in their own backyards." Called "YW-on-Wheels" the mobile unit will go to the outer neighborhoods of New York City to provide informal classes, club-type sessions, and other group activities. Offering such subjects as typing, sewing, art handicrafts, and drama, the program will make use of films, slides, and tape recordings. To let people know about the pending arrival of the "YW-on-Wheels," schools and community leaders will be contacted in advance. After the program gets on a firm basis, it is expected that a regular schedule of visits will be maintained.

(Courtesy of *Channels*)

"The Minds Behind the Movie"

Most of us have arranged or participated in showings of educational films, followed by panels of expert discussants and with quotations from the audience. Something new has been added to that standard format by the Forest Hospital in Des Plaines, Ill. In co-operation with a local movie house, the hospital provides a panel of psychiatrists to discuss aspects of behavior in selected commercial films with the audience at intermissions between regular showings of the film. As people enter the theater, they are given a card explaining the program and asked to note questions for the panel concerning motivations and behavior patterns of characters in the movie.

"At first our audiences seemed bewildered by the procedure because this was all so new to them," the theater manager reports. "But now that we have made the panel a regular feature of the theater schedule, people are warming up to it, and we are getting more participation from the audience." Called "The Minds Behind the Movie," the project has featured such films for discussion as *A Man for All Seasons, In the Heat of the Night* and *The Taming of the Shrew*.

(Courtesy of *Channels*)

Slide Show on Health and Neighborliness

Inner-city youngsters are the stars of a new slide presentation on health and racial harmony produced by the Tuberculosis and Health Society of St. Louis. Designed primarily to be shown to children and adults in the inner city, but suitable for others too, the slides tell the story of neighboring families—one black, one white—who together learned how to build a happy life. The adults and children of the two families are all portrayed by youngsters under eight, in a setting of playhouses furnished with scaled-down furniture. Other cast members are co-operating members of the city's police and fire departments. Among the points made by the slide show is the need for good health, a happy home, kindness and common courtesy, and individual responsibility. To formally introduce the slide program, called "C'mon to My House," the TB Society held a cake and ice cream "cast party."

(Courtesy of *Channels*)

Outdoor "Family Fair"

A unique special event was held by the Community Service Society in New York City. "Family Fair" was run smack in the middle of Manhattan—in the lower plaza of world-famous Rockefeller Center, on and around the picturesque ice-skating rink. Spread over three days, the outdoor activities were roofed by a colorful yellow and white canvas. There were a great many diversions for all family members—including the traditional game and merchandise booths, dancing, puppet shows and other entertainment.

For the fair, the famed Prometheus fountain was converted into a fishpond—with live trout—for those who wanted to go fishing in midtown Manhattan. General admission to the fair was nominal in order to attract as many families as possible.

The event was not intended to be a fund-raiser. Rather, it gave CSS the opportunity to stress a positive value of family life—*family fun*, which can be found even in the midst of a big city of skyscrapers and subways. Involving hundreds of volunteers in the planning and staffing, the event had other practical dividends: demonstrating how new volunteers, both men and women, are recruited as a result of a special project. The thousands who attended, in addition, were given interpretive material about CSS—and in other ways were given a close-up view of the purposes of the organization.

(Courtesy of *Channels*)

Summer Art Festival

The Morosini Boys Club, Children's Aid Society, New York City, hosts each year in late summer a children's Art Festival. On display are art objects, paintings, sculpture and colleges made by boys at each of the society's seven clubs. The festival's emphasis is on art objects made from less traditional materials—everyday items found on the streets and in the children's neighborhoods—rather than those made from the more customary media. The experience helps children begin to see the art that exists in their home areas and how the nature of their community can be expressed through their own imagination. Some children are able to sell their work, giving added recognition to their efforts and abilities. More than 2,000 children and adults, including many from outside New York City, pass through the exhibit annually.

(Courtesy of Boys CLUB and CHILDREN'S
AID SOCIETY)

Three-Day Mental Health Film Festival

A Film Festival was sponsored by the Altrusa Club of Birmingham, Ala., in co-operation with the Jefferson County Association for Mental Health. Six different films were shown each day, some of interest to persons looking for self-help and others designed to aid community and neighborhood leaders to whom troubled persons turn for assistance. Each film was followed by a discussion led·by a competent person provided by the Mental Health Association. Free admission and free coffee were part of the come-on.

(Courtesy of *Channels*)

Film Festival at County Fair

For the second year, the Kern County Health Department in Bakersfield, Calif., and nine voluntary health agencies there have pooled their efforts in order to run a film festival at the county fair. Daily health films were run continuously during the afternoon and evening hours. At the same time, agency volunteers were on duty to answer questions and record requests for literature and other information. Cosponsors with the Health Department were the American Cancer Society, Association for Retarded Children, Heart Association, Epilepsy Society, Mental Health Association, Muscular Dystrophy Association, Multiple Sclerosis Society, National Foundation, and TB and Health Association.

(Courtesy of *Channels*)

Career Exhibition to Recruit Youth

A co-operative effort involving three hospitals in Montclair, N.J., and a local high school attracted 2,000 youngsters and their parents recently to an exhibit-filled health careers program. Students from James Caldwell High School, where the event was held, researched information about the history of medicine, compiled salary statistics for the health industry, and created a variety of posters on health careers. The students also interviewed many hospital workers for a closed-circuit TV program they prepared. Numerous demonstrations were made a part of the program, including electrocardiograph monitoring equipment, prerecorded heartbeats over telephone headsets, food preparation by a microwave oven, a fogging machine used to sanitize patient's rooms, etc. Business firms also brought in computer-related devices and other equipment used in hospital business offices. The Women's Auxiliaries of the three sponsoring hospitals—St. Vincent's, Montclair Community, and Mountainside—helped underwrite the cost of the event and furnished hostesses.

(Courtesy of *Channels*)

Hospital Demonstration in Shopping Center

An excellent way to generate gifts for an institution (Roger Williams Hospital, Providence, R.I., in this case) is to put on a series of well-planned exhibits and demonstrations in a large shopping center pointing out the lifesaving capabilities of the institution. One such exhibit was a cardiac arrest demonstration staged by Roger Williams Hospital at Midland Mall, a shopping center. The spacious mall area attracts thousands of shoppers daily. The hospital's emergency room crew, along with the fire and police departments, was involved, and the dramatic demonstration attracted crowds in the large mall area. This produced excellent publicity in the press, which was then merchandised to the hospital's fund-raising audience.

(Courtesy of ROGER WILLIAMS HOSPITAL)

Health Fair in Department Store

An elaborate event to recruit persons to the health field, a Health Careers Fair, was held in Cleveland, Ohio, for a second year under the auspices of the Cleveland Hospital Council and county medical society. More than 2,600 persons visited the downtown Cleveland department store housing the two-and-one-half-day fair. The store's auditorium was arrayed with fourteen career booths, each representing a different career. Booths were decorated with medical exhibits and equipment and staffed by personnel from the health field. Jobs for the "young at heart" as well as for the young were spotlighted, with a forum highlighting career opportunities in nursing, dietetics, and housekeeping for persons over forty years old. Continuous movies about health occupations were part of the event. Each visitor, in addition, received a ballpoint pen which had printed on its barrel a list of health careers. The 2,600 attendance was double that of the first year.

(Courtesy of *Channels*)

Variety Hour for Shut-ins

The Middle Street Boys Club, Bridgeport, Conn., created a variety program—comedy skits, dance acts, humor and songs—to bring entertainment to patients in hospitals, convalescent homes and homes for the elderly. With more than fifty boys from Bridgeport's inner-city areas involved, the program provided opportunities to display and develop talent, while growing from a fifteen-minute to a two-hour performance. The show was presented to 400 patients at Fairfield Hills State Hospital, and to hundreds more at the Park Avenue Convalescent Home, Carolton Hospital, Roosevelt School and St. Joseph Manor. Eventually performances were given at more than forty hospitals and convalescent homes throughout the state, and before an audience of 5,000 people at a large shopping center.

The Downtown Variety Hour was a success in two ways: First, it provided a community service, bringing entertainment into the lives of people who were often lonely and forgotten; second, it provided the Boys Club members a chance to display their talents in serving others less fortunate than themselves. In addition, of course, it helped interpret to the community the work of the Boys Clubs.

(Courtesy of BRIDGEPORT BOYS CLUBS)

CASE STUDY (FUND-RAISING EVENT)

The June Fete—57th Annual Benefit, Abington (Pa.) Memorial Hospital

This is an outstanding example of imaginative ideas, volunteer and community participation, effective planning and staging. It is outstanding also because of highly successful results—continuous operation as an annual event for more than half a century, the funds it has raised, and the many benefits to the town of Abington as well as to communities in surrounding areas.

This is an event which might appear to be possible only in a very large city, undertaken by a very large organization. But Abington is a small town, ten miles from Philadelphia, with a hospital serving a community of approximately 65,000 persons. Nevertheless, in 1969 the June Fete involved 2,118 volunteers for six months in staging twenty-six Pre-Fete Events which provided "rain insurance" to cover all overhead expenses for the Fete; and a catalogue (souvenir journal) which has earned $75,000 in the past ten years. The 1969 June Fete brought $100,325 to the Abington Memorial Hospital. In total the Fete had raised $2,296,202 up to 1970. June Fete Day 1970 was wet with showers and $88,409 was the net reported after the Fete.

No professional fund raisers have ever taken part. Individual volunteers (over 2,000 in 1970), banks, merchants, business and industry, newspaper, radio and TV stations have contributed to the Fete's success.

In addition to the fund-raising volunteers, the Volunteer Services Department of the hospital provides the continuing year-round life stream of devoted volunteer service. Its 989 volunteers in the fiscal year ending June 30, 1970, gave 65,288 hours to the in-service program, and 10,721 hours to projects outside the hospital.

June 6 was the date for the 1970 "June Fete and Village Fair Day." The timetable, from 8:30 A.M. to 6 P.M., included a Horse and Pony Show; Modern, Sports, and Foreign Car Show; Antique & Classic Car Show; A.K.C. Dog Show; Tea and Fashion Show. There were, also, a Refreshment Tent; Cafeteria; and Lobster Pot. The closing event was a dinner dance at seven o'clock.

Each year a theme is chosen around which to plan printing, decorations, etc. In 1970 it was "The June Fete Round the Clock" and the Village Fair booths featured: *arts and crafts*—"Take Time for A.M.H."; *attic treasures*—"Second Time Around"; *beverages*—"Happy Hour"; *children's activities*—"A Day with Mother Goose"; *country auction*—"Second Hand"; *entertaining ideas*—"Party Time"; *fruit punch*—"A Sip in Time"; *games*—"Beat the Clock"; *garden mart*—"The Early Bird Gets the Worm"; *gourmet corner*—"Thyme and Thyme Again"; *information*—"Ask Anything—Any Time"; *men's booth*—"Watch and Fob"; *occupational therapy*—"A Stitch in Time"; *talent*—"Time on Our Hands"; *the June Fete catalogue*—"Each Shining Hour"; *the June Fete dress and sweater*—"Timely Fashions"; *The Women's Board shop*—"Gifts for All Seasons"; *toys*—"Hickory, Dickory Dock"; *treasure chest*—"Kidd Time."

The events and features listed above provide a stimulating array of ideas for the Special Events Committee of any organization. For readers interested in how such a successful event comes about, copies of the Catalogue (journal) are available upon request for 50 cents postage, which provide in 136 pages a complete story of the June Fete and the twenty-six Pre-Fete Events, with ideas and information about planning, organization, promotion and staging. Address The June Fete Office, Abington Memorial Hospital, Abington, Pa. 19001.

EXPERIENCE REPORTS (FUND-RAISING EVENTS)

A Successful TV Auction

This suggestion for a unique special event on television has been provided through the generosity of the American Heart Association in sharing an experience which may prove of value to other voluntary organizations. In many communities this kind of fund-raising benefit may prove possible and successful.

For eight years the Douglas-Sarpy Heart Association, in Omaha, Neb., has staged with increasing success a TV auction originated by Mrs. Nancy Bounds Moody, who continues to serve as its chairman. Mrs. Moody reports:

The first TV Heart Auction was merchandised and planned with sixteen items which netted $1,600 in proceeds. The confusion of the first show lent to it the spontaneity which is still one of the show's basic elements. The general format proved successful and is still used today as the Auction has grown into a two-hour $10,000 venture.

There are bargain hunters the world over, and everyone loves to participate in a TV auction. We make it fun for them to bid, and fun for them to watch. It is made clear in the opening of the show that the auction is for the Heart Association, for research, community service and education.

This is not a tear-jerking telethon. On the contrary, it is two hours donated to make every merchant look like the greatest guy in the world, to give the audience an opportunity for a possible bargain, and to help the Heart Association.

FRAMEWORK OF THE AUCTION

Here, in summary, are Mrs. Moody's guidelines for the show:

● The on-the-air personnel should include three auctioneers for a two-hour show, or two auctioneers for a one-hour show. Each of the auctioneers is assigned particular items to sell. These people should be professional broadcasters. Even though the key people are called auctioneers, they are not such. The type of presentation and "pitch" on the air puts a great deal of emphasis on brand name, name of donor, possibility of making a bargain purchase, and helping the organization.

• The first ten minutes of each show is spent off camera, with a seven- to ten-second description of the merchandise while the camera pans over each one. This gives the audience an opportunity to see everything and allows them to bid on all items in the show.

• There are two other personalities seen on camera and they are the "tote board" operators. They have two very lovely models as assistants in red leotards and heart aprons. The tote board operators are cut in for a rundown of the latest bids and also work with the two models throughout the show.

ADAPTABILITY OF THE IDEA

This fund-raising special event "on-the-air" will not hold an appeal or be practical for certain organizations. Joint sponsorship is involved: (1) a progressive, community-spirited TV station; (2) a voluntary organization with a program of activities, services or education of community-wide interest and concern. The TV auction offers unusual public relations and public service opportunities for the cosponsors, who are, in addition to the TV station, the merchants who contribute items for the auction. For voluntary agencies, whether health, social welfare or educational, whose services can benefit a substantial percentage of the community population, the public relations, cultivation and fund-raising values of the program should be apparent.

American Heart Associations in communities not already conducting an annual TV auction, and local agencies in other communities where the program does not exist, can obtain a report of the Omaha Heart Association's experience. The report outlines the committees required and the details of organization and planning for: merchandising, air time, promotion, advertising and publicity, TV production, and personnel. Copies of the over-all guidelines, checklists and samples of merchandise donor forms can be purchased by writing to: Mrs. Nancy Bound Moody, Chairman of Special Events, Douglas County Heart Association, Omaha, Nebraska 68102.

(Courtesy of DOUGLAS-SARPY COUNTY HEART ASSOCIATION affiliated with the Nebraska and American Heart Associations)

Merchandise Auction

This is an annual event sponsored by the Cabrillo Civic Club with 25 per cent of the gross proceeds going to the Fresno County, Calif., American Cancer Society branch. Club members collect all the merchandise and conduct the auction. Items include: livestock, hay, puppies, groceries, clothing, jewelry, plants, etc. A free lunch is served at noon. The ACS unit co-operates by mailing out auction notices to board members and to a large list of volunteers, asking them to attend, support and promote the event. The auction is outdoors, slated annually for May. Attendance in 1966 was 700 persons, with a net to ACS of $1,483.

(Courtesy of AMERICAN CANCER SOCIETY)

Rummage Sale

Everyone loves a bargain, and the citizens of Norfolk, Va., are no exception when it comes to the annual Cancer Society Rummage Sale. The event has become a tradition. Tables are set up in Norfolk's spacious Town Hall. Volunteer clerks are on hand to sell merchandise donated by the public. You name it, they sell it—clothing for the entire family, housewares, bric-a-brac, food, plus a special table of new merchandise given by committee members.

Committees are selected well ahead of the event, with a chairman appointed for each table. Over-all chairmen co-ordinate the plans. Letters are sent out asking for donations, with a solid publicity program to follow up the direct contacts. Volunteer workers from outside the local committee are recruited for the two-day project of unpacking, sorting and marking the items, thus making it truly a community affair. The price range is as wide as the list of items to choose from. Some carry price tags as low as a nickel! The day-long event, which annually attracts buyers from a wide area around Norfolk, netted $1,200 for the drive reported here. Over the years the sale has gained great popularity. Fresh, attractive merchandise is important to the success of a rummage sale. If you establish standards, you will have satisfied customers. Such a sale also requires effective publicity, both in contacting donors and in attracting buyers.

(Courtesy of AMERICAN CANCER SOCIETY)

Automobile Auction

The Duval County, Fla., American Cancer Society branch conducted their first Used Car Auction, sponsored by the Used Car Dealers Association, with a twofold purpose: *(1)* to help raise funds; *(2)* to improve the public image of the used car dealers. In a short time the dealers had contributed fifteen cars, arranged with their suppliers to dress them up and called in an auctioneer to sell them. The auction was held in a large parking lot and all proceeds ($3,500) went to ACS. The following year there were fifty cars, and an ad budget and a publicity director, and a goal of $10,000. Admission was free and special entertainment was provided.

(Courtesy of AMERICAN CANCER SOCIETY)

Fashion Show on Skates

The United Hospital Fund of New York, a nonprofit organization, was founded 91 years ago "to obtain benevolent gifts for the hospitals of New York. . . ." In the years since then the Fund, America's oldest federated charity, has raised approximately $96 million in annual campaigns to aid its member voluntary hospitals.

Campaign special events include dinners, luncheons, various meetings and Hospital Week rallies. The United Hospital Fund does not give benefits. Hospital Week comes at mid-campaign and is traditionally launched by one or more rallies, to provide the fullest possible blaze of publicity for hundreds of volunteers collecting coin-box contributions in various indoor and outdoor locations.

The Fund, for about twenty years, has been given the privilege of staging a rally at the Rockefeller Plaza Outdoor Ice Skating Pond. About fifteen years ago, the Fund originated the idea of presenting a fashion show on skates, and has since held about a dozen of these shows, sponsored by fashion stores, magazines, wholesale houses and other high-fashion organizations. Figure skaters also appear. These are young champions who, to preserve their amateur standing, are presented between the acts with no connection to the fashion show. Lunch hour crowds are attracted to the event by music.

Staging of a fashion show on skates takes several months to prepare. No outside person is hired; the Fund's regular public relations and fund-raising staff handle all details. The sponsor agrees to be responsible for the actual fashion segments of the show. The Fund keeps control of all publicity, with Rockefeller Center Incorporated reserving the right to approve releases, and details for the show. Each program must meet the highest standards of good taste of all three organizations. All possible co-operation is given by the staff of the Center to make the show a success. The show is planned so that if it rains on the scheduled date it can be postponed to the following day. This has happened two or three times.

In addition to the skaters and fashion models, those taking part in the event are the chairman of Hospital Week of the United Hospital Fund, who presents a short appeal for the hospitals and then turns over the microphone to a fashion or theatrical celebrity who acts as master of ceremonies. Music is donated or given at union scale. A glee club of about 100 student nurses sings. The Fund's top chairman and the sponsor's VIP's are seated on a dais at pondside.

Other Hospital Week rallies are staged in different parts of Manhattan and Brooklyn. With the large crowds, and a constantly changing audience, no attempt is made at these rallies to present a program as such. One or two good combos, together with an mc who can handle large crowds, make up the entire cast. The mc is given two or three short campaign appeals which he can run into his introductions of the combos. Uniformed student nurses and beribboned volunteers go through the crowds with coin boxes. These rallies are entirely financed by the Fund. Rally expenses include all publicity expenses, plus buses to transport nurses, expenses for props, and food for cold and hungry performers.

(Courtesy of UNITED HOSPITAL FUND of New York)

Arts Fund Festival Week

The Federated Arts Fund, Providence, R.I., staged during the peak of its annual fund drive a Festival Week of four programs at the Midland Mall, a large shopping center in the Warwick area. The opening event was a Sunday afternoon concert presented by the Warwick Civic Orchestra. Performing arts groups associated with the fund presented programs during the week in the spacious mall area, open to the public without charge. The Looking Glass Theater staged *The If Box*, a program for young children. The State Ballet of Rhode Island provided a demonstration of *The World of Classical Ballet* with soloists and members of the ballet performing. The Rhode Island Civic Chorale and Chamber Orchestra of some 150 members closed the series with a Sunday afternoon concert.

Stores on the mall co-operated with window displays, and the Merchants Association provided a budget to cover promotion and production costs. Advance newspaper, radio and TV publicity helped to draw crowds at the times scheduled for performances. The festival and related publicity made people more aware of the Arts Fund organizations during the period that some 300 volunteers were soliciting contributions in the Providence area. The manager of the mall, in a Providence *Sunday Journal* interview explaining reasons for sponsoring such events, said: "The greatest value is to be found in intangibles. Any merchant is looking for increased sales, of course, but there are other elements as well. We like people to wonder what's going on at the mall. We like activities, and we like to be identified with the performing arts."

(Courtesy of Arts Rhode Island)

"Fan Fair"

The Columbus, Ohio, United Appeal decided to let its "Fan Fair," staged by agencies and consisting of exhibits, serve as a kickoff. The purpose was to hold an early kickoff in this fashion to indoctrinate key volunteers prior to the start of solicitations within industry. A disadvantage of this advance date was that a head of steam was worked up which could not be sustained until the opening of the residential campaign. For purposes of publicity only a nominal public kick-off was held in front of the huge electric thermometer at the busiest downtown traffic spot at noon on the actual kickoff day.

More than 10,000 persons attended the "Fan Fair" at the Veterans Memorial in downtown Columbus. It featured fair-type booths and exhibits planned and manned by agency services. Awards were given for the most effective displays and exhibits. At midpoint in the program a pageant of services was held. Dramatic lighting of the auditorium made the pageant particularly vivid. The program featured 70 beneficiaries of the services. The 300-voice Columbus Industrial Chorus sang inspirational songs such as "I Believe" and "You'll Never Walk Alone" and two media personalities shared the narration. Climaxing the pageant was introduction of the poster boy—a three-year-old deaf boy—and Woody Hayes, Ohio State football coach. To maintain interest in late afternoon, a variety show was put on. This featured such agency entertainment as folk singing, an Indian dance, gymnasts and youth choirs.

(Courtesy of *Swaps*, United Way)

Texas-Style Benefit

The Texas Society for the Prevention of Blindness is the happy beneficiary of a Texas-style charity event, the annual Gulf Coast Arabian Open Horse Show. As reported in the Fall, 1969, issue of *News*, published by the National Society for the Prevention of Blindness, Inc., sponsorship of the event was undertaken by the Houston Memorial Chapter of Delta Gamma alumnae, which contracted to sponsor the show for five years—with the Texas Society being the five-year beneficiary. All Delta Gamma chapters are committed to prevention of blindness as their charitable activity.

Rated a "star show" by the American Horse Show Association, the three-day event was held at Houston's Pin Oak Stables, with 2,309 box seats at $2.50 admission and 5,000 grandstand seats at $1. There were five performances, with a total attendance of more than 15,000. Horses from twelve states were entered in over eighty different classes, including halter, equitation, English pleasure, Western pleasure, five-gaited, three-gaited, driving and costume categories.

"Setting the pace," the report reads, "was Mrs. John E. Lyons, who happens to be not only a Delta Gamma but also a board member of the Texas Society. Many other board members volunteered to serve on various committees.

"A goodwill 'kickoff' party, promoting the horse show and announcing the Delta Gamma's sponsorship, was given for Houston's press corps, attended by more than 350 guests.

"Adding to the show's excitement was a giveaway Arabian horse for one lucky ticket holder, contributed to the Society by the president of the Gulf Coast's Arabian Horse Club, David L. Hartman. The horse, named Socquietu, is a dark chestnut, with white mane and tail, valued at $1,500.

"Expenses of the show were defrayed by advertising sales for the souvenir program. Funds were also raised by selling memberships in a 'hospitality club' operated for the show's duration, with dues of $10 entitling members to use the facilities of the club."

The final tally of proceeds from all sources for the 1969 Horse Show provided $8,500 for the Texas Society's coffers.

The Houston event is one of the top 22 horse shows affiliated with the American Horse Show Association. The association has available a brochure "How to Operate a Horse Show." Organizations interested in information about arrangements should write the American Horse Show Association, Inc., 527 Madison Avenue, New York, N.Y. 10022.

(Courtesy of HOUSTON MEMORIAL CHAPTER, DELTA GAMMA SORORITY)

All-Arabian Horse Show

The Arabian Horse Association of Northern California and the San Joaquin County branch of the American Cancer Society cosponsored the annual event for three days of performances as a benefit which attracted approximately 500 persons and netted $575.15 to ACS. The Arabian Horse Association handled the actual program and performances, with ACS responsible only for ticket sales, with proceeds going entirely to ACS. The only expense was for ticket printing, and the only criticism of the event was that earlier publicity would have resulted in more ticket sales.

(Courtesy of AMERICAN CANCER SOCIETY)

Shortest Special Event on Record

Louisville, Ky., kicked off both the 1967 and 1968 United Appeal campaigns with a "Minute to Consider" at 1 P.M. on opening day. It was reported as reminiscent of the old Armistice Day observance. At precisely one o'clock all the civil defense and fire department sirens, church bells, riverboat and factory whistles, radio and TV stations, and store public address systems sounded off with 60 seconds of noise to call attention to this as the "minute to consider . . . the young, the aged, the infirm, the unfortunate . . . to think about all the good your United Appeal pledge can do . . . to consider your own blessings, then make your decision to give generously." Advance newspaper, radio and TV publicity and full-page ads in the Louisville *Times* and *Courier Journal* warned Louisville residents to expect all this and not to become alarmed. (*Authors' Note.* As a public kickoff this assured the attention of the entire population for one minute of concentrated attention and thought. Conceivably such a public kickoff might be planned for a hospital or other organizations which offer their service to the entire community.)

(Courtesy of *Swaps*, UNITED WAY)

Campaign Kickoff, Texas Style

Judging by the nature and results of a recent membership campaign, the YMCA in Arlington, Texas, must be very happy about its unprecedented installation of a woman as boss of the campaign. At the campaign kickoff meeting the leadership was "arrested" by the local police, taken before a justice of the peace and charged with: (1) disturbing the peace and quietude of the city by getting over 150 people worked up and excited enough in behalf of the YMCA to come out on a snowy (yes, snowy) night for a kickoff banquet; (2) disturbing the status quo of the YMCA board by challenging its members to give Arlington the kind of YMCA it rightly deserves; (3) attempting to invade the privacy of the homes and businesses of Arlington to further their scheme of raising money for operation of the YMCA. The campaign's leadership was literally locked up in the city jail for three hours during the first campaign report meeting—pending the raising of $15,000 for a "peace bond." The bond was raised, the prisoners were freed and the lady's gimmick pushed the campaign over the top.

(Courtesy of *Channels*)

Pledges Turn Up in Odd Places

Before one of the report meetings of the Kansas City, Mo., United Campaign, pledges were hidden under chairs, inside coats, under hats, on tabletops and inside shoes. During the meeting "magic pledge finders," wearing magician's hat and cape, passed through the audience and "discovered" the pledges. Each time a pledge was found a bell rang on the magic pledge finder box on the stage, lighting up the word "Pledge." The last pledge was magically discovered on the bald head of the Chief Magician.

(Courtesy of *Swaps*, UNITED WAY)

Scenic Airplane Flights

This is an annual one-day event, cosponsored by the San Diego County Branch of the American Cancer Society and Pacific Southwest Airlines. Planes and crews are made available for flights over the San Diego bay area. ACS handles promotion, the sale of tickets and makeup of flight manifests. Pre-event costs are limited to the printing of tickets, about $30. Tickets are priced at $5 for adults and $2 for children twelve years and under. Ticket sales are stimulated by an intense publicity campaign, including live TV, commencing about two weeks prior to the event.

(Courtesy of AMERICAN CANCER SOCIETY)

Pet Frogs Are Contestants

For four years the members of the Junior Chamber of Commerce in San Diego, Calif., have sponsored a successful Frog Jumping Contest. Several prizes are offered for the frogs which jump farthest and fastest. Before a J.C. member can enter his frog he has to pay an entry fee. Twenty-five per cent of the entry fee goes for the prizes and the other 75 per cent is given to the American Cancer Society. This special event netted $1,500 for the California Division crusade.

(Courtesy of AMERICAN CANCER SOCIETY)

A (Bowling) Strike for Cancer

The Maricopa County Unit of the American Cancer Society in Phoenix, Ariz., arranged a bowling fund-raising event. All Phoenix bowling houses and most of the others in the county set aside a week in April as "Strike Cancer Week." Coin cans were set up at each alley, posters displayed at each house. The idea was for each bowler to drop a contribution into the can each time he or she made a strike. The success of the event naturally depended upon the bowlers getting into the spirit of the thing.

The first step in setting up the event was to contact the Greater Phoenix Bowlers Association and sell the league bowlers on the idea. Their response to it was most enthusiastic. Next, permission was obtained from the owners of the various bowling houses, through the Salt River Bowling Proprietors' Association. Some of the league bowlers went with the volunteers to make the contact. The owners were equally enthusiastic. They agreed to chip in the cost of the 90-minute telecast to promote the event. The owners chose the bowling house which would be the site of the telecast. It was aired on a Sunday afternoon, the first day of "Strike for Cancer Week." Several other notables joined with the Governor, Secretary of State and the Mayor and bowled in competition with all-star bowlers from the area. With the advance publicity the show had received, all the leagues got the word and participated in the event. Many contributions were collected by telephone during the telecast, unsolicited. The net result was $1,800 for the Crusade, a lot of excellent publicity and goodwill, and the event required very little time or effort on the part of staff.

(Courtesty of AMERICAN CANCER SOCIETY)

Figure-Skating Ice Show

"Funorama on Ice" is presented each year by the Essex Skating Club, Inc., of New Jersey, for the benefit of the Hospital Center at Orange, N.J. It has been held for eleven years in West Orange at the South Mountain Ice arena, which has a seating capacity of 3,000 spectators. Peg Fleming, Tim Wood and famous figure-skating stars from over the world have performed.

More than 1,000 volunteers are involved in putting on the event. Included in the group are 200 participants who are members of the Essex Skating Club. Several hundred volunteers from the Hospital Center assist, including trustees, women's auxiliary members, doctors, student nurses, candy stripers, Boy Scouts, church groups, Junior Chamber of Commerce and other community organization members.

For promotion a major insurance company makes available its community service unit, a department store contributes the use of its windows for advertising displays, and many business establishments accept posters produced in a poster-making contest. Country clubs offer combination dinner-Funorama parties to their members. Many organizations, such as Girl Scouts and Boy Scouts, purchase tickets in groups. The Funorama stars visit the hospital to talk with children and adult patients.

The event serves as an excellent public relations vehicle for the Hospital Center and creates considerable goodwill. It receives wide publicity in the local and even New York City newspapers, radio coverage on local stations, and the *Wide World of Sports* TV show aired it one year. A dinner dance, cocktail party and other social festivities are tied in with the event.

Approximately $200,000 has been raised for special hospital projects, which have been selected because of their public appeal—such as equipment for a heart clinic, renovation of the accident room, etc. A number of contributions from individuals and corporations are received each year from people who cannot attend.

Funorama is highly successful, particularly because of the cross section of the local population involved in staging the show. The Funorama team of volunteers includes prominent civic and business leaders, and a wide range of individuals, young and old, of all races, from all economic levels.

Organizations wishing more information may obtain free of charge a copy of the Souvenir Program which contains the complete story of the 1970 Funorama on Ice. Write to Mrs. Laurence Ford, Funorama on Ice, The Hospital Center, 188 South Essex Avenue, Orange, N.J. 07051.

Art Auction in Connecticut

The Stonington, Conn., chapter of the American Cancer Society recently promoted an Art Auction as a departure from previous benefits. The National Arts Gallery, Ltd., 124 Montague Street, Brooklyn, New York 11201, was the agent and exhibitor, furnishing 130 oil paintings, watercolors and original graphics. While contract arrangements vary, in this case the National Arts Gallery management guaranteed the local ACS chapter a commission of 20 per cent of the gross amount of sales. Posters, handbills, engraved invitations, sample news releases and a portion of local publicity expenses were supplied. Also provided were a work of art as a door prize, transportation and insurance for the art objects, an auctioneer and assistant.

The ACS chapter was responsible for all local arrangements—a suitable place for the auction (the local high school); microphone and public address system; police protection; personnel to assist the auctioneer; and volunteers to assist in setting up the art items for display. The auction was an evening affair, held from six o'clock to eleven-thirty. A local catering service provided a mobile snack bar. Three committees carried responsibility for invitations, advertising, publicity and promotion.

Difficulties encountered included the necessity of compiling a mailing list of 2,000 art-minded individuals and potential purchasers; a rainy night; and a band rehearsal taking place in the school at the same time.

The report of the ACS chairman pointed out some essentials for a future auction with more substantial proceeds: "An art auction needs to be instigated and promoted by knowledgeable individuals in the world of art, who have the necessary contacts with art-educated buyers, and who can arouse public interest. Merely advertising and publicizing an Art Auction, no matter how worthy the cause, will not bring out the necessary attendance of potential purchasers."

(Courtesy of AMERICAN CANCER SOCIETY, Stonington, Conn. Chapter)

Raised More Than Money

"The High Cost of Hunger," a public forum sponsored by the Metropolitan Council for Community service in Denver, Colo., featured a luncheon costing 17 cents a plate, although those attending were charged one dollar. The 17-cent plate, according to the flyer promoting the conference, was what is allowed for a person's meal in the current Colorado grants for the Aid to Families with Dependent Children program. The luncheon proceeds beyond the basic 17 cents went to the Denver Welfare Rights Organization whose members helped serve the meal.

(Courtesy of *Channels*)

Thousands of Miles of Spaghetti

Spaghetti twirlers had a feast in Waterbury, Conn., when the American-Italian Civic Club sponsored a supper for the benefit of the American Cancer Society fund drive. The event was held in the club rooms, with two servings: 11:30 A.M. to 1:30 P.M., and 5 P.M. to 8 P.M.

The club originated the idea of having the benefit supper. Their offer was accepted with enthusiasm by the Waterbury ACS Branch. The club formed committees, dividing responsibility for the different activities. Splendid publicity helped insure success. Hearty appetites were matched by healthy receipts. The spaghetti supper netted $885 for the fund drive.

(Courtesy of AMERICAN CANCER SOCIETY)

Annual Benefit Dinner

Dinner at a local inn was cosponsored by the owner and a service club. The specific year reported here involved cosponsorship with the Capitol Lions Club. All details were handled by the sponsors with minimum assistance from the Santa Cruz County Branch ACS. The event was held with 350 persons attending. Gross income, derived from ticket sales, was $2,680. Expenses—mainly food costs—amounted to $960. The net to ACS was $1,720.

(Courtesy of AMERICAN CANCER SOCIETY)

Annual Emerald Lake Dinner

This event, started a dozen years ago, is sponsored by the San Mateo County Branch, American Cancer Society, and the Emerald City Unit, involving about

25 volunteers. Preparation time is from six to ten months and requires approximately eight meetings for planning and organizing.

Held each April, the dinner promotes income primarily from ticket sales. A 35-member Ticket Committee begins sales ($3.50 per person) about a month in advance, turning in the unsold tickets a week before the event. Publicity is sustained through the ticket-selling period, and considerable follow-up publicity comes through media coverage. For several years the dinner has been held at the Redwood City Elks Club. The only major cost is for meat, with remaining items donated by local merchants. The most recent dinner drew an attendance of 700 persons. The initial dinner netted $200 for ACS. The most recent one grossed $2,640, with expenses of $400, netting $2,240.

(Courtesy of AMERICAN CANCER SOCIETY)

Dinner Meetings for Prospects

Roger Williams Hospital, Providence, R.I., has for several years held successful evening dinner meetings and tours of the hospital for selected prospects. Board members invite people they know who have the financial means to become contributors to the hospital. Guests are told why they are there, shown what the hospital is doing and what it is offering to the community, and then asked to become contributors. This new interested group of prospects also serves as a source of possible board members for the hospital.

(Courtesy of ROGER WILLIAMS HOSPITAL)

Pancake Breakfast

A breakfast featuring that old standby was held in Chico, Calif., during YMCA Week. More than 1,000 breakfasts were served from 6:30 A.M. to 2 P.M. The event netted over $1,000 since all help and supplies were donated.

(Courtesy of NATIONAL COUNCIL YMCA)

"Bunny Girls" for Breakfast

The United Fund in Pontiac, Mich., served up real live Bunny Girls, courtesy of the Detroit Playboy Club, to greet volunteers at the Advance Gifts Kickoff Breakfast. In addition to their primary duties of being seen, the girls handed out instructional materials and gave away live rabbits to astonished unit heads. A live orchestra added to the enjoyment of the event. The Bunnies, incidentally, wore pleated skirts and playboy sweaters.

(Courtesy of *Swaps*, UNITED WAY)

Cooking Demonstration

Sponsored by Omega Nu Sorority, a well-known cooking expert was obtained from San Francisco through the Pacific Gas & Electric Company to conduct afternoon and evening cooking demonstrations, featuring Continental cuisine in the afternoon and the art of Mexican cooking in the evening.

The benefit for the local branch of the American Cancer Society was held at the Episcopal Church Parish Hall, with a $2 per person admission. Door prize was a new stove donated by the manufacturer and again obtained through the assistance of Pacific Gas and Electric Company. The Stanislaus-Toulumne County Branch of ACS helped publicize the event and assisted in selling tickets. There were no costs, and the net to ACS was $452.

(Courtesy of AMERICAN CANCER SOCIETY)

Bacon and Eggs Meeting for Media

The national public relations department of Goodwill Industries of America held a special breakfast event in New York City for the national communications media. Purpose of the event was "to inform the press, radio, television, and magazine professionals of the scope, variety, and importance of the Goodwill program." Speakers at the breakfast included a panel representing the rehabilitation field, business and government.

(Courtesy of *Channels*)

Parisienne Holiday Show

Annually the Town & Country Women's Club sponsors a very elegant fashion luncheon, using the facilities of a private club in Santa Barbara to benefit the American Cancer Society county and unit branches. The event is invitational and usually held in June. The invitation list is compiled from names suggested by several groups: the Women's Club, the Santa Barbara Fashion Guild, Chamber of Commerce, and a group of ACS volunteers. A major attraction for the event is the celebrity who serves as master of ceremonies.

Six months of planning precede the event, but most of this is done by the sponsoring group, who also advance and handle pre-event expenses. ACS staff assistance is required as the show approaches, with approximately one month of active, regular contact and follow-through on clerical and other assignments. Show themes vary from year to year. There were 1,000 people present at the last one. Gross income was $6,777. Costs, primarily for luncheon, and some for decorations and ticket printing amounted to $2,094. Net proceeds were $4,782.45.

(Courtesy of AMERICAN CANCER SOCIETY)

ANNOTATED BIBLIOGRAPHY

Channels. New York: National Public Relations Council.

A twice-a-month roundup of ideas and trends in health and welfare, public relations and education.

Evaluating Your Public Relations Program. New York:
The National Public Relations Council.

A useful handbook for staff members who have the responsibility for developing a broad-based public relations program.

Levine, Howard and Carol. *Effective Public Relations for Community Groups*. New York: Association Press, 1969.

Adapts concepts and techniques, successfully used in business, industry and education, to the special requirements of voluntary organizations and special agencies involved in community action.

Making the Most of Radio-Television. New York: The National Public Relations Council.

A guide for developing productive TV and radio relationships, programs, announcements, etc.

Productive Press Relations. New York: The National Public Relations Council.

A handbook for volunteers and staff members in developing relationships with newspapers. How to prepare news releases, and other information important in meeting the requirements of newspaper editors.

Public Relations News, New York: Public Relations News.

While its reporting primarily is related to public relations problems and news of business and industry, this weekly four-page news letter is always full of experience reports and stimulating ideas. Its "Case Study" reports frequently describe examples of public service projects conducted in co-operation with public service organizations and community agencies. Expensive for small voluntary organizations, but a good source of information about public-service-minded companies for staff members of national and large city organizations.

Your Annual Meeting. New York: The National Public Relations Council.

A guide for planning annual meetings effective in content and staging.

Authors' Appreciations

Numerous individuals and organizations have contributed to the preparation of this book and to its usefulness, providing information and offering suggestions based on their professional experience.

The authors wish to express gratitude especially to David M. Church for his review of chapters and to Harold N. Weiner, formerly Executive Director, National Public Relations Council of Health and Welfare Services, Inc., for frequent consultations in identifying sources for needed information.

Appreciation is also expressed to the following individuals and organizations for their cooperation in many ways:

ABINGTON HOSPITAL, Abington, Pennsylvania
   Miss Dorothy Hammer
AMERICAN ALUMNI COUNCIL
   Mrs. Jean Mercker
AMERICAN CANCER SOCIETY, New York City
   Irving Rimer, *Director of Public Relations*
AMERICAN COLLEGE PUBLIC RELATIONS ASSOCIATION
   James K. Blake, *Director of Communication Services*
AMERICAN HEART ASSOCIATION, New York City
   Philip W. Ellard, *Development Coordinator*
AMERICAN SOCIETY FOR THE PREVENTION OF CRUELTY
   TO ANIMALS, New York City
   Mrs. George Hayman, *Special Events*
BARTON-GILLET CO., New York City & Baltimore
MRS. LEONARD BERNHEIM
BOYS CLUBS OF AMERICA, New York City
   Edward J. Stapleton, *Director of Public Relations*
BROWN UNIVERSITY
   Howard W. Curtis, *Secretary*
CORNELL WOMEN'S CLUB, New York City
DOUGLAS-SARPY HEART ASSOCIATION of the Nebraska
   Heart Association, Inc.
   Mrs. Nancy Bounds Moody

FAMILY SERVICE ASSOCIATION OF AMERICA
   Alfred S. Taylor, formerly *Director of Public Relations*
IRVINGTON HOUSE, New York City
   Mrs. Loraine M. Sternberg, *Director of
   Special Events*
LENOX HILL HOSPITAL, New York City
   Miss Alice Z. McHugh, *Assistant Director
   of Development*
MAUDEEN MARKS PUBLIC RELATIONS AND ADVERTISING,
   Houston, Texas
MARTS & LUNDY, INC., New York City
   Melvin D. Brewer, *President*
   Harry Staley
McBURNEY YMCA, New York City
   Paul Stone
PLAYS FOR THE LIVING, New York City
   Miss Ann Booth, *Executive Director*
PUBLIC RELATIONS NEWS, New York City
   Mrs. Denny Griswold, *Publisher*
PREVENTIVE MEDICINE INSTITUTE-STRANG CLINIC,
   New York City
   Mrs. Maxine V. Foshay, *Director of Public
   Relations*
PUBLIC RELATIONS SOCIETY OF AMERICA, New York City,
   Milton Fairman, formerly *Editor, Public Relations Journal*
LOUIS QUINN ASSOCIATES, Los Angeles, California
RECORDING FOR THE BLIND, New York City
   William Wilkinson, *Director of Development*
MARY ALICE RICE, *Fashion Show Coordinator,* New
   York City
SOCIETY OF MEMORIAL-SLOAN KETTERING CANCER
   CENTER, New York City
LENORE TOBIN, *Theater Parties Specialist,* New
   York City
UNITED HOSPITAL FUND, New York City
   Gordon Nugent, *Director, Women's Division*
UNITED WAY, INC.
   Philip Tracy, *Director of Public Relations*
YMCA, National Council
   John R. Burkhart, formerly *Director of Public Relations Services*
YMCA, Greater New York
   Francois Sheets, *Director of Public Relations*
Special recognition is due the organizations—national and local—which made available more than five hundred reports of successful special events. Literally scores of these have been selected for inclusion in the book for their variety of ideas and practical suggestions which should prove valuable to voluntary organizations, large and small, in their fields of service.

                                                          E.R.L.
                                                          B.E.S.